CHURCH OF THE NAZARENE
MESOAMERICA

CHILDREN'S BIBLE QUIZZING MINISTRY

Joshua Judges Ruth

Be strong and very courageous.

Bible Studies and quizzing for children from 6-12 years

Children's Bible Quizzing Ministry - Joshua, Judges, and Ruth

Published by: Discipleship Ministries of the Mesoamerica Region

www.discipleship.MesoamericaRegion.org

www.SdmiResources.MesoamericaRegion.org

Translated from Spanish and edited by Monte Cyr

Copyright © 2022 - All rights reserved

ISBN: 978-1-63580-310-5

The people who participated in the original idea and production of the games and activities portion of this book are:

Carolina Ambrosio
Eva Velazquez
Patricia Picavea
Patricia Zamora

Adapted by: Pamela Vargas Castillo, with love for the children of the Church of the Nazarene

Mesoamerica Region

KidzFirst Bible Studies for Children: Joshua, Judges, and Ruth

REVISED 2021-08-18

Copyright © 2021 Global Nazarene Publications

kidzfirstpublications.org

ISBN 978-1-56344-948-2

Editor for US English version: Kimberly D. Crenshaw

Editor for Global English: Leslie M. Hart

Editorial Committee: Leslie M. Hart, William J. Hart, Kathy Lewis, and Scott Stargel

Cover Art: Megan Goodwin

Published by KidzFirst Publications
an Imprint of Sunday School and Discipleship Ministries International
Church of the Nazarene, 17001 Prairie Star Parkway, Lenexa, KS 66220 (USA)

This edition published by arrangement with Nazarene Publishing House, Kansas City, Missouri USA

The first Children's Bible Quiz event, created by Rev. William Young, was introduced with a demonstration at the 1968 General Nazarene Young People's Society Convention Kansas City, Missouri (USA). Three Nazarene churches sent teams for the demonstration: Kansas City First, Kansas City St. Paul's, and Overland Park.

Welcome to the marvelous ministry of Children's Bible Quizzing

In this book you will find:

1. Bible Study Lessons (p. 12)

2. Guide for leading Children's Bible Quizzing using games and activities (p. 98)

3. Guide for leading Children's Bible Quizzing using questions and answers (p. 168)

4. Quizzing Competition Questions and Answers (p. 176)

NOTE: It's important that you work with only one type of quizzing for competitions.

CONTENTS

WELCOME AND OVERVIEW

Welcome to the *Bible Studies for Children* series that celebrates genuine discipleship through God's transforming Word!

These studies help children, ages 6 through 12, to gain a practical understanding of the Bible. Through this series, the children view the story of God through the lives of real people and historical events. They see God's love revealed through words, actions, and miracles. They learn how God works through ordinary people, and they discover their place in God's plan to redeem the world.

Each lesson includes the Bible context, content and review activities. In addition, the lesson provides the teacher with discussion questions and review questions. Red and blue level review questions prepare children to participate in an optional Bible Quiz event.

SUMMARY OF THE *BIBLE STUDIES FOR CHILDREN* SERIES

GENESIS

This study provides the foundation for the entire series. It describes God's relationship to all creation and his desire to establish a people to worship him. The study explains how God created the world from nothing, formed a man and a woman, and created a beautiful garden for their home. It reveals how evil, sin, and shame came into the world and the consequences of bad choices. Genesis introduces the plan of God to reconcile the broken relationship that is caused by sin. It introduces Adam, Eve, Noah, Abraham, Isaac, and Jacob. It tells about the covenant God made with Abraham and how Jacob became known as Israel. Genesis tells the story of Joseph, who saves the Egyptians from famine. It ends as the Israelite people move to Egypt to escape the famine.

EXODUS

Exodus explains how God continued to keep his promise to Abraham. It describes how Pharoh enslaved the Israelites. It reveals how God used Moses to rescue the Israelites from slavery. In Exodus, God establishes his authority over the Israelites. He leads them through the priesthood, the Tabernacle, the Ten Commandments, and other laws. God prepares the Israelites to be his people and to enter the Promised Land. As Exodus ends, only a part of God's covenant with Abraham is complete.

JOSHUA, JUDGES, & RUTH

This study explains how God fulfilled his promise to Abraham. When Moses was near the end of his life, God chose Joshua to lead the Israelites. Joshua led the 12 tribes of Israel to conquer the Promised Land and to live in it. After Joshua's death the Israelites struggled to obey God. They would obey, then disobey, and then suffer the consequences of disobedience. As the people suffered by their unfaithful choices, God called judges to lead the Israelites to faithfully obey the Lord. This study focuses on the judges Deborah, Gideon, and Samson. The story of Ruth takes place during this time of suffering. Ruth, Naomi, and Boaz show God's love and compassion in the middle of difficult circumstances. God blesses their faithfulness and redeems their circumstances. Ruth becomes the great-grandmother of King David.

1 & 2 SAMUEL

The study of 1 and 2 Samuel begins with the life and ministry of Israel's last judge, Samuel. Samuel followed God as he led Israel. The Israelites demanded a king like the nations around them. With the Lord's guidance, Samuel anoints Saul as the first king of Israel. Saul begins his reign well, but then he turns away from God. Because of this, David is chosen and anointed as the next king of Israel. David trusts God to help him to do impossible things. David is dedicated to God. But David is tempted, and he chooses to sin. Unlike Saul, David mourns because of his sin. He asks God to forgive him. God restores his relationship with David, but the consequences of sin remain with David, his family, and the nation of Israel. Throughout these stories of turmoil, God's presence remains constant. King David prepared the way for a new kind of King—Jesus.

MATTHEW

This study is the focal point of the entire series. The previous studies point to Jesus as the promised Messiah and the Son of God. This study focuses on the birth, the ministry, the crucifixion, and the resurrection of Jesus. Jesus ushered in a new era. The children learn about this new era in several events: the teachings of Jesus, the mentoring of his disciples, his death, and his resurrection. Jesus teaches what it means to live in the kingdom of heaven. Through Jesus, God provides a new way for all people to have a relationship with him.

ACTS

Acts records the birth of the church and its growth, especially through the ministries of Peter and Paul. At the beginning of this study, Jesus ascends to heaven and God sends the Holy Spirit to all believers. The good news of salvation through Jesus Christ spreads to many parts of the world. The apostles preach the gospel to the Gentiles and missionary work begins. The message of the love of God transforms both the Jews and the Gentiles. A direct connection can be seen between the evangelism of Paul and Peter and the lives of people today.

SIX-YEAR CYCLE

The following cycle is included for those who participate in the Bible Quiz event option of Bible Studies for Children.

The annual cycle is based on the school year of each country. The World Quiz event happens every four years in June.

Joshua, Judges, & Ruth (2022)
1 & 2 Samuel (2023)
Matthew (2024)
Acts (2025)
Genesis (2026)
Exodus (2027)

TEACHER PREPARATION

It is important to prepare thoroughly for each lesson. The children are more attentive and gain a better understanding when the study is presented well. If a teacher prepares well, he or she will also present the lesson well.

LESSON ELEMENTS

Each lesson contains the following elements.

Memory verse: Each lesson includes scripture for the children to memorize. These verses support the "Truth about God." The children will know the God of the Bible through his Word.

Truths about God: These truths help the teacher to recognize and emphasize how God's actions reveal his character and love for all people. The teacher should emphasize the "truths about God" as he or she teaches the lesson.

Lesson focus and summary: This section highlights the major ideas, events, and scriptures that the lesson covers.

Bible background: This section provides the teacher more information about the Bible story. It will help the teacher to understand better the scripture passage. The information enriches the teacher's knowledge and abilities.

Did you know?: This provides an interesting fact about the context of the story.

Vocabulary: These words and definitions will help the teacher to explain the meaning of the words used in the Bible.

Story-telling: This section suggests a storytelling method to connect the children to the Bible story.

Biblical lesson: This focuses on reading the scripture and discussion questions. This will help the children to apply the story to their lives.

Memory verse practice: This activity helps the children to memorize the verse for each lesson.

Additional activities: This section provides a game, craft, or other activity to connect the children to the lesson. These activities reinforce the main points.

Activities for older children: These activities are designed to engage older children with the main point.

Practice for a Bible Quiz event: Time to review and prepare the children to participate in an optional Games and Activities (MEBI) (p. 98) or Questions and Answers (p. 168) Bible Quiz event.

PREPARATION SEQUENCE

The following steps outline the recommended preparation sequence for the teacher.

STEP 1: LESSON REVIEW

You should thoroughly read the entire lesson. Give special attention to the memory verse, truths about God, lesson focus and summary, and the biblical lesson teaching tips.

STEP 2: BIBLE PASSAGE AND BIBLICAL BACKGROUND

Study the verses in the Bible, the biblical background, and the vocabulary sections.

STEP 3: STORY-TELLING

The **bold text** in each study suggests the words for you to say to the children.

This section includes a game or other activity to prepare the children for the biblical lesson. Become familiar with the activity, the instructions, and the supplies. Prepare and bring the necessary supplies to the class. Prepare the activity before the children arrive.

STEP 4: BIBLICAL LESSON

Review the lesson and learn it well enough to tell the story so that the children will understand the major points. Learn the definitions of the vocabulary words. When the vocabulary words appear, pause to explain them. After the story, ask the discussion questions. This will help the children to understand and to apply the story to their lives.

STEP 5: MEMORY VERSE

Memorize the verse before you teach it to the children. Page 120 contains a list of the memory verses. Pages 94-97 contain suggested memory verse activities. Choose an activity to help the children to learn the memory verse. Prepare the supplies that you will bring to class. Become familiar with the activity, and practice the way you will instruct the children.

STEP 6: ADDITIONAL ACTIVITIES

The purpose of any activity is to connect children to the lesson. Be creative! Make adjustments or substitutions in games and supplies so that they fit your culture and context. The additional activities are optional. They enhance the children's study if you choose to use them. Many of these activities require additional supplies, resources, and time. Become familiar with an activity before you choose it. Read the instructions and prepare the supplies that you will bring to class.

STEP 7: PRACTICE FOR A BIBLE QUIZ

A Bible Quiz event is an optional part of Bible Studies for Children. If you choose to participate in a Bible Quiz event, you should plan enough time to prepare the children for it. This book provides for two types of Bible Quizzing: Games based quizzing or Question and Answer based Quizzing. Each of these types is explained in it's respective section.

SUGGESTED SCHEDULE

You should plan for one to two hours of class time. The following is a suggested schedule for each lesson with options for 90 minutes and 2 hours. You may adjust the schedule as needed.

1½ hour	2 hours	
5 minutes		You should review the previous week's lesson with any children who arrive early. You may also choose to preview memory verses, stories, or vocabulary words for today's lesson.
5 minutes	10 minutes	Story-telling opening activity
10 minutes	10 minutes	Bible story
5 minutes	10 minutes	Review
10 minutes	15 minutes	Optional activity
10 minutes	15 minutes	Biblical lesson
10 minutes	15 minutes	Memory verse activity
	10 minutes	Optional activity
30 minutes	30 minutes	Bible Quiz event practice
5 minutes	5 minutes	Review of the main points and prayer

JOSHUA, JUDGES & RUTH

DO NOT BE AFRAID
Joshua 1:1-18

MEMORY VERSE

Have I not commanded you? Be strong and courageous. Do not be afraid; do not be discouraged, for the Lord your God will be with you wherever you go.

Joshua 1:9

TRUTHS ABOUT GOD

*This lesson will teach the following truths about God. The asterisk * indicates the primary truth that you should teach the children.*

* God gives us strength and courage to do his will.

- God is faithful to fulfill his promises.

- God will never leave those who love him.

LESSON FOCUS AND SUMMARY

In this study, the children will learn that God wanted the Israelites to be his holy, covenantal people.

1. After Moses died, Joshua became the leader of the Israelites.

2. God told Joshua to lead the Israelites into the land that he promised to give to them.

3. God promised to help Joshua to do this big job.

4. The people promised to obey Joshua as their new leader.

🗺 BIBLICAL BACKGROUND

In Exodus, God gave Moses the Law and provided for the Israelites in miraculous ways. After Moses died, Joshua served as God's representative and led the nation of Israel into a new era. The Israelites waited many long years for a place to call home. Now those years were finally over, and the people waited at the border to enter Canaan, the Promised Land.

In chapter 1, the Lord assured Joshua of victory over the Canaanites. God gave Joshua these commands: be strong and courageous, obey the Law, speak about the Law, and meditate on the Law. These commands worked together to accomplish God's greater purpose to create a holy, covenantal people.

God wanted the Israelites to love him with all their heart, soul, mind, and strength (Deuteronomy 6:4-5) and serve him as a kingdom of priests for all the earth (Exodus 19:5-6). It would be difficult for Israel to conquer Canaan. But, the Israelites would succeed if they trusted God, followed Joshua, and did not quit. Israel's struggle would strengthen them. They would develop godly character and gain a land of their own.

DID YOU KNOW?

Shortly before his death, God allowed Moses to glimpse the promised land of Canaan from Mt. Nebo. God buried him nearby. From there, Joshua led the Israelites to conquer the land that God promised to Abraham's descendants many years earlier (Genesis 15).

VOCABULARY

Faith words

Obedience means to do what God tells us to do. The Bible helps us understand what God wants us to do.

People

Joshua helped Moses throughout the years in the wilderness. Before Moses died, God chose Joshua to lead the Israelites. Joshua led the people into the Promised Land.

The officers were the leaders who listened to what Joshua commanded and told his commands to the people.

The Reubenites, the Gadites, and the half-tribe of Manasseh were three of the Israelite tribes.

Places

Jericho was a large and important city. A tall, thick wall protected this city.

The Jordan River was a large river in Canaan. It connected the Sea of Galilee to the Dead Sea.

Terms

The Book of the Law, sometimes referred to as **the Law**, is the first five books of the Bible. The Lord directed Moses to begin to write it when he was on Mt. Sinai. God gave these instructions to the people so that they knew how to obey him.

Forsake means to reject, to abandon, or to turn away from someone.

Courageous means brave. It describes a person who acts bravely even when fear, danger, or difficulty are present.

STORYTELLING

Each week you will need the following items.

1. A carrier like a small travel bag

2. A storage container for each week's story items (It can be a bag, basket, or box.)

For today's story, you will also need the following items.

3. A walking stick or a stick to represent one.

4. A map or a small gift box or bag filled with dirt

5. A Bible, tablets, or a scroll that represents the Law or the Book of the Law

Before class

1. Read Joshua 1:1-18.

2. Gather today's story items. Substitute a picture for any unavailable items.

3. Place today's story items inside the travel bag. Place the travel bag in the storytelling area.

Follow the leader

Tell the children to stand in a straight line, one behind the other. Choose a child to be the leader. Tell the children that they must watch the leader and mimic everything that he or she does. The leader then leads the group around the room. He or she must use different hand gestures, sounds, or motions for the children to imitate. For example, the leader can walk with baby steps, large steps, or skips. End the game at the storytelling area.

Story time

Read these instructions before you begin.

1. Focus on the main points as you tell the story in your own words. Remove an item from the bag as you illustrate each point. If you are comfortable, include more details. If needed, you may use the suggested script.

2. As you tell the story, display each item in order. Place the item where the children can see it.

3. After you tell the story, place all the items inside the bag again.

4. To review the story, ask a volunteer to remove an item from the bag and then tell what it represents. Repeat this process with all the items until the children are able to retell the story completely.

5. Review the "Memory motion" described below. Demonstrate this motion any time you mention what it represents. This week includes two memory motions.

Main points in order

Say, **We are on an epic expedition. I packed our travel bag with tools that will help us explore the book of Joshua. Each week we will search inside the bag for the tools that we will need for our journey. Today we begin with...** Unpack the items as you tell the story.

1. A walking stick or a stick to represent one – Use the stick as you walk back and forth in front of the children. Say, **In the book of Exodus, Moses served God and led the people with his helper Joshua. After many years, they finally came to the Promised Land. Before Moses died, God chose Joshua to be the next leader of the Israelites (Deuteronomy 31:1-8).**

2. A map or a small gift box or a bag filled with dirt to represent the land – Say, **Now it was time for Joshua to lead God's people into the Promised Land. God told Joshua to get ready to cross the Jordan River. God promised to give to the Israelites the land that he promised to Moses and their ancestors. Everywhere the Israelites walked would belong to them.**

3. Memory motion #1: Be strong and courageous! – There are two motions. 1. "Be strong" - Show the children how to make a fist in the air and flex their arm muscles or some other culturally appropriate gesture to show their strength. 2. "Be courageous" - Next, show the children how to lower their fists to their hips and stand with feet apart or

some other culturally appropriate gesture as a brave stance, to imitate a super hero. Or, invite the children to think of another motion. Say, **God promised Joshua that he would never leave or forsake Joshua. God also promised to help Joshua lead the Israelites into the Promised Land. God told Joshua to be strong and courageous. As I tell the story, do this motion every time you hear what it represents. Count the number of times that someone says this phrase to Joshua.**

4. The Bible, two tablets or a scroll that represents the Book of the Law – Say, **God said that he would be with Joshua like he was with Moses. But, Joshua must obey the Book of the Law that God gave to Moses. God told Joshua to study the law so completely that he was able to obey everything that was in it. As long as Joshua obeyed God's law, he would be successful and God would be with him.**

BIBLICAL LESSON

Tips for the teacher

As you lead the Bible study, emphasize these ideas.

- Explain that the story of Joshua is a continuation of the history of God's people. In Genesis 15, God promised the land to Abraham. Many years later, Joshua prepared to lead the Israelites to take possession of that same land.

- Remind the children that the land was not a free gift. The Israelites fought fierce enemies. They were required to follow God's instructions exactly. They trusted that he would help them succeed.

5. Memory motion #2– Salute or Handshake – This represents a promise or an agreement to obey or to follow someone. Say, **Joshua told the people to gather their supplies. In three days, they would cross the Jordan River and conquer the land God promised to their ancestors. The Israelite leaders promised to obey Joshua in the same way that they obeyed Moses.**

Say, **Now it is your turn to tell the story.** Return the items to the bag. Invite the children to take turns. A child will choose an item from the bag without looking and then explain what it means/ represents. Or, they may choose to review one of the memory motions and explain what it represents. After the children remove all the items and explain them, ask a volunteer to place them in the correct story order.

- If possible, use a Bible map to show the children the places mentioned in these stories.

Read the Scripture

Before you tell the story, Say, **Today we begin our study of a book in the Bible called Joshua. Joshua is also the name of one of the greatest heroes of our faith.**

We met Moses when we studied the book of Exodus. With Joshua by his side, Moses led the Israelites out of Egypt and through the desert for forty years. The Israelites finally completed their journey to the land that God promised to give them. After Moses died, the Lord told Joshua to lead the people into the new land.

The land was not easy to conquer. Sometimes the enemies outnumbered the Israelites. The Israelites had to obey God and follow his instructions exactly. Then, God would give them victory over all the enemies.

Read Joshua 1:1-18 aloud. You may choose to use the items and the motions to emphasize the main points.

Discussion questions

Discuss the story and ask the children the following questions. Remember that there might not be a right or wrong answer.

1. **Why do you think God told Joshua to be strong and courageous? Why might he feel afraid?**

2. **How would knowledge about the Book of the Law help the Israelites?**

3. **What did the Lord know about the people who lived in Canaan?** Read Genesis 15:12-21.

4. **The Lord knew it would not be easy. What were some of the difficulties that the Israelites would experience?**

5. **The Lord provided help to the Israelites. How does the Lord provide help to us when we face difficult situations? What must we do?**

Final thoughts

This is the thought that you want the children to remember.

Say, **Do you remember your first day of school? How did you feel? Were you excited or a little nervous? The Israelites went on an adventure into a new place. They needed strength and courage to remain faithful to the Lord. The Lord promised that he would never leave Joshua. It is the same for you and for me. God does not always take away our problems, but he is faithful. That means that he will always be with us. He will provide for us if we obey him. We must be strong and say "yes" to the Lord. We must be courageous and remain faithful to him.**

MEMORY VERSE PRACTICE

See the "Memory Verse Activities" for suggestions to help the children learn the memory verse.

ADDITIONAL ACTIVITIES

Play a game or do an activity in the CBQM section that relates to this lesson (p. 103ff)

PRACTICE FOR BIBLE QUIZ

Practice for Bible Quizzing with games and activities OR questions and answers.

SEEK AND HIDE

Joshua 2:1-24

MEMORY VERSE

Then Peter began to speak: "I now realize how true it is that God does not show favoritism but accepts from every nation the one who fears him and does what is right."

Acts 10:34-35

TRUTHS ABOUT GOD

*This lesson will teach the following truths about God. The asterisk * indicates the primary truth that you should teach the children.*

* God made it possible for anyone to know him.

• God wants a personal relationship with everyone.

• God accepts anyone who believes that he is the one true God and entrusts his or her life to him.

LESSON FOCUS AND SUMMARY

In this study, the children will learn that God keeps his promises. He provides for his people who entrust their lives to him.

1. Joshua sent spies to explore the Promised Land, especially Jericho.

2. A woman named Rahab hid the spies and helped them escape from Jericho.

3. The people of Jericho felt terrified of the Israelites.

4. The spies promised to save Rahab and her family when they returned to destroy Jericho.

BIBLICAL BACKGROUND

In this lesson, we meet Rahab. She is an unexpected ally and a special person in Israel's history. She shows us that anyone is able to believe that the one true God exists and to trust him.

Although Rahab was not a descendant of Abraham, she believed that the God of the Israelites was the Lord of the heavens and the earth. Since the time of the Exodus, the nation of Israel included people who were not descended from Abraham. However, a covenant member of Israel must believe in Yahweh, which is God's name, and live faithfully.

Everyone in Jericho knew that the God of Israel defeated Egypt and provided miraculously for his people. They knew that God gave the Israelites victory over the great armies of the Amorite kings. However, Rahab alone chose to join God's people. Everyone else in the city resisted them.

This passage does not approve of Rahab's lies to protect the spies. Remember that Rahab was not an Israelite and did not know how to live a life that pleased God. She did not know about the

Ten Commandments. Although not all of her behaviour was good, Rahab believed in the God of Israel. Because she chose to help God's people, Joshua spared her and her family.

What was true for Rahab is also true today. God does not expect us to be holy before we join his kingdom. God gives us the power to live holy lives after we become his people.

DID YOU KNOW?

The ancient city of Jericho was an area that measured about six-acres. One acre is approximately the size of a modern football field. The wall that surrounded the city was 5 meters high and 2 meters thick.

VOCABULARY

Faith words

Choices are decisions we make. All choices have consequences. When we obey God, we make right choices. When we know the right choice and decide to choose differently, we disobey God.

People

The spies were men that Joshua sent to gather resources in Canaan and Jericho.

Rahab was a woman who lived in Jericho and hid the two spies.

The Amorites lived in the country of Ammon that was located east of Jericho.

Places

Shittim was a town that was located east of Jericho.

Things

Flax is a plant that grows 1 to 2 meters tall and is good for many things. The seeds are very nutritious, and people used the fiber to make cloth and paper. Rahab hid the spies under the stalks of flax that lay on her roof.

STORYTELLING

Each week you will need the following items.

1. A carrier like a small travel bag

2. A storage container for each week's story items (It can be a bag, basket, or box.)

For today's story, you will also need the following items.

3. A spyglass, a pair of binoculars, or eyeglasses

4. A broad leaf or a small branch

5. A map or a sword

6. A red string, a rope or a ribbon

Before class

1. Read Joshua 2:1-24.

2. Gather today's story items. You may substitute a picture for any unavailable items.

3. Transfer all previous lesson items from the travel bag to the storage container. Place this container beside the storytelling area.

4. Place today's story items inside the travel bag, and place the travel bag in the storytelling area.

Optional activity: follow the leader or other activity.

Lesson review

Ask a volunteer to select an item from the storage container and explain what it represented in the previous lesson.

Story time

Read these instructions before you begin.

1. Focus on the main points as you tell the story in your own words. Remove an item from the bag as you illustrate each point. If you are

comfortable, include more details. If needed, you may use the suggested script.

2. As you tell the story, display each item in order. Place the item where the children can see it.

3. After you tell the story, place all the items inside the bag again.

4. To review the story, ask a volunteer to remove an item from the bag and then tell what it represents. Repeat this process with all the items until the children are able to retell the story completely.

5. Review the "Memory motion" described below. Demonstrate this motion any time you mention what it represents.

Main points in order

Say, **Today we continue to explore the book of Joshua. Each week I pack our travel bag with the tools that we need for our journey. Today we begin with...** Unpack as you tell the story.

1. Look through the spyglass, binoculars, or eyeglasses, or shade your eyes with your hand as if you see a distant land. Say, **Joshua secretly sent two spies to learn about the resources in the land and in the city of Jericho.**

2. Hold up the broad leaf or a small branch - Say, **Rahab hid the spies on the roof of her house under some stalks of flax. When the King's messengers looked for the Israelite spies, she said the men left when the city gates closed.**

3. Take out a map or a sword - Say, **The people of Jericho felt terrified of the Israelites. They heard about the signs and wonders that God did in Egypt and how he provided for the Israelites. They also heard that the Israelites destroyed the kings east of the Jordan River.**

4. A red string, a rope, or a ribbon – Say, **In exchange for the safety she provided, the spies agreed to spare Rahab and her family when they returned to conquer Jericho. If Rahab tied a red rope in her window and brought her family into her house, then the spies would save them.**

5. Memory motion - Rope Climb - Show the children how to close both fists around a vertical, imaginary rope. Put one fist in front of your face and the other in front of your chest. Reach down with the top hand and close your fist around the rope, as the bottom fist moves up the rope. Imagine and move as if you are climbing down a rope. Or, invite the children to think of another motion. Say, **After the spies promised to save Rahab and her family, she lowered the men on the rope through her window in the city wall. As I tell the story, do this motion when you hear what it represents.**

Say, **Now it is your turn to tell the story.** Return the items to the bag. Invite the children to take turns. Choose a volunteer to choose an item from the bag without looking and then explain what it means/ represents. Or, they may choose to review one of the memory motions and explain what it represents. After the children remove all the items and explain them, ask a volunteer to place them in the correct story order.

BIBLICAL LESSON

Tips for the teacher

As you lead the Bible study, emphasize these ideas.

- Do not be afraid of the tough questions that might come from this story. Many things about it may seem wrong to the children. Before the class, tell the parents that the scripture in today's Bible story includes the word "prostitute" and tell them how you plan to discuss it. Pray for wisdom as you plan a response. Do not offer an explanation unless your students ask. If the children ask, "What is a prostitute?" keep your answer simple. One possibility is to Say, **A prostitute lived a sinful life with many men.** If this seems inappropriate for your group Say, **The details are not important or appropriate to talk about right now. Today it is important** to remember that Rahab did not know God. She did not know about the Ten Commandments. Although some of her behaviour was bad, God helped Rahab to believe in him and to choose to help God's people. From Rahab we learn that God does not expect us to be holy before we know and accept him. God gives us the power to live holy lives after we become his people.

- Help the children focus on the important parts of the story, particularly the fact that a foreigner could become part of the people of God.

Read the Scripture

Say, **Do you know someone with a bad reputation? Sometimes all we know about a person is a rumor. This week, we meet Rahab. She was a woman with two problems: a bad reputation, and a hometown called Jericho in Canaan. Most Canaanites lived wicked lives and worshiped false gods. However, the Lord helped Rahab believe that he was the one true God.**

Read Joshua 2:1-24 aloud. You may choose to use the items and the motions to emphasize the main points.

Discussion questions

Discuss the story and ask the children the following questions. Remember that there might not be a right or wrong answer.

1. **What did the people of Jericho and Canaan think about God and the Israelites? What did they know? How did the Canaanites feel about the Israelites and God?**

2. **Why do you think the king of Jericho wanted to find the Israelite spies?**

3. **Why was it such a brave thing for Rahab to hide and protect the Israelite spies?**

4. **Do you think it was right for Rahab to lie to protect the spies? Why or why not? What were some other choices for Rahab?**

5. **How would this situation be different if all of Jericho asked to become part of God's people?**

Final thoughts

This is the thought that you want the children to remember.

Say, **The Lord helped Rahab believe that he was the one true God. Because she believed in him and his power, she helped the Israelite spies. In return, the Lord showed Rahab kindness. The Lord worked through the spies to save Rahab and her family.**

Does it surprise you that the Lord showed kindness to someone with a bad reputation? Do you wonder why God provided for a person who was not a member of the nation of Israel and whom the Israelites considered an enemy? God loves all people, good and bad. Because of this love, God made it possible for anyone to trust in him. Like Rahab, all people can become part of the people of God if they will choose him.

MEMORY VERSE PRACTICE

See the "Memory Verse Activities" for suggestions to help the children learn the memory verse.

ADDITIONAL ACTIVITIES

Play a game or do an activity in the CBQM section that relates to this lesson (p. 103ff)

PRACTICE FOR BIBLE QUIZ

Practice for Bible Quizzing with games and activities OR questions and answers.

WHAT HAPPENED TO THE RIVER?

Joshua 3:1-17

MEMORY VERSE

Joshua told the people, "Consecrate yourselves, for tomorrow the Lord will do amazing things among you."

Joshua 3:5

TRUTHS ABOUT GOD

*This lesson will teach the following truths about God. The asterisk * indicates the primary truth that you should teach the children.*

* * God is able to do the impossible.

* • God instructs his people.

* • God has power over nature.

LESSON FOCUS AND SUMMARY

In this study, the children will learn that when God's people followed his instructions, they saw powerful miracles.

1. Joshua led the Israelites to the banks of the Jordan River.

2. The priests carried the Ark of the Covenant and led the Israelites across the Jordan.

3. When the priests stepped into the Jordan River, the water stopped and did not flow.

4. The Israelites crossed the Jordan on dry ground.

BIBLICAL BACKGROUND

In this lesson, we will learn how the nation of Israel left the wilderness and entered Canaan, the Promised Land. The Israelites arrived at the Jordan River, but because the river was at flood stage and there was no bridge, it was impassable. This was not the only problem. They had many belongings to move. Traditionally, the Ark of the Covenant led the Israelite army into battle. However, it was large and very heavy. It seemed impossible for the Israelites to cross the flooded river.

Once again, the Lord did the impossible. When the feet of the priests who carried the Ark of the Covenant touched the water, the flow of the river water stopped. The nation of Israel crossed the Jordan River on the dry ground.

The Lord performed many miracles to benefit Israel. He saved them, taught them, and revealed himself to them through miracles. This miracle accomplished three things. First, it allowed the people to cross a river that they could not cross on their own. The second effect was spiritual. In verse 10, Joshua explained that the Lord stopped the flow of the river to prove that he was with the people of Israel as they entered the land. God's presence assured the Israelites of their future victory over the people of Canaan. A third purpose for the miracle was to show that God had chosen Joshua as Israel's new leader. God would work through Joshua in the same way that God had worked through Moses.

🔖 DID YOU KNOW?

The Ark of the Covenant was very heavy, weighing 80 to 120 kilograms. Six men accompanied it; four men carried it and two extra men allowed the others to take turns to rest. In ancient Israel, priests often carried the Ark of the Covenant into battle ahead of the warriors. This symbolized that God's presence led Israel into battle.

❓ VOCABULARY

Faith words

Consecrate means to choose and prepare an object or a person for God's use only.

People

The Levites were the people from the tribe of Levi who helped the priests with their duties.

The Priests were the descendants of Aaron, a Levite. God chose the priests to serve as the worship leaders of Israel. They served in the Tabernacle.

Places

Adam was a town that was located near Zarethan. It was located approximately 30 kilometers up the river from the place where the Israelites crossed the Jordan River.

The Sea of Arabah was another name for the Dead Sea.

📖 STORYTELLING

Each week you will need the following items.

1. A carrier like a small travel bag

2. A storage container for each week's story items (It can be a bag, basket, or box.)

For today's story, you will also need the following items.

3. A container of water or a picture of a river

4. A small toy chest or a special keepsake box

5. A container of dry sand or dirt

Before class

1. Read Joshua 3:1-17.

2. Gather today's story items. You may substitute a picture for any unavailable items.

3. Transfer all previous lesson items from the travel bag to the storage container. Place this container beside the storytelling area.

4. Place today's story items inside the travel bag. Place the travel bag in the storytelling area.

Optional activity: follow the leader or other game

Lesson review

Ask a volunteer to select an item from the storage container and explain what it represented in the previous lesson.

Story time

Read these instructions before you begin.

1. Focus on the main points as you tell the story in your own words. Remove an item from the bag as you illustrate each point. If you are comfortable, include more details. If needed, you may use the suggested script.

2. As you tell the story, display each item in order. Place the item where the children can see it.

3. After you tell the story, place all the items inside the bag again.

4. To review the story, ask a volunteer to remove an item from the bag and then tell what it represents. Repeat this process with all the items until the children are able to retell the story completely.

5. Review the "Memory motion" described below. Demonstrate this motion any time you mention what it represents.

Main points in order

Say, **Today we continue to explore the book of Joshua. Each week I pack our travel bag with the tools that we need for our journey. Today we begin with...** Unpack as you tell the story.

1. Hold up the container of water or picture of a river. Say, **Joshua led the Israelites to the banks of the Jordan River. They camped for three days before Joshua gave them the Lord's instructions to prepare to cross over the river.**

2. A small toy chest or a special memento box - Say, **This is a special, small box to represent the Ark of the Covenant. It was the Israelites' most prized possession. It was big and very heavy. It took four priests to carry it. It was important, because it was a symbol of God's presence. The Israelites carried it with them through the desert. They would carry it across the Jordan River and into the Promised Land.**

3. Memory motion: Stop sign - Show the children how to put one hand up with the palm out to represent that God stopped the flood waters of the Jordan River. Or, invite the children to think of another appropriate motion. Say, **As I tell the story, do this motion when you hear what it represents.**

4. Say, **The Jordan River was at flood stage. When the priests stepped into the water, the flow of water stopped and piled up in a heap all the way to the city of Adam, a long way from where the Israelites crossed. Therefore, the water that flowed to the sea stopped.**

5. A small container of dirt or sand to represent dry land - Say, **The priests carried the Ark of the Covenant and stood on dry ground in the middle of the Jordan River. This symbolized that the Lord went ahead of the Israelites and was in the place of danger and protected them. All the Israelites crossed on the dry ground similar to when they crossed the Red Sea when they were escaping from Pharaoh and his army.**

Say, **Now it is your turn to tell the story.** Return the items to the bag. Invite the children to take turns. Choose a volunteer to take an item from the bag without looking and then explain what it means/ represents. Or, they may choose to review one of the memory motions and explain what it represents. After the children remove all the items and explain them, ask a volunteer to place them in the correct story order.

✠ BIBLICAL LESSON

Tips for the teacher

As you lead the Bible study, emphasize these ideas.

- Remind the children that the word consecrate means to set something apart for God's use only. The phrase, to consecrate themselves, means the people prepared themselves to represent God in the land.

- The Lord clearly led his people. The Ark represented God's presence and always traveled in front of the people. After the people consecrated themselves, they followed the ark and waited for God to provide all they would need.

- Joshua told the people not to go near the ark. He said to maintain a distance of about two thousand cubits between the people and the ark. Two thousand cubits is about 900 meters.

- Talk about how God speaks to each of us in different ways. Sometimes he directs each of us but allows us to choose different options.

Sometimes he directs us through other people. He often directs us through prayer. When we pray we should listen for God to direct our thoughts and questions. Sometimes we must be patient and wait for an answer.

Read the Scripture

Show the students the small toy chest or special memento box that you used in the storytelling activity and Say, **The priests carried the Ark of the Covenant as they led the Israelites into the waters of the Jordan River. When the people saw the priests and the Ark they knew where to go, but Joshua warned them to maintain a distance between them and the Ark and not go near it.**

Read Joshua 3:1-17 aloud. You may choose to use the items and the motions to emphasize the main points.

Discussion questions

Discuss the story and ask the children the following questions. Remember that there might not be a right or wrong answer.

1. **Why do you think the Lord wanted the Ark of the Covenant to go in front of the people?**

2. **Why was it important for the people to consecrate themselves before they crossed the Jordan River?**

3. **How would the Canaanites know that the Israelite's God was the one, true, living God?**

4. Read Exodus 14:13-22 and Joshua 3:14-17. Ask, **How are the miracles that happened at the Jordan River and the Red Sea similar?**

5. **What did the Israelites know and not know about God's plan for them to enter the Promised Land? Why did they have to trust him?**

Final thoughts

This is the thought that you want the children to remember.

Say, Water that stood in a heap all by itself! Thousands of people that walked across a dry riverbed where water once flowed freely! It sounds impossible! In Exodus, the Lord parted the Red Sea so that the Israelites were able to cross safely. Forty years later, he helped their children cross the Jordan River in the same way. He was faithful and committed to the Israelites. He was able to provide anything that they needed, even the things that seemed impossible.

The good news is that God does not help us only when we have a huge need. He is there for us every day, throughout our lives, in the same way that he was there for the Israelites. When it was necessary, he did the impossible for them. He is also able to do the impossible for you.

MEMORY VERSE PRACTICE

See the "Memory Verse Activities" for suggestions to help the children learn the memory verse.

ADDITIONAL ACTIVITIES

Play a game or do an activity in the CBQM section that relates to this lesson (p. 103ff

PRACTICE FOR BIBLE QUIZ

Practice for Bible Quizzing with games and activities OR questions and answers.

A TALE OF TWELVE STONES

Joshua 4:1-24; 5:10-12

MEMORY VERSE

He said to the Israelites, "In the future when your descendants ask their parents, 'What do these stones mean?' tell them, 'Israel crossed the Jordan on dry ground.'"

Joshua 4:21-22

TRUTHS ABOUT GOD

*This lesson will teach the following truths about God. The asterisk * indicates the primary truth that you should teach the children.*

* If we remember what God did in the past, it helps us to trust him today.

• God honors those who trust him.

• God wants his people to remember what he did for them.

LESSON FOCUS AND SUMMARY

In this study, the children will learn that God wants us to remember what he did for us in the past. This will help us to know that he is trustworthy. He will always be with us and will provide for our needs.

1. God directed Joshua to tell one person from each of the 12 Israelite tribes to take a stone from the Jordan River.

2. When the priests stepped out of the Jordan, the water returned to flood stage.

3. Joshua made a memorial with the twelve stones to remind the Israelites of what God did for them.

4. At Gilgal, the manna stopped after the Israelites ate food from Canaan.

BIBLICAL BACKGROUND

Why bother to remember the past? Why should the events of the Old Testament be important to us? Today's lesson provides the answer. If we remember what God did in the past, it will help us to trust him today and always. God is the same yesterday, today, and forever. His abilities, his character, and his desires for us never change. What was true about him in the past is true about him today. God wants us to remember what he did so that we will know him, trust him, and love him.

Last week, we learned that one goal of the miracle at the Jordan River was to help Israel to recognize that Joshua was God's chosen leader. However, God did not want the people to think that Joshua had the power to make the waters stop on his own. God showed that his power was the source of the miracles they witnessed. He filled the ark, the clouds, and the fire with his presence. He spoke and acted through them. He made them holy for his use. But, God was not limited to the confines of a physical object. He transcended everything that he used to communicate with Israel.

Israel revered Joshua. However, God's presence went before the people with the ark carried by the priests. The Israelites knew that the Lord was the source of the victory.

🔍 DID YOU KNOW?

The men of the tribes of Reuben, Gad, and the half-tribe of Manasseh asked Moses if they and their families could stay on the east side of the Jordan and not cross into the Promised Land. Moses agreed. However, he required that the men must cross the Jordan to help their brothers fight for their land.

❓ VOCABULARY

Faith words

A miracle is an impossible act that only God is able to do. God's miracles show people his character and help them to trust him.

People

Descendants are a person's children, grandchildren, great-grandchildren, and all the following generations.

Places

Gilgal was Israel's first campsite in Canaan. It was not far from Jericho.

Terms

A memorial is an object, event, or place that helps people to remember a special event or person.

The Passover is a special feast to celebrate how God delivered the Israelites' from Egypt. God protected their firstborn sons from death when he passed over the Israelite homes in the last plague.

Manna was the special bread God provided for the Israelites in the desert. Manna means, "What is it?"

📖 STORYTELLING

Each week you will need the following items.

1. A carrier like a small travel bag

2. A storage container for each week's story items (It can be a bag, basket, or box.)

For today's story, you will also need the following items.

3. A stone with the number twelve written on it or twelve small stones.

4. A container of water

5. A small toy chest or a special keepsake box to represent the Ark

6. A piece of bread or a cracker

Before class

1. Read Joshua 4:1-24 and 5:10-12.

2. Gather today's story items. You may substitute a picture for any unavailable items.

3. Transfer all previous lesson items from the travel bag to the storage container. Place this container beside the storytelling area.

4. Place today's story items inside the travel bag. Place the travel bag in the storytelling area.

Optional activity: follow the leader

Tell the children to stand in a straight line, one behind the other. Choose a child to be the leader. Tell the children that they must watch the leader and mimic everything that he or she does. The leader leads the group around the room. He or she uses different hand gestures, sounds, or motions for the children to imitate. For example, the leader walks with baby steps, large steps, or skips. End the game at the storytelling area.

Lesson review

Ask a volunteer to select an item from the storage container and explain what it represented in the previous lesson.

Story time

Read these instructions before you begin.

1. Focus on the main points as you tell the story in your own words. Remove an item from the bag as you illustrate each point. If you are comfortable, include more details. If needed, you may use the suggested script.

2. As you tell the story, display each item in order. Place the item where the children can see it.

3. After you tell the story, place all the items inside the bag again.

4. To review the story, ask a volunteer to remove an item from the bag and then tell what it represents. Repeat this process with all the items until the children are able to retell the story completely.

5. Review the "Memory motion" described below. Demonstrate this motion any time you mention what it represents.

Main points in order

Say, **Today we continue to explore the book of Joshua. I packed our travel bag with the tools that we need for our journey. Today we begin with...** Unpack the items as you tell the story.

1. Hold up the twelve small stones or the stone with the number twelve written on it. Say, **The whole nation of Israel crossed over the Jordan River. God wanted one man from each of the twelve tribes to choose a stone from where the priests stood in the middle of the river. The stones would remind them that God stopped the water and they crossed on dry ground.**

✝ BIBLICAL LESSON

Tips for the teacher

As you lead the Bible study, emphasize these ideas.

- God used the twelve stones to remind the Israelites that God miraculously helped all the people of Israel cross the Jordan River on dry

2. The small toy chest or keepsake box – Say, **This special box represents the Ark of the Covenant. The priests carried the Ark and stood in the middle of the Jordan River until everything that the Lord commanded happened. The Ark reminded the people that God went before them in a place of danger.**

3. A container of water - Say, **Once the priests who carried the Ark of the Covenant stepped out of the Jordan River, the water returned to flood stage.**

4. Memory motion: Build the altar - Demonstrate how to pound one fist on top of the other and to alternate this motion with the other fist. Say, **This motion represents that Joshua built an altar with the twelve stones from the Jordan River. When they saw it, the Israelites remembered what God did. As I tell the story, do this motion when you hear what it represents.** Or, invite the children to think of another motion.

5. A piece of bread or a cracker - Say, **When the Israelites reached Gilgal they celebrated the Passover and ate the manna. The next day they ate roasted grain and bread from the produce of the land. This represents the food that God provided.**

Say, **Now it is your turn to tell the story.** Return the items to the bag. Invite the children to take turns. Choose a volunteer to choose an item from the bag without looking and then explain what it represents. Or, they may choose to review one of the memory motions and explain what it represents. After the children remove all the items and explain them, ask a volunteer to place them in the correct story order.

ground. The people acted in faith and obeyed God's instructions.

- It may seem that this event was easy to remember, however the Israelites quickly forgot that their obedience was important.

- In these miracle-filled stories, the most important lessons are to remember that God provides and that we must always obey him.

Read the Scripture

Say, **In our last lesson, the Jordan River flooded and it seemed impossible to cross. However, God provided a way.**

Read Joshua 4:1-24 and 5:10-12 aloud. You may choose to use the items and the motions to emphasize the main points.

Discussion questions

Discuss the story and ask the children the following questions. Remember that there might not be a right or wrong answer.

1. **What does it mean to fear the Lord?**

2. **Why did the Lord want the Israelites to make a memorial with the 12 stones? Why do you think that it was important for the Israelites to remember what God did?**

3. **What are some ways that we might build personal memorials that will help us remember God's goodness to us?**

4. **How do you think Joshua felt when God spoke to him? If you were Joshua, how would you feel if the Lord told you that he would make you into a heroic leader of Israel?**

5. **The Israelites waited to receive the Promised Land for many generations (over 450 years).**

How do you think they felt when they finally reached Canaan?

Final thoughts

This is the thought that you want the children to remember.

Say, **It might seem strange to read that a pile of rocks was very important. However, God directed the leaders to choose those special stones. God wanted something that would last and that the people would be able to see, touch and remember. They would know that what had happened was real. It was not a dream or a memory that would fade. Every time the people saw the rocks, or when their children asked them about the rocks, the Israelites would share about how God had provided for them.**

God kept his promise. Abraham's descendants were now in the Promised Land. The future would include challenges. However, when difficult things happened, the rocks would remind Israel that God is faithful. They could trust God with their lives.

Do you remember a time when God helped you? When you get home, find a stone to remind you that God provides for you. Place it where you will see it often and remember that God is trustworthy. When you remember something new that God has provided, add another stone and build your personal memorial.

☑ MEMORY VERSE PRACTICE

See the "Memory Verse Activities" for suggestions to help the children learn the memory verse.

🧩 ADDITIONAL ACTIVITIES

Play a game or do an activity in the CBQM section that relates to this lesson (p. 103ff

❓ PRACTICE FOR BIBLE QUIZ

Practice for Bible Quizzing with games and activities OR questions and answers.

OH, NO, JERICHO!

Joshua 5:13—6:25

MEMORY VERSE

Obey the Lord your God and follow his commands and decrees that I give you today.

Deuteronomy 27:10

TRUTHS ABOUT GOD

*This lesson will teach the following truths about God. The asterisk * indicates the primary truth that you should teach the children.*

* God is always at work in the world. We participate in God's work when we obey him.

- God sometimes uses unusual ways to accomplish his will.

- God rewards those who obey him.

LESSON FOCUS AND SUMMARY

In this study, the children will learn that God invites us to join him as he works in the world. However, we must obey him to experience his blessing.

1. A heavenly commander of God's army met with Joshua.

2. The heavenly commander told Joshua how to conquer Jericho.

3. The Israelites obeyed God's directions and destroyed Jericho.

4. The spies fulfilled their promise and Joshua saved Rahab and her family.

BIBLICAL BACKGROUND

After the Israelites crossed the Jordan, a man with a sword surprised Joshua. Joshua asked him if he was on the side of Israel or its enemies. The man said he was the commander of the army of the Lord, and he was not on either side. Joshua fell on his face and asked for instructions. The man told Joshua to take off his sandals because he was on holy ground.

This event was important because it demonstrated that Joshua's attitude was humble, respectful, and reverent toward the Lord. God wanted Joshua to understand that God was the leader, and Joshua served him and his plan. God did not want Israel to forget this and think that Joshua led them by his own strength without God's help. Yahweh did not give his unconditional approval to Israel's actions. God made it clear that Israel served him and acted upon his plan. Joshua honored God's presence and authority. He humbly submitted to the Lord.

Joshua was not only humble, he was obedient. He asked God to instruct him. Obedience was crucial for victory because Yahweh required Israel's participation with him in the battle. If they disregarded his instructions, they would fight for themselves, not Yahweh. He would not fight for them if they did not follow and obey him completely. Israel's role was necessary even though it was clearly God's power, not Israel's, that guaranteed victory. Divine power was abundant when Israel humbly obeyed. God gave them the victory he had promised.

🔍 DID YOU KNOW?

Seven is an important number in this story (and in the Bible). There were seven priests with seven trumpets. The battle ended on the seventh day when they marched around the city seven times. Seven symbolizes completeness or perfection. Another example is the seven days of creation.

❓ VOCABULARY

Faith words

God's work means everything that God does. **God's work** also means anything that God asks people to do.

Places

Jericho was an ancient city with a long history. Some archaeologists call it the oldest walled city in the world. It was built more than 7,000 years before Abraham lived. In ancient times, another name for Jericho was the City of Palm Trees.

Terms

The devoted things were gold, silver, and other valuable objects that people gave to their god or gods. They never used those things again for any other purpose. Sometimes God told the Israelites to destroy the "devoted things" after a victory.

A war cry was a loud shout that was a part of the ritual of war.

The Lord's treasury was probably located near or in the Tabernacle. The people stored all the gold, silver, and valuable items there, until the priests used them in service to the Lord.

📖 STORYTELLING

Each week you will need the following items.

1. A carrier like a small travel bag

2. A storage container for each week's story items (It can be a bag, basket, or box.)

For today's story, you will also need the following items.

3. A sandal or Shoe

4. A small toy Chest or special Keepsake box, to represent the Ark of the Covenant

5. A horn with the number seven attached

6. A red rope, string, or ribbon

7. Gold or silver coins or valuable metal items

Before class

1. Read Joshua 5:13-6:25.

2. Gather today's story items. You may substitute a picture for any unavailable items.

3. Transfer all previous lesson items from the travel bag to the storage container. Place this container beside the storytelling area.

4. Place today's story items inside the travel bag. Place the travel bag in the storytelling area.

Optional activity: follow the leader

Tell the children to stand in a straight line, one behind the other. Choose a child to be the leader. Tell the children that they must watch the leader and mimic everything that he or she does. The leader leads the group around the room. He or she uses different hand gestures, sounds, or motions for the children to imitate. For example, the leader walks with baby steps, large steps, or skips. End the game at the storytelling area.

Lesson review

Ask a volunteer to select an item from the storage container and explain what it represented in the previous lesson.

Story time

Read these instructions before you begin.

1. Focus on the main points as you tell the story in your own words. Remove an item from the bag as you illustrate each point. If you are comfortable, include more details. If needed, you may use the suggested script.

2. As you tell the story, display each item in order. Place the item where the children can see it.

3. After you tell the story, place all the items inside the bag again.

4. To review the story, ask a volunteer to remove an item from the bag and then tell what it represents. Repeat this process with all the items until the children are able to retell the story completely.

5. Review the "Memory motion" described below. Demonstrate this motion any time you mention what it represents.

Main points in order

Say, **Today we continue to explore the book of Joshua. Each week I pack our travel bag with the tools that we need for our journey. Today we begin with...** Unpack the items as you tell the story.

1. Hold up the sandal or shoe. Say, **God sent a commander of the heavenly armies to meet with Joshua. When Joshua asked the commander if he had a message from the Lord, the commander said, "Take off your sandals, because the place where you stand is holy." Joshua obeyed.**

2. A small toy Chest or special keepsake box - Say, **The Lord told Joshua how to conquer Jericho. In this battle, the Lord not only wanted Joshua to conquer the Canaanite city, but also their false religion. Joshua told the Israelites to march around the city once in this order: the armed guard, the seven priests with horns, the Ark of the Covenant**

and the rear guard. They were to do that for six days.

3. A horn with the number seven written or attached to it – Say, **On the seventh day, the Israelites marched around Jericho seven times. After the seventh time, the Priests blew a long blast on their horns and the people loudly shouted ... and the walls of Jericho fell down.**

4. Memory motion: March and Shout – Demonstrate for the children how to march in place as you count to seven. When you say "seven" give a shout. Or, invite the children to think of another motion. Say, **As I tell the story, do this motion when you hear what it represents.**

5. A red rope, string, or ribbon - Say, **Rahab knew the Israelites had arrived so she brought her family into her home and placed the red rope outside her window in the city wall. The spies kept their promise and saved her and her family. They brought them out of the city before they destroyed it.**

6. Gold or silver coins or valuable metal items – Say, **Everything was destroyed except the devoted things. These were items of gold, silver, bronze and iron to use in the Lord's service. The people devoted these to the Lord and kept them in the Lord's treasury.**

Say, **Now it is your turn to tell the story.** Return the items to the bag. Invite the children to take turns. Choose a volunteer to choose an item from the bag without looking and then explain what it represents. Or, they may choose to review one of the memory motions and explain what it represents. After the children remove all the items and explain them, ask a volunteer to place them in the correct story order.

BIBLICAL LESSON

Tips for the teacher

As you lead the Bible study, emphasize these ideas.

- Remind the children that God wants us to obey him. It is important to listen to God and follow his commands.

- If you have time, discuss the similarities between Joshua's experience with the commander of the Lord's army and Moses's experience at the burning bush.

Read the Scripture

Show the sandal or shoe to the children and say, **This shoe reminds us that Joshua was humble before the Lord. He showed respect for God when he removed his sandals and bowed low. Joshua had the right attitude. He listened carefully to God's instructions so that he would be able to obey every detail.**

Read Joshua 5:13-6:25 aloud. You may choose to use the items and the motions to emphasize the main points.

Discussion questions

Discuss the story and ask the children the following questions. Remember that there might not be a right or wrong answer.

1. **Who did Joshua really honor when he bowed to the commander of the Lord's army and removed his sandals?**

2. **When the Israelites gave a battle cry, they expressed joy, which came from their faith and trust in the Lord. How do you express your faith and trust in God?**

3. **What do you think would have happened at Jericho if the Israelites had not obeyed God's directions completely?**

4. **Imagine you were an Israelite and saw the walls of Jericho fall down. What would you think?**

5. **The Israelites kept their promise to rescue Rahab and her family. What do you think Rahab learned from that?**

Final thoughts

This is the thought that you want the children to remember.

Say, **The Israelites defeated Jericho. They obeyed God and won a great victory. What might have been different if they had disobeyed the Lord's instructions and followed their own plan? Obedience to the Lord was the key to their success. When we obey, our hearts are open as we listen to and follow the Lord. We want the same things he does. When we disobey, we want our own way instead of God's way and we miss the blessings that he wants us to experience. The Israelites chose to follow the Lord's instructions. They took part in his plan. Choose today to follow the Lord. His plans may surprise you!**

MEMORY VERSE PRACTICE

See the "Memory Verse Activities" for suggestions to help the children learn the memory verse.

ADDITIONAL ACTIVITIES

Play a game or do an activity in the CBQM section that relates to this lesson (p. 103ff

PRACTICE FOR BIBLE QUIZ

Practice for Bible Quizzing with games and activities OR questions and answers.

THE SIN OF ACHAN

Joshua 7:1-26

MEMORY VERSE

There is a way that appears to be right, but in the end it leads to death.

Proverbs 14:12

TRUTHS ABOUT GOD

*This lesson will teach the following truths about God. The asterisk * indicates the primary truth that you should teach the children.*

* God does not disregard sin.

• God requires people to obey him completely.

• God provides a way for people to repent of their sins and restore their relationship with him.

LESSON FOCUS AND SUMMARY

In this study, the children will learn that sin breaks our relationship with God and often affects others. However, God provides a way to restore the broken relationship.

1. Achan disobeyed God's commands and took some things from Jericho.

2. Because of Achan's disobedience, the Israelites were defeated at Ai.

3. God told the Israelites they could not defeat their enemies until they destroyed the stolen things.

4. The Israelites punished Achan and destroyed the things he took.

BIBLICAL BACKGROUND

God does not overlook sin. The story of Achan's sin and punishment illustrates this point vividly. It reminds us that there are consequences when we sin.

Israel knew sin was a serious matter. Defiant sins were particularly serious because they were intentional violations of God's covenant law. There was no sacrifice for such sins. Numbers 15:30-31 tells us that the proper punishment for defiant sins was to cut off the sinner from the people. A man's life continued, in a sense, through his descendants. They would continue his work, maintain his property, and keep his possessions. To be cut off, then, was very much like a death sentence because it affected a man's legacy. Such a punishment, then, was very harsh. It was as if Yahweh said, "If you break the covenant vows and reject me, you will lose everything. It means ultimate death. Yes, it is that serious."

Achan's story also demonstrates that a person's sin affects an entire community. God halted Israel's progress until the community dealt with the sin. Mercifully, God provided a way for Israel to repent. He loved them enough to guide, warn, justly punish, and restore the community to relationship with him.

DID YOU KNOW?

The Israelites would sometimes "cast lots" to determine God's will. This was a process that seemed to be random, such as throwing bits of bones or stones, similar to dice. For the Israelites, this was not a random, risky action or magic. They believed that God guided this process.

VOCABULARY

Faith words

Sin means to disobey God. We sin when we do something that God says we must not do. We also sin when we do not do what God says we must do.

People

The Clan of Judah includes all the families that descended from Jacob's son Judah. It is also one of the 12 tribes of Israel.

Places

Ai was a city that was located north of Jericho. The name **Ai** means "The Ruin."

The Valley of Achor was located between Jericho and Jerusalem. It is where Achan was stoned. Achor means "trouble."

Terms

A shekel was a common Hebrew coin that weighed about half an ounce. 200 shekels was a lot of money.

The devoted things were people or items that belonged completely to Yahweh God or idol gods.

Phrases

"The Lord's anger burned against Israel" means that God's anger was so strong that it was like a fire that consumed everything. This anger did not stop unless the offender made restitution.

"They tore their clothes" describes the way ancient people expressed deep sorrow, worry, repentance, and other strong emotions.

STORYTELLING

Each week you will need the following items.

1. A carrier like a small travel bag

2. A storage container for each week's story items (It can be a bag, basket, or box.)

For today's story, you will also need the following items.

3. Gold or silver coins and fancy cloth

4. A cloth or something to hide the coins or valuable items described above

5. A torn clothing item

6. A rock

Before class

1. Read Joshua 7:1-26.

2. Gather today's story items. You may substitute a picture for any unavailable items.

3. Transfer all previous lesson items from the travel bag to the storage container. Place this container beside the storytelling area.

4. Place today's story items inside the travel bag. Place the travel bag in the storytelling area.

Optional activity: follow the leader or other activity.

Lesson review

Ask a volunteer to select an item from the storage container and explain what it represented in the previous lesson.

Story time

Read these instructions before you begin.

1. Focus on the main points as you tell the story in your own words. Remove an item from the bag as you illustrate each point. If you are comfortable, include more details. If needed, you may use the suggested script.

2. As you tell the story, display each item in order. Place the item where the children can see it.

3. After you tell the story, place all the items inside the bag again.

4. To review the story, ask a volunteer to remove an item from the bag and then tell what it represents. Repeat this process with all the items until the children are able to retell the story completely.

5. Review the "Memory motion" described below. Demonstrate this motion any time you mention what it represents.

Main points in order

Say, **Today we continue to explore the book of Joshua. Each week I pack our travel bag with the tools that we need for our journey. Today we begin with...** Unpack the items as you tell the story.

1. Hold up the gold or silver coins and fancy cloth then cover them under the cloth to hide them. Say, **When Israel defeated Jericho, God instructed the Israelites to destroy everything except the devoted things. However, an Israelite man named Achan kept some of the things that God said to destroy and hid them in his tent. So the Lord became very angry because of Israel's disobedience.**

2. A torn clothing item - Say, **After the Israelite victory over Jericho, Joshua sent a small army to defeat the city of Ai because it was not very large. However, the soldiers of Ai defeated the Israelite army! The Israelites**

lost their courage and became afraid. Joshua tore his clothes to show his dismay. He was confused and did not understand why God had allowed this defeat. He was afraid that the Canaanites would hear about their defeat and attack them.**

3. Memory motion: A posture of prayer - Show to the children how to clasp their hands, to close your eyes, to bow your head, or to kneel or bow low to show reverence to God when we pray. Or, invite the children to think of another appropriate motion. Say, **As I tell the story, do this motion when you hear what it represents. When Joshua heard about the defeat at Ai, he immediately tore his clothes and bowed low before the Ark of the Covenant. He told God about his fear and confusion. God told Joshua that Israel had sinned and an Israelite stole some devoted things.**

4. A stone - Say, **Eventually, Achan admitted that he had stolen the devoted things. His sin brought guilt and punishment upon the Israelites. God said that he would not continue to be with them until the Israelites destroyed whatever among them was devoted to destruction. The Israelites punished Achan and his household. They followed God's instructions, stoned them, and burned everything. Afterwards, they piled rocks on top of them.**

Say, **Now it is your turn to tell the story.** Return the items to the bag. Invite the children to take turns. Choose a volunteer to choose an item from the bag without looking and then explain what it represents. Or, they may choose to review one of the memory motions and explain what it represents. After the children remove all the items and explain them, ask a volunteer to place them in the correct story order.

✝ BIBLICAL LESSON

Tips for the teacher

As you lead the Bible study, emphasize these ideas.

- Be prepared to answer questions about why God punished Achan and his family so severely. This is not easy even for adults to understand.

- Help the children understand that repentance is more than just when we say the words, "I am sorry. I did it." The sorrow comes because we understand that we dishonor God when we sin. Repentance is a strong determination that we will never do such a thing again.

- Achan showed no sign of repentance. He only confessed when Joshua confronted him. Assure the children that although sin is serious, God eagerly forgives those who repent.

Read the Scripture

Say, **Today's story is difficult because it teaches us that sin is very serious and brings destruction. Because God is holy, he does not tolerate sin. Sin results in punishment because it is willful disobedience to God. Sometimes one person's sin affects other people. Sin breaks our relationship with God, but there is hope. God always provides a way to restore our relationship with him. He eagerly forgives us when we repent.**

Read Joshua 7:1-26 aloud. You may choose to use the items and the motions to emphasize the main points.

Discussion questions

Discuss the story and ask the children the following questions. Remember that there might not be a right or wrong answer.

1. **When Achan stole the devoted things, he broke the Israelites' covenant with God. Why do you think Achan did this?**

2. **Joshua could not understand why they were defeated in the battle at Ai. What did Joshua expect to happen?**

3. **Read Joshua 7:6-9. Joshua worried about the future. What did he think might happen? If you were Joshua, would it be easy to trust the Lord again? Why?**

4. **If you were Achan, how difficult would it be to admit your sin? How do you think he felt?**

5. **If you were an Israelite, how would you have reacted to Achan and his sin?**

Final thoughts

This is the thought that you want the children to remember.

Say, **What does it mean, that God is unable to overlook sin? It is true that God is pure love. However, God does not ignore sin. When God's people sin, they betray and dishonor him. This is especially so if they deliberately disobey God. That is what Achan did.**

Do we have to be afraid that we might do something God will not forgive? The answer is both no and yes! Jesus died for every sin, and if we repent, God gladly forgives us. However, if we refuse to repent, God allows us to remain in our sin, and sin always brings destruction. We repent when we confess that we did something wrong, we are sorry, and we are determined to do what is right in the future.

Do not be like Achan. Try to honor God in everything that you do. If you sin, remember that although God does not ignore your sin, he promises to forgive you if you repent.

☑ MEMORY VERSE PRACTICE

See the "Memory Verse Activities" for suggestions to help the children learn the memory verse.

🧩 ADDITIONAL ACTIVITIES

Play a game or do an activity in the CBQM section that relates to this lesson (p. 103ff

⊗❓ PRACTICE FOR BIBLE QUIZ

Practice for Bible Quizzing with games and activities OR questions and answers.

BYE BYE, AI
Joshua 8:1-35

MEMORY VERSE

Be strong and very courageous. Be careful to obey all the law my servant Moses gave you; do not turn from it to the right or to the left, that you may be successful wherever you go.

Joshua 1:7

TRUTHS ABOUT GOD

This lesson will teach the following truths about God. The asterisk * indicates the primary truth that you should teach the children.

* God restores his people when they return to him.

• God wants his people to return to him.

• God is eager to restore those who return to him.

LESSON FOCUS AND SUMMARY

In this study, the children will learn that God's purpose for punishment was to transform and make Israel holy so that he would be able to enjoy a relationship with them. The same is true for us today.

1. After Israel punished Achan, God gave the Israelites a new plan to defeat Ai.

2. The Israelites obeyed God and completely defeated Ai.

3. After the battle, Joshua built an altar, and the Israelites worshiped God.

4. The Israelites renewed their covenant with God at Mount Ebal.

BIBLICAL BACKGROUND

Israel wrestled with a difficult thought … victory did not happen automatically. Their success depended upon Yahweh's leadership and Israel's relationship to him. Achan's sin violated the covenant. Unfaithfulness to the covenant was a sin that God would not tolerate. The consequence for sin was the same for the Israelites and the Canaanites alike. This was a very serious situation. Israel gave God a reason to destroy them. Instead, he offered a path to restoration.

Because God's nature is to love, he willingly forgives a sinner without holding a grudge. When Joshua displayed faithfulness and obedience, God responded with words of reassurance and encouragement. If someone broke the covenant agreement, the rules and the consequences remained uncompromised. However, that person was also able to repent and resume life with God.

Through Israel's experiences with Achan's punishment, the battle of Ai, and the renewal of the covenant, the people learned that a relationship with God was not primarily about the blessing of accumulated riches. God had a more important purpose when he rescued Israel and made a covenant with them. He wanted to transform their lives and make them holy. Then, he could enjoy a deeper relationship with them and all humanity. When the nation of Israel was unfaithful, God did not grant them victory. However, when Israel obeyed God, repented, and made restitution, God eagerly forgave them and welcomed them back into the covenant relationship.

📋 DID YOU KNOW?

At this time, the nation of Israel included other people who had joined them when they left Egypt and as they wandered in the wilderness. The Israelites knew them as foreigners, because they were originally from another country. Although they were not Israelites, Israel accepted them into the community and included them in God's covenant.

❓ VOCABULARY

Faith words

A covenant is an agreement between God and his people. Both God and his people make promises to each other. God's covenants offer us a relationship with God so that we experience his love and presence. We agree to live faithfully, in reverence and obedience, to him.

People

A fugitive is a person who runs away from danger or punishment.

A survivor is a person who lives through a terrible accident or a dangerous event. At Ai, there were no fugitives or survivors. The Israelites killed everyone.

Places

Mount Ebal was a mountain that was located near Ai. At this mountain, Joshua built an altar to the Lord and renewed the covenant.

Bethel was a city that was located northwest of Ai. During the battle, some of the Israelites waited between Bethel and Ai to ambush Ai.

Mount Gerizim was a mountain that was located near Mount Ebal. When a person spoke from this mountain or Mount Ebal, people in the valley below could hear them.

Terms

A javelin is a long thin piece of wood with a pointed end. In biblical times, a person used it as a weapon.

The Book of the Law includes the five books that Moses wrote. The Hebrews also called it the Pentateuch or the Torah.

A blessing is a statement that proclaims God's favour or goodness to those who obey him.

A curse is a statement or prayer that describes bad things that will happen to those who disobey God.

An ambush is a surprise attack from a hidden place.

A burnt offering is an offering that showed the Israelites' surrender and obedience to God.

A fellowship offering is an offering to thank God and celebrate his goodness.

📖 STORYTELLING

Each week you will need the following items.

1. A carrier like a small travel bag

2. A storage container for each week's story items (It can be a bag, basket, or box.)

For today's story, you will also need the following items.

3. A spear or a stick to represent a spear

4. A stone or several stones

5. Tablets to represent the copy of the law of Moses that Joshua wrote for the people

Before class

1. Read Joshua 8:1-35.

2. Gather today's story items. You may substitute a picture for any unavailable items.

3. Transfer all previous lesson items from the travel bag to the storage container. Place this container beside the storytelling area.

4. Place today's story items inside the travel bag. Place the travel bag in the storytelling area.

Optional activity: follow the leader or other activity.

Lesson review

Ask a volunteer to select an item from the storage container and explain what it represented in the previous lesson.

Story time

Read these instructions before you begin.

1. Focus on the main points as you tell the story in your own words. Remove an item from the bag as you illustrate each point. If you are comfortable, include more details. If needed, you may use the suggested script.

2. As you tell the story, display each item in order. Place the item where the children can see it.

3. After you tell the story, place all the items inside the bag again.

4. To review the story, ask a volunteer to remove an item from the bag and then tell what it represents. Repeat this process with all the items until the children are able to retell the story completely.

5. Review the "Memory motion" described below. Demonstrate this motion any time you mention what it represents.

Main points in order

Say, **Today we continue to explore the book of Joshua. Each week I pack our travel bag with** the tools that we need for our journey. Today we begin with...** Unpack as you tell the story.

1. Memory motion: Hide in ambush - Show the children how to crouch down and hide behind their hands. Or, invite the children to think of another motion. Say, **As I tell the story, do this motion when you hear what it represents.**
Say, **God gave Joshua a plan to defeat Ai. Some of the soldiers hid in ambush behind the city and they waited for Joshua's signal to attack.**

2. A spear or a stick that represents the spear. Say, **After the men of Ai ran out of the city to attack the Israelites, Joshua held out his spear toward the city. This was the signal that it was time to attack.**

3. A stone or stones - Say, **Because the Israelites completely obeyed God's plan, they defeated Ai. Then Joshua built an altar to the Lord. He followed all of Moses's instructions as he built it. Then the people worshipped the Lord and gave offerings at the altar.**

4. Tablets to represent the Law of Moses - Say, **All the people and the leaders gathered around the Ark of the Covenant as Joshua copied the law of Moses onto stones. Then Joshua read what he wrote to all the people.**

Say, **Now it is your turn to tell the story.** Return the items to the bag. Invite the children to take turns. Choose a volunteer to choose an item from the bag without looking and then explain what it represents. Or, they may choose to review one of the memory motions and explain what it represents. After the children remove all the items and explain them, ask a volunteer to place them in the correct story order.

✛ BIBLICAL LESSON

Tips for the teacher

Be prepared to lead the children in the prayer of salvation if you feel prompted by the Holy Spirit.

If needed, utilize the "Leading a child to Christ" resource.

As you lead the Bible study, emphasize these ideas.

- Explain why it was important for the covenant to be renewed. God's covenant did not change or expire. The Israelites needed to renew their commitment to fulfill their part of the covenant.

- Encourage the children to obey God in all things.

Read the Scripture

Before you tell the story say, **Israel began to understand that their victory depended on their faithfulness to God and their relationship with him. God restored the covenant because of their absolute obedience. Now he gave Joshua a new battle plan.**

Read Joshua 8:1-35 aloud. You may choose to use the items and the motions to emphasize the main points.

Discussion questions

Discuss the story and ask the children the following questions. Remember that there might not be a right or wrong answer.

1. **After Ai defeated Israel, how do you think Joshua felt about another battle against Ai?**

2. **What did the Lord say to comfort Joshua? Would those words help you to be brave? Why?**

3. **Why was it important for the Israelites to follow the Lord's instructions?**

4. **What does the Israelites' success in the battle tell you about the Lord?**

5. **Why do you think Joshua and the Israelites chose to renew their covenant with the Lord?**

Final thoughts

This is the thought that you want the children to remember.

Ask, **Why was it important for Israel to renew the covenant? Did it expire?** Allow time for discussion, but guide the conversation so that everyone understands that the renewal would help Israel.

When God revealed the Israelites' sin, they obeyed his directions completely. This demonstrated that they wanted to return to him. Joshua 8 tells what happened next. First, God spoke words of encouragement to Joshua. Next, he gave Joshua a new battle plan. Then, he gave the Israelites victory over Ai.

Did you notice what God did not do? God did not stay angry at the Israelites. He did not remind them of their sin and disobedience anymore. It was as though the sin had never happened.

That is how God responds when someone repents. God restores the once broken relationship. Have you disobeyed God? The Lord wants a relationship with you! First, confess what you did and tell God you are sorry. Ask the Lord to forgive you for your disobedience. Then decide to change the way that you think and act. Next, do it! Like the Israelites, you will experience the joy of a restored relationship with God!

If you feel prompted by the Holy Spirit, lead the children in a prayer for salvation. If needed, you may use the resource, "Leading a Child to Christ."

☑ MEMORY VERSE PRACTICE

See the "Memory Verse Activities" for suggestions to help the children learn the memory verse.

🧩 ADDITIONAL ACTIVITIES

Play a game or do an activity in the CBQM section that relates to this lesson (p. 103ff

❓ PRACTICE FOR BIBLE QUIZ

Practice for Bible Quizzing with games and activities OR questions and answers.

A TRICK AND A TREATY

Joshua 9:1—10:15

MEMORY VERSE

All the ways of the Lord are loving and faithful toward those who keep the demands of his covenant.

Psalm 25:10

TRUTHS ABOUT GOD

*This lesson will teach the following truths about God. The asterisk * indicates the primary truth that you should teach the children.*

* God honors us when we fulfill our promises.

• God wants us to ask him to give us wisdom and discernment before we make major decisions.

• God expects his people to do as they promise.

LESSON FOCUS AND SUMMARY

In this study, the children will learn that God keeps his promises and wants us to keep our promises. When we ask, God gives us wisdom and help.

1. The Gibeonites lied and coerced the Israelites to make a peace treaty.

2. The Gibeonites were able to deceive the Israelites because the Israelites did not consult God.

3. When the five kings attacked, the Israelites kept their promise to protect the Gibeonites.

4. God miraculously stopped the sun until the Israelites won the battle.

BIBLICAL BACKGROUND

Israel was "between a rock and a hard place." The Gibeonites, who lived in Canaan, lied and convinced the Israelites that they were from a distant land. They pleaded with Israel to agree to a peace treaty. The Israelites established the agreement because they believed the lie. However, Israel disobeyed God's command because they entered into a covenant with a group of Canaanites. Once a covenant was made in the name of Yahweh, it could not be broken without the consequence of divine wrath. The fact that Israel agreed to the covenant was bad. It was also bad for Israel to break the covenant. Both options were bad ones.

Joshua found a solution. He cursed the Gibeonites for their deception. He assigned them to a subservient role among Israel and in the worship of Yahweh. The Lord honored this decision and personally intervened in the fight to protect Gibeon from the Canaanite kings.

Joshua's solution reflects several important things. First, Israel must maintain God's reputation and his standard of faithfulness to a covenant agreement. Second, God told the Israelites to destroy the people of Canaan because of their wickedness. He wanted to protect Israel from this sinful influence. Gibeon's subservient role removed this threat and incorporated the Gibeonites into Israel. Third, God established a pattern to welcome foreigners who converted from their old beliefs and wished to join the covenant community of Israel. Fourth, when the Gibeonites lied, they sinned. However, the punishment for their sin worked to Gibeon's advantage.

👁️🗹 DID YOU KNOW?

It was a miracle when God stopped the sun, which allowed the Israelites to defeat their enemies. The Book of Jashar includes this story. This book, which no longer exists, was a collection of songs and poems that commemorated Israel's significant events. It also included David's funeral song for Saul and Jonathan (2 Samuel 1:17-27).

❓ VOCABULARY

Faith words

Faithful means a person is dependable and trustworthy. God is always faithful. We can trust him to fulfill his promises. God expects his people to be faithful to him and to others.

People

The Gibeonites were people who lived close to Jerusalem and were afraid of the God of Israel.

The Hivites were a people group who lived in Canaan.

Adoni-Zedek was the king of Jerusalem whose name meant "lord of righteousness."

The Amorites were a famous, wealthy, Canaanite tribe.

Places

Gibeon was an important city located north of Jerusalem.

The Valley of Aijalon was a place on a trade route where many battles took place.

Goshen was a town that was located south of Hebron.

Terms

A delegation is a smaller group of people that makes decisions for a larger group of people.

A peace treaty is a covenant that said one group would serve the other group rather than be killed.

The woodcutters and water carriers were servants.

Hailstones are lumpy ice balls of frozen rain that fall from the sky.

📖 STORYTELLING

Each week you will need the following items.

1. A carrier like a small travel bag

2. A storage container for each week's story items (It can be a bag, basket, or box.)

For today's story, you will also need the following items.

3. An old, broken and dirty sandal, or old, dirty and torn clothes, and a piece of old moldy bread or fruit

4. A crown

5. A piece of ice or an ice tray, or clear glass marbles to represent the hailstones

6. A flashlight or something that is bright yellow to represent the bright sun

Before class

1. Read Joshua 9:1-10:15.

2. Gather today's story items. You may substitute a picture for any unavailable items.

3. Transfer all previous lesson items from the travel bag to the storage container. Place this container beside the storytelling area.

4. Place today's story items inside the travel bag. Place the travel bag in the storytelling area.

Optional activity: follow the leader or other activity.

Lesson review

Ask a volunteer to select an item from the storage container and explain what it represented in the previous lesson.

Story time

Read these instructions before you begin.

1. Focus on the main points as you tell the story in your own words. Remove an item from the bag as you illustrate each point. If you are comfortable, include more details. If needed, you may use the suggested script.

2. As you tell the story, display each item in order. Place the item where the children can see it.

3. After you tell the story, place all the items inside the bag again.

4. To review the story, ask a volunteer to remove an item from the bag and then tell what it represents. Repeat this process with all the items until the children are able to retell the story completely.

5. Review the "Memory motion" described below. Demonstrate this motion any time you mention what it represents.

Main points in order

Say, **Today we continue to explore the book of Joshua. Each week I pack our travel bag with the tools that we need for our journey. Today we begin with...** Unpack the items as you tell the story.

1. Hold up the broken sandal, torn clothing, and moldy piece of food. Say, **Even though Gibeon was very close to the Israelites, the Gibeonites pretended that they had travelled many days from a distant land. They feared God and the Israelites. They did not want the Israelites to conquer them as they had conquered Jericho and Ai. Therefore, the Gibeonites deceived Israel. They compelled the Israelites to enter into a peace treaty so that the Gibeonites could avoid destruction.**

2. Memory motion: a handshake or an appropriate signal to make a promise or agreement with someone - Show the children how to turn to the person sitting next to him or her and shake hands. Or, invite the children to think of another appropriate motion. Say, **As I tell the story, do this motion when you hear what it represents. The Israelites were on God's mission. But, they did not consult him before they made an important decision. Instead, they believed the Gibeonites' lie and agreed to make a peace treaty with this group of Canaanites.**

3. A crown - Say, **Because they feared the Israelites, five kings in the area combined their armies to fight them. When the five kings attacked Gibeon, the Gibeonites sent a desperate message to Joshua. They needed him to defend them against the kings.**

4. The pieces of ice – Say, **Israel defeated the enemy armies, and as they began to flee from Israel, the Lord caused hailstones to fall from the sky. This killed many of the enemy.**

5. A flashlight or something bright yellow to represent the sun - Say, **When he was in the battle, Joshua asked the Lord to make the sun stand still. The sun did not go down for about a full day. This allowed Israel to defeat the enemy kings.**

Say, **Now it is your turn to tell the story.** Return the items to the bag. Invite the children to take turns. Choose a volunteer to choose an item from the bag without looking and then explain what it means/ represents. Or, they may choose to review one of the memory motions and explain what it represents. After the children remove all the items and explain them, ask a volunteer to place them in the correct story order.

BIBLICAL LESSON

Tips for the teacher

As you lead the Bible study, emphasize these ideas.

- It is important to fulfill an agreement or a promise, even when the circumstances are difficult. Explain that when they make promises, they should make room for an exception if someone is in danger, for example when someone faces harm, injury or abuse. In most situations, we should do what we agree to do.

- It was important for the Israelites to honor their promise. The Israelites represented God to the Canaanites, and their actions reflected on God's character.

- Remind the children that God always fulfills his promises, and so should we.

Read the Scripture

Say, **Today we are learning that it is important to obey God and to honor our promises.**

Read Joshua 9:1—10:15 aloud. You may choose to use the items and the motions to emphasize the main points.

Discussion questions

Discuss the story and ask the children the following questions. Remember that there might not be a right or wrong answer.

1. Read Joshua 9:14. **What did the Israelites fail to do? Why is this always important?**

2. **The Israelites did not attack the Gibeonites because of their treaty. How difficult do you think it was to fulfill that promise?**

3. **Suppose you were an Israelite soldier. What would you have thought when Joshua asked you to go into battle to protect the Gibeonites? How would you have felt?**

4. **What miracles did the Lord perform in Joshua 10?**

5. Read today's memory verse, Psalm 25:10. **What are some ways that the Lord shows love and faithfulness to you?**

Final thoughts

This is the thought that you want the children to remember.

Ask, **What happened when the Israelites forgot to consult with God before they made a treaty with the Gibeonites?** (They were deceived.) **What happened when the Israelites fulfilled their promise to protect the Gibeonites?** (The sun stood still to help them win the battle.)

The Israelites did not thoroughly consider the possible results of their decision. First, they made a peace treaty before they consulted with the Lord. Then they promised to help those tricky Gibeonites fight against the five Canaanite kings. Although the Israelites made a mistake, the Lord helped them.

God does not overlook sin because he is holy. But, he is full of love, grace and forgiveness. God wants us to fulfill our promises. Joshua honored his word to help the Gibeonites. When Joshua needed help, the Lord heard his prayer and honored Joshua because Joshua had fulfilled his promise. Proverbs 21:3 says, "To do what is right and just is more acceptable to the Lord than sacrifice." Remember to talk to God about your decisions. Honor God and fulfill your promise to do the right thing.

MEMORY VERSE PRACTICE

See the "Memory Verse Activities" for suggestions to help the children learn the memory verse.

ADDITIONAL ACTIVITIES

Play a game or do an activity in the CBQM section that relates to this lesson (p. 103ff

PRACTICE FOR BIBLE QUIZ

Practice for Bible Quizzing with games and activities OR questions and answers.

LAND AT LAST

Joshua 13:1-7; 14:1-15

MEMORY VERSE

And whatever you do, whether in word or deed, do it all in the name of the Lord Jesus, giving thanks to God the Father through him.

Colossians 3:17

TRUTHS ABOUT GOD

*This lesson will teach the following truths about God. The asterisk * indicates the primary truth that you should teach the children.*

* God blesses those who serve him wholeheartedly.

• God provides peace and rest for his people.

• God keeps his promises.

LESSON FOCUS AND SUMMARY

In this study, the children will learn that God keeps his promises and blesses those who serve him.

1. After many years of battle and conquest, Joshua divided the land of Canaan among the 12 tribes of Israel.

2. The tribes received land on both the east and the west sides of the Jordan River.

3. Caleb reminded Joshua that they were the faithful spies (Numbers 13:27-30). Following the promise of God, Joshua rewarded Caleb for his faithfulness by assigning him a special portion of the land.

4. The land and the people rested from war.

BIBLICAL BACKGROUND

The land of Canaan was firmly, although not completely, under the Israelites' control. Some Canaanites remained in the remote regions. Joshua's era of leadership was almost finished, for he was old and soon he would die. Yahweh comforted Joshua with a promise. After Joshua died, the Lord would continue to drive out the Canaanites, but Joshua needed to complete one final task. He needed to divide the land and give the rest of the tribes of Israel their inheritance.

Caleb reminded Joshua that Moses promised to give to Caleb a special portion of the land. When God sent him to investigate the land, Caleb was faithful. Now, forty-five years later, he would receive his reward, a prime area of the Promised Land. He did not hesitate to claim his territory, although the powerful Anakim people still occupied it. He believed the Lord would give him victory over them. Interestingly, the text skips Caleb's victorious battle with the Anakites and tells us that the land experienced rest from war. This intentionally emphasized the point that rest was the direct result of Caleb's wholehearted confidence in God and reliance on him.

Caleb's life was an example to all of Israel of what they could expect if they would only trust and obey God. All of Israel could experience the fullness of God's blessing if they continued to walk faithfully with him.

⊟ DID YOU KNOW?

Joshua and Caleb shared a special relationship. They were the only two people who were adults when Israel left Egypt and whom God allowed to settle in the Promised Land (Numbers 31:11). All those who settled in the Promised Land after the conquest were born within the 40 years that the Israelites wandered in the wilderness or afterwards.

⑦ VOCABULARY

Faith words

A conviction is a strong belief that guides a person's actions.

People

Caleb was one of the twelve spies from the Israelites' first spy mission into Canaan. He remained faithful to the Lord.

Anakites were the people from Anakim who survived a previous battle with the Israelites and moved into Hebron. The 12 Israelite spies reported them as unusually large people.

Places

Kadesh Barnea was an area located southwest of the Dead Sea. The Israelites camped there on their way to Canaan when Moses sent the twelve spies into Canaan to see what the land was like.

Hebron was a city that Caleb received as part of his inheritance. It is located west of the Dead Sea.

Terms

An inheritance is property or possessions that a person receives from a family member or friend. The Israelites received Canaan as their inheritance from God.

Allocate means to distribute intentionally among people. It was Joshua's job to allocate the land among the tribes.

⊞ STORYTELLING

Each week you will need the following items.

1. A carrier like a small travel bag

2. A storage container for each week's story items (It can be a bag, basket, or box.)

For today's story, you will also need the following items.

3. The map that was used previously

4. A pair of scissors

5. A scroll, a Bible or the tablets that were used previously

Before class

1. Read Joshua 13:1-7 and 14:1-15.

2. Gather today's story items. You may substitute a picture for any unavailable items.

3. Transfer all previous lesson items from the travel bag to the storage container. Place this container beside the storytelling area.

4. Place today's story items inside the travel bag. Place the travel bag in the storytelling area.

Optional activity: follow the leader

Tell the children to stand in a straight line, one behind the other. Choose a child to be the leader. Tell the children that they must watch the leader and mimic everything that he or she does. The leader leads the group around the room. He or she uses different hand gestures, sounds, or motions for the children to imitate. For example, the leader walks with baby steps, large steps, or skips. End the game at the storytelling area.

Lesson review

Ask a volunteer to select an item from the storage container and explain what it represented in the previous lesson.

Story time

Read these instructions before you begin.

1. Focus on the main points as you tell the story in your own words. Remove an item from the bag as you illustrate each point. If you are comfortable, include more details. If needed, you may use the suggested script.

2. As you tell the story, display each item in order. Place the item where the children can see it.

3. After you tell the story, place all the items inside the bag again.

4. To review the story, ask a volunteer to remove an item from the bag and then tell what it represents. Repeat this process with all the items until the children are able to retell the story completely.

5. Review the "Memory motion" described below. Demonstrate this motion any time you mention what it represents.

Main points in order

Say, **Today we continue to explore the book of Joshua. Each week I pack our travel bag with the tools that we need for our journey. Today we begin with...** Unpack the items as you tell the story.

1. Hold up the map. Say, **There was still land that the Israelites needed to conquer. The Lord told Joshua that he would drive the people out of the land. Then Joshua would be able to divide the land among the tribes of Israel.**

2. The pair of scissors - Say, **Joshua, the priests, and the heads of the tribes divided the land together. They followed the instructions God gave to Moses. The tribes that remained all received their inheritance. Before the** Israelites had crossed the river, Joshua had divided the land east of the Jordan.

3. The scroll or tablets - Say, **Many years earlier, Moses sent Caleb to explore the land of Canaan with 11 other spies. Because Caleb told the truth about the land, Moses promised to give him the land his feet walked on. Now Caleb reminded Joshua of his faithfulness and Joshua gave him the land of Hebron.**

4. Memory motion: Rest - Show the children how to place their palms together and to rest their cheek on the back of their hands. Or, invite the children to think of another appropriate motion. Say, **As I tell the story, do this motion when you hear what it represents. After Joshua divided the land among the tribes, the land experienced rest from war.**

Say, **Now it is your turn to tell the story.** Return the items to the bag. Invite the children to take turns. Choose a volunteer to choose an item from the bag without looking and then explain what it means/ represents. Or, they may choose to review one of the memory motions and explain what it represents. After the children remove all the items and explain them, ask a volunteer to place them in the correct story order.

BIBLICAL LESSON

Tips for the teacher

As you lead the Bible study, emphasize these ideas.

- Connect the idea of inheritance to modern life. Explain that people receive an inheritance from a family member. The Israelites were heirs because they were the family of Abraham and the family of God.

- The land was Israel's earthly inheritance. But, Israel also received a spiritual inheritance in which we are able to share when we live a life of faithfulness to God.

Read the Scripture

Say, **In today's scripture, we are finding out how the Israelite tribes received their inheritance in the Promised Land. We are also finding out who received a special inheritance and why.**

Read Joshua 13:1-7 and 14:1-15 aloud. You may choose to use the items and the motions to emphasize the main points.

Discussion questions

Discuss the story and ask the children the following questions. Remember that there might not be a right or wrong answer.

1. **How do you think the Israelites felt when Joshua and the other leaders began to give them their land?**

2. **Caleb waited 45 years for the land of Hebron as his inheritance. How do you think he felt? Do you think that he ever doubted that he would receive it?**

3. **Unusually large, strong, and fierce men populated the land Caleb received. Why did Caleb feel confident that he could drive out those people?**

4. **What are some ways you can follow the Lord wholeheartedly, like Caleb?**

5. **What do you think the people did when the land rested from war?**

Final thoughts

This is the thought that you want the children to remember.

Say, **Caleb followed the Lord with all his heart. He courageously gave a good report about the land he explored even when others did not. Caleb stepped forward and followed God without fear of the consequences. He did not care if he disagreed with the other men.**

God wants us to follow him wholeheartedly, and not feel afraid of what other people may think. He wants us to remember everything that he did for us and then to trust him when we face new experiences or difficulties.

Because Caleb followed the Lord, the Lord blessed him. When we serve the Lord, he blesses us. Sometimes that blessing is as simple as a sense of peace because we know he is near. At other times, he blesses us because he provides for our needs. What are some ways that God blesses you or has blessed you in the past?

MEMORY VERSE PRACTICE

See the "Memory Verse Activities" for suggestions to help the children learn the memory verse.

ADDITIONAL ACTIVITIES

Play a game or do an activity in the CBQM section that relates to this lesson (p. 103ff

PRACTICE FOR BIBLE QUIZ

Practice for Bible Quizzing with games and activities OR questions and answers.

EVERY PROMISE KEPT
Joshua 20:1-9; 21:1-8, 43-45

MEMORY VERSE

Not one of all the Lord's good promises to Israel failed; every one was fulfilled.

Joshua 21:45

TRUTHS ABOUT GOD

This lesson will teach the following truths about God. The asterisk * indicates the primary truth that you should teach the children.

* God fulfills his promises to his faithful people.

- God always fulfills his promises.

- God cares about justice and mercy.

LESSON FOCUS AND SUMMARY

In this study, the children will learn that God is faithful and loves us. When we sin, he looks at the intent of our hearts and provides both justice and mercy.

1. God established six cities of refuge to provide protection for people who unintentionally killed someone.

2. As the Lord commanded, the Israelites gave the Levites towns and pasturelands of their own.

3. God fulfilled his promise to give the Israelites the land of Canaan.

4. The tribes whose land was east of the Jordan returned to their homes.

BIBLICAL BACKGROUND

In this lesson, Joshua finishes his task of dividing the land among the tribes of Israel. We also learn about the cities of refuge, the Levites' inheritance, and the main point of the entire book.

The cities of refuge were safe zones for people who accidentally killed someone. Their function taught Israel that there were two elements to sin, the act and the intent. Killing an innocent person was an act of sin that required punishment. But, when there was no hate or harmful intent that motivated it, the action was an accident. This was not the same as murder. Intention was very important, and it meant the difference between life and death. Israel needed to learn to practice justice. This meant that they must look beyond the appearance of the facts and consider the heart and motivation of the person who committed the act.

Finally, the purpose of the book of Joshua is clear. The story of the conquest of Canaan is an encouragement for Israel to believe, trust, and obey God and rely wholeheartedly on him. If they did so and followed the covenant, they would continue to experience the blessings of rest and peace as they took possession of their full inheritance.

🔍 DID YOU KNOW?

The Levites did not receive large parcels of land. God wanted them dispersed throughout the Promised Land, to settle near each tribe so that they were able to assist in spiritual matters. Because of this, they received cities and pasturelands among all the other tribes. They would serve as spiritual leaders and teachers for all of Israel.

❓ VOCABULARY

Faith words

To promise means to honor your word that you will or will not do something. It means you do what you say you will do. God always does what he says he will do.

People

Eleazar was the high priest who served under Aaron. He also served Moses and Joshua.

The Kohathite, Gershonite, and Merarite clans were descendants of Jacob's son Levi. These Levite families received cities and pasturelands from Eleazar and Joshua (21:3-7).

Places

The cities of refuge were six cities that God set apart for the protection and safety of those who accidentally killed someone. There were three cities on each side of the Jordan River so that anyone from any tribe could get to one of the cities quickly.

Terms

A city gate was a place where the people held trials. The elders of the city gathered there to decide whether a criminal or a fugitive was guilty or not.

The avenger of blood was the closest family member to a person whom someone had killed. The avenger would try to kill their relative's killer in revenge.

📖 STORYTELLING

Each week you will need the following items.

1. A carrier like a small travel bag

2. A storage container for each week's story items (It can be a bag, basket, or box.)

For today's story, you will also need the following items.

3. The map that was previously used

4. A Bible or the tablets that were used previously

5. A pillow or blanket

Before class

1. Read Joshua 20:1-9; 21:1-8, 43-45.

2. Gather today's story items. You may substitute a picture for any unavailable items.

3. Transfer all previous lesson items from the travel bag to the storage container. Place this container beside the storytelling area.

4. Place today's story items inside the travel bag. Place the travel bag in the storytelling area.

Optional activity: follow the leader

Tell the children to stand in a straight line, one behind the other. Choose a child to be the leader. Tell the children that they must watch the leader and mimic everything that he or she does. The leader leads the group around the room. He or she uses different hand gestures, sounds, or motions for the children to imitate. For example, the leader walks with baby steps, large steps, or skips. End the game at the storytelling area.

Lesson review

Ask a volunteer to select an item from the storage container and explain what it represented in the previous lesson.

Story time

Read these instructions before you begin.

1. Focus on the main points as you tell the story in your own words. Remove an item from the bag as you illustrate each point. If you are comfortable, include more details. If needed, you may use the suggested script.

2. As you tell the story, display each item in order. Place the item where the children can see it.

3. After you tell the story, place all the items inside the bag again.

4. To review the story, ask a volunteer to remove an item from the bag and then tell what it represents. Repeat this process with all the items until the children are able to retell the story completely.

5. Review the "Memory motion" described below. Demonstrate this motion any time you mention what it represents.

Main points in order

Say, **Today we continue to explore the book of Joshua. Each week I pack our travel bag with the tools that we need for our journey. Today we begin with...** Unpack items as you tell the story.

1. Memory motion: Shield - Show the children how to close their fits and cross their arms in front of their chest to form a shield in the form of an "X" and not a cross. Or, invite the children to think of another motion. Say, **As I tell the story, do this motion when you hear what it represents. The Israelites set up six cities of refuge as places where those who unintentionally killed someone could go for safety. These cities protected and shielded that person from the revenge of an avenger of blood.**

2. A map - Say, **The Levites reminded Joshua, the priests, and the tribal leaders that the Lord commanded through Moses for the Israelites to provide for them. The Israelites gave cities and pasturelands of their own to the Levites. Each tribe gave from their inheritance.**

3. A Bible - Say, **This represents God's words to us. They are true because God is trustworthy. God fulfilled his promise to give the land of Canaan to the Israelites. The Lord also protected the Israelites from their enemies. God did not fail to carry out any of the promises that he made to Israel. He fulfilled every one.**

4. Pillow or blanket - Say, **The people settled in the land the Lord gave to them. They experienced rest from war and enjoyed peace on every side.**

Say, **Now it is your turn to tell the story.** Return the items to the bag. Invite the children to take turns. Choose a volunteer to choose an item from the bag without looking and then explain what it means/ represents. Or, they may choose to review one of the memory motions and explain what it represents. After the children remove all the items and explain them, ask a volunteer to place them in the correct story order.

BIBLICAL LESSON

Tips for the teacher

As you lead the Bible study, consider these ideas.

- Summarize Joshua 22:1-9 to give to your students some further background to this story. Explain that the Israelites fulfilled their obligations and were able to return and collect their lands.

- Explain to your students what the word "refuge" means, so that they can fully comprehend what a city of refuge was. When an Israelite fled to the city for protection, he would stand outside the city gate and plead his case. Then the city officials would give him a place to live.

- The Levites provided spiritual guidance for the nation of Israel. They lived throughout the land among all the tribes so that almost no one was farther than one day of travel from a Levitical city.

Read the Scripture

Say, **Today we are learning that God provided protection from injustice, especially in cases of revenge. As God had directed Moses, Joshua and the leaders designated cities of refuge to ensure fair treatment for those who killed someone accidentally. The Levites were the leaders of those cities. God provided for the Levites and gave them cities and pasturelands. God fulfilled his promises and proved that he was trustworthy and faithful to his people. The people would look back at this time in their history and be encouraged as they enjoyed the blessing of rest from the conquest of Canaan.**

Read Joshua 20:1-9; 21:1-8, 43-45 aloud. You may choose to use the items and the motions to emphasize the main points.

Discussion questions

Discuss the story and ask the children the following questions. Remember that there might not be a right or wrong answer.

1. **Why did God create the cities of refuge for the Israelites? In those cities, the avenger of blood could not exercise revenge for the** unintentional death of a family member. **Why? Do you think that was fair?**

2. **Why did the Israelite leaders designate the location of the cities of refuge where they did?**

3. **The Levites received their towns and pasturelands after the other Israelites received their inheritances. Do you think it was difficult for them to wait for their land? Why?**

4. Read Genesis 15:18-21 and Joshua 21:43-45. **What do these verses tell you about God?**

5. **The Lord did not fail to keep any of his promises to Israel. What are some promises that the Lord has given to you? Has he fulfilled them yet?**

Final thoughts

This is the thought that you want the children to remember.

Say, **Today we learned how God kept his promises to the Israelites. He had made some of the promises over 500 years earlier! He provided land for his people. In biblical times, land was one of the greatest gifts people could receive. He provided a place for them to live and rest.**

We can trust God to keep his promises to us. The Bible tells us about the promises God makes to his people. One promise is to provide for our needs (Philippians 4:19). **He also promised to forgive our sins if we confess them to him. You can trust God to keep all of his promises. He did not fail the Israelites and he will not fail you.**

MEMORY VERSE PRACTICE

See the "Memory Verse Activities" for suggestions to help the children learn the memory verse.

ADDITIONAL ACTIVITIES

Play a game or do an activity in the CBQM section that relates to this lesson (p. 103ff

PRACTICE FOR BIBLE QUIZ

Practice for Bible Quizzing with games and activities OR questions and answers.

JOSHUA SAYS FAREWELL

Joshua 23:1-16; 24:14-32

MEMORY VERSE

Now fear the Lord and serve him with all faithfulness.

Joshua 24:14a

TRUTHS ABOUT GOD

*This lesson will teach the following truths about God. The asterisk * indicates the primary truth that you should teach the children.*

* God calls his people to always remain faithful to him.

* God deserves respect, love, and worship.

* God wants people to choose to follow him.

LESSON FOCUS AND SUMMARY

In this study, the children will learn that God is faithful and expects his people to be faithful.

1. When Joshua was old, he summoned all of the people of Israel.

2. Joshua reminded the people of what God had done for them.

3. Joshua warned the people of what would happen if they did not obey God.

4. Joshua and the people renewed their commitment to only serve the Lord.

BIBLICAL BACKGROUND

In his farewell speech to the people of Israel, Joshua reminded them of the Lord's faithfulness and urged them to remain faithful to the Lord. The blessings that they enjoyed were the result of their covenantal relationship with him. If Israel treated God with the opposite of faithfulness, they could only expect the opposite of blessing.

Joshua reminded Israel of what God had done for them. In every way, God was worthy of their loyalty. God fought for them and helped them defeat their enemies. God brought them to Canaan and gave each tribe an inheritance in the land. God proved that he was trustworthy. He always wanted the best for them and he always guided them to be their best. They could expect more of the same if they remained faithful to the covenant.

God's command to worship only him was unusual. At that time, it was common to worship many gods. Many legal and cultural interactions with other nations involved the recognition and worship of their gods. Under no circumstances was this acceptable for Israel. The Lord is a jealous God, and though his love was unconditional, the covenant was not. The covenant was clear. Israel must obey it, or they would experience the negative consequences. God would never abandon Israel. Whether the Lord blessed or punished, his purpose was always to bring them back into a deeper relationship with himself. He knew they must live by the covenant to experience the fulfilment that only comes from a holy life with him.

🔍✓ DID YOU KNOW?

Joshua gave his speech at Shechem. It was a very important city in Israel's history. Both Abraham and Jacob built altars to the Lord there. Shechem symbolized a place of God's faithfulness.

❓ VOCABULARY

Faith words

To fear God means to have deep respect and reverence for God and a strong desire to not offend him.

Places

The River was another name for the Euphrates River. It was one of four rivers which flowed from the Garden of Eden.

The Euphrates formed the northern border of the land that God promised to Israel.

Terms

The gods your ancestors worshipped may have included the worship of Apis, the sacred bull of Egypt, and Nanna, the moon god of Ur.

📖 STORYTELLING

Each week you will need the following items.

1. A carrier like a small travel bag

2. A storage container for each week's story items (It can be a bag, basket, or box.)

For today's story, you will also need the following.

3. A map

4. The tablets or scroll from previous lessons

5. A stone

Before class

1. Read Joshua 23:1-16; 24:14-32.

2. Gather today's story items. You may substitute a picture for any unavailable items.

3. Transfer all previous lesson items from the travel bag to the storage container. Place this container beside the storytelling area.

4. Place today's story items inside the travel bag. Place the travel bag in the storytelling area.

Optional activity: follow the leader

Tell the children to stand in a straight line, one behind the other. Choose a child to be the leader. Tell the children that they must watch the leader and mimic everything that he or she does. The leader leads the group around the room. He or she uses different hand gestures, sounds, or motions for the children to imitate. For example, the leader walks with baby steps, large steps, or skips. End the game at the storytelling area.

Lesson review

Ask a volunteer to select an item from the storage container and explain what it represented in the previous lesson.

Story time

Read these instructions before you begin.

1. Focus on the main points as you tell the story in your own words. Remove an item from the bag as you illustrate each point. If you are comfortable, include more details. If needed, you may use the suggested script.

2. As you tell the story, display each item in order. Place the item where the children can see it.

3. After you tell the story, place all the items inside the bag again.

4. To review the story, ask a volunteer to remove an item from the bag and then tell what it represents. Repeat this process with all the items until the children are able to retell the story completely.

5. Review the "Memory motion" described below. Demonstrate this motion any time you mention what it represents.

Main points in order

Say, **Today, we finish the first book in our study, and end this portion of our expedition. So, I packed our travel bag with the tools that we will need to complete our journey with Joshua. Today we begin with...** Unpack the items as you tell the story.

1. Hold up the map and say, **Our map. Israel enjoyed rest from all their enemies, and Joshua grew old. He called the leaders and all the people together one last time. He reminded them that God had given them the entire land of Canaan. God continued to fulfill his promises. God had fought for them and had protected them, and he would continue to do so. God promised to drive out the nations who still lived in the land that he had promised as an inheritance.**

2. A scroll or the tablets - Say, **Joshua reminded the people that the Lord had made a covenant with them. God had promised to drive out the nations and give the Israelites their land. However, Israel had promised to obey all that was in the Book of the Law of Moses. The Lord gave them success because they obeyed God and worshipped him only. If Israel did not continue to fulfill their promise then their success would not continue.**

3. Memory motion: A house and worship one God - Show the children how to place their hands over their heads to represent a roof, and then point up with the index fingers of both hands. This represents that a person's household would worship the one true God. Or, invite the children to think of another appropriate motion. **As I tell the story, do this motion when you hear Joshua's words.** Say, **Joshua continued to caution the people about the temptation to worship other gods. He reminded them again that the Lord had proved to be trustworthy because of all he had done for them. He told them to throw away the gods that their ancestors had worshipped and that their fathers had worshipped in Egypt. But he knew that the people must decide for themselves who they would serve. Joshua said, "As for me and my house, we will serve the Lord."**

4. A stone - Say, **The people renewed the covenant to always serve God and to worship him only. Joshua wrote the people's covenant in the book of the Law. Then he set up a large stone to remind all the people of their promise to love, obey, and worship God only.**

Say, **Now it is your turn to tell the story.** Return the items to the bag. Invite the children to take turns. Choose a volunteer to choose an item from the bag without looking and then explain what it means/ represents. Or, they may choose to review one of the memory motions and explain what it represents. After the children remove all the items and explain them, ask a volunteer to place them in the correct story order.

BIBLICAL LESSON

Tips for the teacher

As you lead the Bible study, emphasize these ideas.

-   If you have time, highlight the importance of Shechem in Israel's history. Abraham came to Shechem on his journey into Canaan. God promised Abraham that he would give that land to his descendants. Abraham built an altar there. Jacob, Abraham's grandson, also built an altar there. Jews believed that Jacob dug a well there, called Jacob's Well. When the Israelites conquered Canaan, Joshua built an altar and held a covenant renewal ceremony at Shechem (Joshua 8:30-35).

At the end of his life, Joshua held another covenant renewal ceremony at Shechem. In addition, Joseph's bones were buried in Shechem. Jesus visited Jacob's Well in Shechem and ministered to the Samaritan woman there (John 4).

Read the Scripture

Say, **As we say farewell to Joshua, he reminds the people of all the mighty things that the Lord had done for them. He warns them to obey the Law of Moses or they would experience God's wrath. He emphasizes that they should not worship the other gods in the land of Canaan. He challenges the people and says, "But if serving the LORD seems undesirable to you, then choose for yourselves this day whom you will serve. But as for me and my household, we will serve the LORD." We will see how the people responded.**

Read Joshua 23:1-16 and 24:14-32 aloud. You may choose to use the items and the motions to emphasize the main points.

Discussion questions

Discuss the story and ask the children the following questions. Remember that there might not be a right or wrong answer.

1. **Joshua reminded the Israelites of God's faithfulness to them. What events do you think the people remembered?**

2. **Why do you think God did not want the Israelites to associate with the other nations?**

3. **What challenges might the Israelites experience as they try not to associate with other nations in Canaan?**

4. **Joshua set up a large stone as a symbol of the people's covenant. How do you think this reminder helped them?**

5. **What are some ways to show that you love God?**

Final thoughts

This is the thought that you want the children to remember.

Say, **God showed kindness to his people in a time of trouble.**

God did not want the Israelites to associate with other nations. Were God's actions mean or unfair? Those wicked nations worshipped other gods. If the Israelites associated with them, they might marry them and begin to follow their customs and wicked practices. They might begin to worship the Canaanite idol gods. God's covenant gave the people guidelines so that they would obey and worship the Lord alone. Then they would become a holy people that God would use to influence the world. God knew how hard it would be for the Israelites to follow him while surrounded by those temptations. He put those boundaries in place to help them, so they would always remain faithful to him. He wants us to remain faithful too!

✓ MEMORY VERSE PRACTICE

See the "Memory Verse Activities" for suggestions to help the children learn the memory verse.

ADDITIONAL ACTIVITIES

Play a game or do an activity in the CBQM section that relates to this lesson (p. 103ff

PRACTICE FOR BIBLE QUIZ

Practice for Bible Quizzing with games and activities OR questions and answers.

DISOBEDIENCE AND DISASTER

Judges 2:1-23

MEMORY VERSE

Lord our God, you answered them; you were to Israel a forgiving God, though you punished their misdeeds.

Psalm 99:8

TRUTHS ABOUT GOD

*This lesson will teach the following truths about God. The asterisk * indicates the primary truth that you should teach the children.*

* God is both just and merciful to those who disobey him.

* God does not force obedience but he allows consequences of sin.

* God is faithful and merciful to provide help when we ask.

LESSON FOCUS AND SUMMARY

In this study, the children will learn that God will not force us to obey him. Yet, there are consequences for sin. God is merciful and will always provide help when we turn to him and obey.

1. The Israelites disobeyed God when they did not drive out all the people of Canaan.

2. After Joshua and his generation died, the people began to worship idols.

3. When the people disobeyed him, God allowed their enemies to defeat and oppress them.

4. When the Israelites cried out for help, God gave them a judge who helped them defeat their enemies and brought them back to obedience. After the judge died, Israel disobeyed again and experienced the consequences again. This cycle repeats itself in the book of Judges.

BIBLICAL BACKGROUND

After Joshua died, God's people began the process of making the Promised Land (Canaan) their permanent home. For about 200 years, they struggled to establish themselves. The current residents, the Canaanites, dominated the land with their religious beliefs and practices. During this period, there was no national leader to unite the tribes of Israel or to remind them of their promise to follow God. Without a leader like Joshua to keep them focused on God, the Israelites struggled to fulfill their covenant promises. The Book of Judges tells us how difficult it was.

In chapter two, a new generation of Israelites, who did not know the Lord nor what he had done for Israel, grew up. They worshipped other gods. They served the "Baals" and "Ashtoreths," the gods and goddesses of the Canaanites. They broke their covenant with the Lord. It is hard to understand why they would forsake God after all that he had done for them.

We should be careful before we judge the Israelites too harshly. There is more than one way to forsake God. It is idolatry to treasure anything or anybody above God. We can forsake God through busyness if we are too busy to pray, to read God's Word, or to worship him. It could be that we do not notice other people in need because we are too distracted by things we want. One of the reasons we study the Bible is because it reminds us to keep our promises to God.

DID YOU KNOW?

• Bochim is a place that the Bible mentions only once. It is located near Bethel. Bochim means "weepers." Even though the people of Israel wept, they soon forgot about the angel's warning. Some people think that Bochim does not appear elsewhere because the people forgot about the warning and their tears.

• The Israelites built houses that had a room for their animals.

VOCABULARY

Faith words

To show mercy means to cancel or reduce a righteous punishment, or to forgive. When God shows us mercy, he does not treat us in the way that we deserve.

People

A judge was a person chosen by God to lead the Israelites to obey God and rescue them from their enemies.

An angel of the Lord was a messenger sent by God.

Terms

The ancestors were a person's grandparents, great-grandparents, and other past family members.

Baals were Canaanite gods that the people believed controlled the weather and increased the abundance of crops and the productivity of livestock.

The plunder was money or possessions that victorious soldiers took from their defeated enemies.

A thorn in someone's side is a phrase that describes a source of constant suffering. It describes the nations that God allowed to defeat the Israelites repeatedly because of their cycle of disobedience.

STORYTELLING

Each week you will need the following items.

1. A carrier like a small travel bag

2. A storage container for each week's story items (It can be a bag, basket, or box.)

For today's story, you will also need the following items.

3. The Ten Commandment tablets or a scroll

4. A tissue or handkerchief

5. A sword

Before class

1. Read Judges 2:1-23.

2. Gather today's story items. You may substitute a picture for any unavailable items.

3. Transfer all previous lesson items from the travel bag to the storage container. Place this container beside the storytelling area.

4. Place today's story items inside the travel bag. Place the travel bag in the storytelling area.

Optional activity: follow the leader

Tell the children to stand in a straight line, one behind the other. Choose a child to be the leader. Tell the children that they must watch the leader and mimic everything that he or she does. The leader leads the group around the room. He or she uses different hand gestures, sounds, or motions for the children to imitate. For example, the leader walks with baby steps, large steps, or skips. End the game at the storytelling area.

Lesson review

Ask a volunteer to select an item from the storage container and explain what it represented in the previous lesson.

Story time

Read these instructions before you begin.

1. Focus on the main points as you tell the story in your own words. Remove an item from the bag as you illustrate each point. If you are comfortable, include more details. If needed, you may use the suggested script.

2. As you tell the story, display each item in order. Place the item where the children can see it.

3. After you tell the story, place all the items inside the bag again.

4. To review the story, ask a volunteer to remove an item from the bag and then tell what it represents. Repeat this process with all the items until the children are able to retell the story completely.

5. Review the "Memory motion" described below. Demonstrate this motion any time you mention what it represents.

Main points in order

Say, **Today we begin to explore the book of Judges. Each week I pack our travel bag with the tools that we need for our journey. Today we begin with...** Unpack as you tell the story.

1. Hold up the tablets. Say, **The Israelites did not obey God and drive out the people of Canaan or tear down their altars. Instead, they began to worship the idols of the Canaanites. They did not keep their covenant promise. The Lord said, "You have disobeyed me. Why have you done this?" The Lord told them that because they disobeyed, his covenant was no longer in effect. He would no longer protect them from the people of the land. The people of Canaan and their idols would become a trap to the Israelites.**

2. A tissue or a handkerchief - Say, **When the angel of the Lord delivered this message, the people wept and gave offerings to God. As long as Joshua lived, the people obeyed God. After Joshua and that generation died, the next generation of Israelites worshipped the Canaanite idol gods, Baal and Ashtoreth.**

3. A sword – Say, **Because they were disobedient, God allowed the Israelites' enemies to defeat them when they went to battle.**

4. A tissue or a handkerchief - Say, **When the Israelites were defeated, the Canaanite rulers would oppress them. Then, the people would cry to the Lord for help.**

5. Tablets and sword – Say, **The Lord heard the people's cries and felt compassion for them. He sent leaders, called judges, to lead the people. The judges helped the Israelites obey the Lord and keep their covenant. The judge also helped them defeat their enemies.** Hold up the tablet and the sword together. **But when the judge died, the people returned to their evil ways.** Put down the tablet and the sword.

6. A sword – Say, **When the people rebelled, the Lord removed his protection and allowed their enemies to defeat them.**

7. A tissue or a handkerchief - Say, **When their enemies oppressed them, the people cried out to the Lord again, until God raised up a new judge.**

8. Memory motion: Stubborn disobedience - Show the children how to place their palm in front of them (or other appropriate gesture) as if to Say, "Stop!" Then tell the children to cover their ears and to turn around. Or, invite the children to think of another appropriate motion. Say, **As I tell the story, do this motion when you hear what it represents.** Say, **This action represents that the Israelites did not listen to God. Instead, they did what they wanted to do and turned away from him.**

Say, **Now it is your turn to tell the story.** Return the items to the bag. Invite the children to take turns. Choose a volunteer to choose an item from the bag without looking and then explain what it means/ represents. Or, they may choose to review one of the memory motions and explain what it represents. After the children remove all the items and explain them, ask a volunteer to place them in the correct story order.

BIBLICAL LESSON

Tips for the teacher

As you lead the Bible study, emphasize these ideas.

- Explain how the Israelite judges differed from today's judges.
- Explain that God sent judges to Israel as a gift of mercy and grace, not as a punishment.

Read the Scripture

Say, **After Joshua's death, the Israelites ignored the covenant and God withdrew his promise to help them in battle. But, God did not abandon his people. He sent them judges to remind them of their covenant and to lead them in battle. The people obeyed until the judge died.**

Read Judges 2:1-23 aloud. You may choose to use the items and the motions to emphasize the main points.

Discussion questions

Discuss the story and ask the children the following questions. Remember that there might not be a right or wrong answer.

1. **Who broke their covenant with God? What were the consequences?**

2. **Do you think the Israelites were truly sorrowful and repentant, or were they just upset because they were punished?**

3. **What happened when the Israelites forgot who God was and what God had done?**

4. **How did God show mercy to the Israelites?**

5. **The Israelites worshipped false gods instead of the one true God. What are some "false gods" people worship today?**

Final thoughts

This is the thought that you want the children to remember.

Say, **We see a pattern in Judges: The Israelites disobeyed God and experienced bad consequences. Then they cried out to God. He rescued them and sent them a judge. They repented and obeyed until the judge died. Then the cycle repeated again. No matter how often God showed mercy and helped them, the Israelites returned to worshipping other idol gods.**

But, even when they forgot about God entirely, God still wanted them to return to him. God allowed nations to defeat Israel to show the Israelites how lost they were without him. That is why God gave them judges. He did not want them to continue suffering. He wanted to guide them back to him.

God loves you too! His greatest desire is for you to love and obey him. Learn from the mistakes of the Israelites and stay true to God!

MEMORY VERSE PRACTICE

See the "Memory Verse Activities" for suggestions to help the children learn the memory verse.

ADDITIONAL ACTIVITIES

Play a game or do an activity in the CBQM section that relates to this lesson (p. 103ff

PRACTICE FOR BIBLE QUIZ

Practice for Bible Quizzing with games and activities OR questions and answers.

THE BEE AND THE THUNDERBOLT

Judges 4:1-24

MEMORY VERSE

I know that you can do all things; no purpose of yours can be thwarted.

Job 42:2

TRUTHS ABOUT GOD

This lesson will teach the following truths about God. The asterisk * indicates the primary truth that you should teach the children.

*   God makes things possible when they seem completely impossible.

•   God is greater than anyone can imagine.

•   God sometimes uses unlikely people to accomplish his will.

LESSON FOCUS AND SUMMARY

In this study, the children will learn that God sometimes demonstrates his power and strength through faithful people who may seem weak and powerless.

1. The Israelites cried to the Lord for help after 20 years of cruel oppression under Jabin, the Canaanite king.

2. Deborah was a prophet and Israel's judge.

3. Through Deborah, God commanded Barak to fight Sisera's army, which included 900 iron chariots.

4. Barak insisted that Deborah go with him into the battle.

5. The Israelites defeated a much stronger enemy through the power of God.

BIBLICAL BACKGROUND

Judges 4 continues the tragic, familiar theme: Israel forgets God; Israel sins against God; God allows a wicked enemy to conquer and oppress Israel. When the Israelites cry out for help, God instructs Israel's judge to rescue them.

The judges were often ordinary people empowered by God to do extraordinary things. The book of Judges reveals that God often demonstrates his strength through the weak and powerless.

In today's lesson, Israel disobeyed again, and God allowed Jabin, a Canaanite king, to defeat the Israelites. For twenty years, Jabin cruelly oppressed them. The people sought God's help, and God called on Deborah, the fourth judge of Israel. Deborah was a prophet and Israel's only female judge. The people trusted her to settle their disputes, and now they needed a strong leader to seek God's help.

Deborah sent for Barak and told him that the Lord would deliver king Jabin's general, Sisera, and his entire army into Barak's hands. But, Barak refused to fight unless Deborah agreed to go with him. Deborah agreed, but said that because of his lack of faith, the Lord would deliver Sisera into a woman's hands, not his. Barak was victorious and Sisera fled. A woman named Jael killed Sisera in his sleep and received the honor of the victory.

Once more, God used the powerless to turn an impossible situation into a glorious display of his power.

🔍 DID YOU KNOW?

Several names in this lesson mean something special.

• Deborah's name means "bee." Bees are small insects, but Deborah the "bee" had stronger faith than Barak.

• Barak's name means "thunderbolt." A thunderbolt is powerful, but sadly, Barak's trust in God was weak.

• Jael's name meant "mountain goat." The milk she gave Sisera was probably goat's milk.

❓ VOCABULARY

Faith words

God's power is a phrase that means the power of God is greater and stronger than anyone or anything. God can do all things.

People

Jabin was a Canaanite king.

Sisera was the commander of Jabin's army.

Deborah was a prophet and Israel's fourth judge. She called Israel to battle the Canaanites. Her name means "bee."

Barak was the commander of the Israelite army. His name means "thunderbolt."

Jael was the wife of Heber the Kenite. The Kenites were allies with King Jabin. Jael urged Sisera to rest in her family's tent, and then she killed him in his sleep. Sisera's death guaranteed Jabin's downfall.

Places

The Palm of Deborah was the place where Deborah held court. It was located in the hill country of Ephraim.

Naphtali was an area that belonged to the tribe of Naphtali. It was located northwest of the Sea of Galilee. The Canaanites were strong in this area.

Zebulun was the area that belonged to the tribe of Zebulun. It was located close to Naphtali.

Mount Tabor was a mountain that was almost 400 meters tall. It was located southwest of the Sea of Galilee.

Terms

A prophet is one who receives God's messages and shares them with others.

To hold court means to be in charge of a court when it carries out its tasks. When Deborah held court, people brought their disputes to her for resolution.

To honor someone means to show respect and acknowledge his or her greatness. To be honored and respected was very important to people in ancient cultures.

📖 STORYTELLING

Each week you will need the following items.

1. A carrier like a small travel bag

2. A storage container for each week's story items (It can be a bag, basket, or box.)

For today's story, you will also need the following.

3. A tissue or handkerchief

4. A palm or tree branch

5. A sword

Before class

1. Read Judges 4:1-24.

2. Gather today's story items. You may substitute a picture for any unavailable items.

3. Transfer all previous lesson items from the travel bag to the storage container. Place this container beside the storytelling area.

4. Place today's story items inside the travel bag. Place the travel bag in the storytelling area.

Optional activity: follow the leader

Tell the children to stand in a straight line, one behind the other. Choose a child to be the leader. Tell the children that they must watch the leader and mimic everything that he or she does. The leader leads the group around the room. He or she uses different hand gestures, sounds, or motions for the children to imitate. For example, the leader walks with baby steps, large steps, or skips. End the game at the storytelling area.

Lesson review

Ask a volunteer to select an item from the storage container and explain what it represented in the previous lesson.

Story time

Read these instructions before you begin.

1. Focus on the main points as you tell the story in your own words. Remove an item from the bag as you illustrate each point. If you are comfortable, include more details. If needed, you may use the suggested script.

2. As you tell the story, display each item in order. Place the item where the children can see it.

3. After you tell the story, place all the items inside the bag again.

4. To review the story, ask a volunteer to remove an item from the bag and then tell what it represents. Repeat this process with all the items until the children are able to retell the story completely.

5. Review the "Memory motion" described below. Demonstrate this motion any time you mention what it represents.

Main points in order

Say, **Today we continue to explore the book of Judges. Each week I pack our travel bag with the tools that we need for our journey. Today we begin with...** Unpack items as you tell the story.

1. Hold up the tissue or handkerchief. Say, **The Canaanite king Jabin treated the Israelites badly for twenty years. So, the Israelites cried out to the Lord for help.**

2. A palm or tree branch - Say, **God called a woman named Deborah to be the judge and leader of the Israelites. Deborah sat under a palm tree and gave wise advice, and the people listened to her. She heard their cries to God for help.**

3. A sword – Say, **Deborah sent for a strong soldier named Barak. She gave Barak a message from the Lord. Barak would lead an army to defeat King Jabin's commander, Sisera, who had 900 chariots.**

4. Memory motion: Muscle flex – as appropriate show the children how to clinch their fists and raise their arms as they flex their arm muscles. Invite the girls to stand first and flex their muscles. Then ask the boys to join them and flex their muscles. Or, invite the children to think of another appropriate motion. Say, **As I tell the story, do this motion when you hear what it represents.**

Say, **Barak told Deborah that he would go if she went with him. Deborah agreed but told Barak that a woman would receive the honor for the victory. A woman named Jael killed Sisera, king Jabin's commander. The Lord helped Israel's weak army defeat Jabin's strong army.**

Say, **Now it is your turn to tell the story.** Return the items to the bag. Invite the children to take turns. Choose a volunteer to choose an item from the bag without looking and then explain what it represents. Or, they may choose to review one of the memory motions and explain what it represents. After the children remove all the items and explain them, ask a volunteer to place them in the correct story order.

BIBLICAL LESSON

Tips for the teacher

As you lead the Bible study, emphasize these ideas.

- Contrast the power of Jabin's army with the power of Israel's army. Emphasize that God's power made the difference.

- Consider how many times you see something that is unexpected in our story. Challenge the children to notice each time this happens. Help the children see that God does the unexpected to accomplish the impossible.

- Barak refused to go unless Deborah went with him. Perhaps Barak felt that the army would only follow him if they saw Deborah lead them. This shows how much the people trusted and respected Deborah.

Read the Scripture

Say, **Today's Bible story includes some unusual things. God does not always make things happen in the way we expect. He is greater than anything we are able to imagine. He makes the impossible possible!**

Read Judges 4:1-24 aloud. You may choose to use the items and the motions to emphasize the main points.

Discussion questions

Discuss the story and ask the children the following questions. Remember that there might not be a right or wrong answer.

1. **Why did the Israelites cry out to God for help? Did they deserve God's help?**

2. **A soldier's honor was very important to him. What is honor? How can someone gain or lose it?**

3. **Barak was afraid to fight Sisera's army because it was much more powerful than Israel's army. What should Barak have remembered to help him be brave?**

4. **Do you think what Jael did to Sisera was wrong? Why?**

5. **How do you think the story would have ended if Barak had trusted God from the start?**

Final thoughts

This is what you want the children to remember.

Say, **Several names mean something special in this story.**

Deborah's name means "bee." Bees are small insects, but Deborah the "bee" had stronger faith than Barak. Barak's name means "thunderbolt." A thunderbolt is powerful, but sadly, Barak's trust in God was not very strong. The bee was stronger than the thunderbolt.

Were you ever in a situation that seemed impossible? From a human viewpoint, Sisera's army was too strong for the Israelites to defeat because Israel had no iron chariots. How could they possibly win against an army with 900 iron chariots? Yet God told Deborah that Barak would win. When Deborah and Barak trusted and obeyed God, he did something greater than the Israelites imagined. Not only was Sisera defeated, not a single enemy soldier escaped to fight Israel again! If God destroyed a powerful army, think about what he is able to do when your situation seems impossible. Trust him to guide you because our God makes the impossible possible!

MEMORY VERSE PRACTICE

See the "Memory Verse Activities" for suggestions to help the children learn the memory verse.

ADDITIONAL ACTIVITIES

Play a game or do an activity in the CBQM section that relates to this lesson (p. 103ff

PRACTICE FOR BIBLE QUIZ

Practice for Bible Quizzing with games and activities OR questions and answers.

GET A GRIP, GIDEON!

Judges 6:1-40

MEMORY VERSE

The Lord your God is with you, the Mighty Warrior who saves. He will take great delight in you; in his love he will no longer rebuke you, but will rejoice over you with singing.

Zephaniah 3:17

TRUTHS ABOUT GOD

*This lesson will teach the following truths about God. The asterisk * indicates the primary truth that you should teach the children.*

* God often works through our weaknesses.

- God's power is greater than human weakness.

- God is patient with people.

LESSON FOCUS AND SUMMARY

In this study, the children will learn that God helps us to do anything he asks us to do, even when it seems impossible to us.

1. God allowed the Midianites to harass the Israelites for seven years because the Israelites disobeyed him.

2. God sent an angel to Gideon. The angel told Gideon to save Israel, but Gideon did not think he was able to do it.

3. Gideon did as the Lord commanded and tore down Baal's altar and the Asherah pole.

4. Gideon tested God with the wool fleece.

BIBLICAL BACKGROUND

The cycle continued. Israel's disobedience led to defeat. The Midianites cruelly oppressed Israel for seven years. They taunted the Israelites, burned their crops, and stole their cattle. The Israelites cried out again to God for help, so God raised up a judge named Gideon to deliver his people. Gideon's story is another example of God's love and patience with his people, despite their repeated disobedience.

Like many people God calls, Gideon felt inadequate. He made excuses and gave many reasons why he could not do what God asked of him. Gideon believed that he was not important enough to lead Israel. God told Gideon, "You can do it, because I will help you" (6:16). This episode in Israel's history repeats a familiar pattern and promise in the Bible. God will help us accomplish whatever he asks us to do.

Like Gideon, many of God's people want to make a difference, but they feel inadequate. God says, "You can do it because I will help you!" This is an important truth about whom God calls and how he works. When we trust and obey God, he makes the impossible possible!

DID YOU KNOW?

This is the first Bible story to talk about camels as war animals (Judges 6:5).

? VOCABULARY

Faith words

To trust God means to believe that God is always good, always dependable, and he always fulfills his promises.

People

The Midianites lived in Midian, which was located east of the Jordan River. Even though they were also descendants of Abraham, the Midianites were enemies of Israel.

Gideon was the judge that God called to save the Israelites from the Midianites. His name means, "One who cuts down the enemy."

Joash was Gideon's father. He had an altar to Baal and an Asherah pole. Those symbols indicate that he worshipped other gods.

Places

Manasseh was the name of land that was located on both sides of the Jordan River. It was given to the tribe of Manasseh.

Ophrah was a city that was located southwest of the Sea of Galilee. An angel of the Lord visited Gideon under an oak tree in Ophrah.

Terms

A mountain cleft is a small gap or crevice in the mountain. The Israelites built shelters in mountain clefts to hide from the Midianites.

A winepress was a large stone enclosure where the people squeezed grapes and turned them into juice and wine.

An Asherah pole was a large pole to honor the Canaanite goddess Asherah.

A fleece was a sheep's hide with wool on 1 side.

STORYTELLING

Each week you will need the following items.

1. A carrier like a small travel bag

2. A storage container for each week's story items (It can be a bag, basket, or box.)

For today's story, you will also need the following items.

3. A scrap of food – a piece of bread, a vegetable or a piece of fruit.

4. A tissue or handkerchief

5. A rock

6. A small rug, cloth, or towel

Before class

1. Read Joshua 6:1-40.

2. Gather today's story items. You may substitute a picture for any unavailable items.

3. Transfer all previous lesson items from the travel bag to the storage container. Place this container beside the storytelling area.

4. Place today's story items inside the travel bag. Place the travel bag in the storytelling area.

Optional activity: follow the leader

Tell the children to stand in a straight line, one behind the other. Choose a child to be the leader. Tell the children that they must watch the leader and mimic everything that he or she does. The leader leads the group around the room. He or she uses different hand gestures, sounds, or motions for the children to imitate. For example, the leader walks with baby steps, large steps, or skips. End the game at the storytelling area.

Lesson review

Ask a volunteer to select an item from the storage container and explain what it represented in the previous lesson.

Story time

Read these instructions before you begin.

1. Focus on the main points as you tell the story in your own words. Remove an item from the bag as you illustrate each point. If you are comfortable, include more details. If needed, you may use the suggested script.

2. As you tell the story, display each item in order. Place the item where the children can see it.

3. After you tell the story, place all the items inside the bag again.

4. To review the story, ask a volunteer to remove an item from the bag and then tell what it represents. Repeat this process with all the items until the children are able to retell the story completely.

5. Review the "Memory motion" described below. Demonstrate this motion any time you mention what it represents.

Main points in order

Say, **Today we continue to explore the book of Judges. Each week I pack our travel bag with the tools that we need for our journey. Today we begin with...** Unpack items as you tell the story.

1. Hold up the scrap of food, bread, vegetable, or fruit. Say, **When the Israelites planted crops, the Midianites would steal or destroy them. God allowed the Midianites to bully Israel because the Israelites had disobeyed him.**

2. A tissue or handkerchief - Say, **Because of the Midianite raids on their crops, the Israelites became poor and hungry, so they cried out to the Lord for help.**

3. Memory motion: Crouch and hide - Show to the children how to pretend as though they were hiding behind something. Demonstrate a crouched position and place your hands in front of your face to hide it. Or, invite the children to think of another motion. Say, **As I tell the story, do this motion when you hear what it represents. "An angel of the Lord came to see Gideon when he hid in the winepress to thresh his wheat. He did not want the Midianites to find him or his grain."**

4. A rock - Say, **The angel of the Lord told Gideon to save Israel, but Gideon did not believe that he was able to do it. The Lord commanded Gideon to tear down his father's altars to Baal. Gideon obeyed and then he built a new altar to the Lord.**

5. A small rug, cloth, or towel – Say, **Gideon was not sure if the Lord would help him, so he tested God twice. The first time, he laid a fleece on the ground and asked the Lord to cover it with dew but keep the ground dry. The second time, Gideon asked God to cover the ground with dew but keep the fleece dry. Both times, God granted Gideon's request.**

Say, **Now it is your turn to tell the story.** Return the items to the bag. Invite the children to take turns. Choose a volunteer to choose an item from the bag without looking and then explain what it represents. Or, they may choose to review one of the memory motions and explain what it represents. After the children remove all the items and explain them, ask a volunteer to place them in the correct story order.

BIBLICAL LESSON

Tips for the teacher

As you lead the Bible study, emphasize these ideas.

- Help the students understand that God often calls weak people to do mighty things. That makes it clear to everyone that God is the source of his or her abilities.

- Why was Gideon afraid? The Israelites believed that no one could see God and live. (See Exodus 33:20.) Gideon probably thought that this also applied to God's angels.

- After Gideon saw the first miracle of the wet fleece, he asked for a second miracle. Perhaps he thought the results of the first miracle could have happened naturally. A thick fleece could retain moisture long after the sun dried the ground that surrounded it. This is a poor way to make a decision. Today we have the Bible to guide us when we hear God's call.

Read the Scripture

Say, **When Moses and the Israelites wandered in the wilderness, they battled the Midianites and nearly destroyed them. But many years later, the Midianites regained their strength and began to oppress Israel.**

Read Judges 6:1-40 aloud. You may choose to use items and motions to emphasize the main points.

Discussion questions

Discuss the story and ask the children the following questions. Remember that there might not be a right or wrong answer.

1. **Why did the Israelites continue to disobey God and worship false gods?**

2. **What would you do if an angel appeared and told you that God intended to save your entire country through you?**

3. **Who went with Gideon to defeat the Midianites?** (Read Judges 6:16)

4. **Was Gideon a coward because he destroyed the altar and Asherah pole at night?**

5. **Have you ever heard the expression "put out a fleece"? What do you think this means?**

Final thoughts

This is the thought that you want the children to remember.

Say, **You might expect a powerful God to pick only powerful people to do his will. That is what people usually do. But God does the opposite. Gideon said that his tribe was weak and that he was the youngest, least important person in his family. Yet God chose this timid, uncertain man to fulfill his purposes. Why? If God used the strongest people, who would get the credit?**

In 2 Corinthians 12:10, Paul said, "I delight in weaknesses, in insults, in hardships, in persecutions, in difficulties. For when I am weak, then I am strong." You do not have to be a super-Christian for God to use you. God does not look for ability. He looks for availability.

MEMORY VERSE PRACTICE

See the "Memory Verse Activities" for suggestions to help the children learn the memory verse.

ADDITIONAL ACTIVITIES

Play a game or do an activity in the CBQM section that relates to this lesson (p. 103ff

PRACTICE FOR BIBLE QUIZ

Practice for Bible Quizzing with games and activities OR questions and answers.

THE MIDIANITES MEET THEIR MATCH

Judges 7:1-25; 8:28

MEMORY VERSE

Wait for the Lord; be strong and take heart and wait for the Lord.

Psalm 27:14

TRUTHS ABOUT GOD

*This lesson will teach the following truths about God. The asterisk * indicates the primary truth that you should teach to the children.*

* God sometimes does a mighty work in an unusual way that surprises us.

• God asks his people to trust him.

• God works in powerful, unexpected ways.

LESSON FOCUS AND SUMMARY

In this study, the children will learn that God sometimes works through people in unusual ways. Even when it does not seem likely, God is faithful and trustworthy.

1. God directed Gideon to reduce his army from 32,000 to 300 men.

2. God sent Gideon on a spy mission to learn how scared of the Israelite army the Midianites were.

3. With God's help, Gideon's tiny army defeated the Midianites with trumpets, empty jars, and torches.

4. After the battle, the Israelites enjoyed peace for 40 years.

BIBLICAL BACKGROUND

God had a strange plan for victory over the Midianites. Gideon had raised an army of 32,000 soldiers, but God told him to reduce it. Gideon allowed anyone who felt afraid to return home. Then the Lord gave him a special test to select the best of the men who remained. In the end, Gideon's army included only 300 soldiers. Yet God promised to rescue his people with this small band of men.

That night, Gideon and his servant Purah spied on the Midianite camp. They heard about one Midianite's dream. In it, a round loaf of barley bread rolled into the camp. It struck a tent with a force that caused the tent to collapse. Because barley was an inferior grain, the Midianite's friend believed that God had already given the Midianites into Gideon's hands (7:14). Gideon praised God for this information and told his men to prepare for battle.

Gideon's strategy was simple: surprise the enemy. He divided his men into three groups. He gave each man a trumpet and a jar that contained a torch. When Gideon gave the signal, they blew their trumpets and broke their jars to reveal their torches. The Midianites thought there was a huge army, because normally, only a few soldiers carried a trumpet and the rest carried weapons. In their confusion and fear, the Midianites fought each other or they fled. Gideon and his men pursued the Midianites and captured their leaders.

Gideon's success amazed the people. They begged him to be their king, but he refused (8:23). Because the Midianites were defeated, Israel enjoyed 40 years of peace during Gideon's lifetime (8:28).

🔍 DID YOU KNOW?

The name Harod means trembling or terror. The Spring of Harod was where Gideon chose the 300 soldiers. This small army caused the much larger Midianite army to shake with fear.

❓ VOCABULARY

Faith words

Faith is a trust in God that leads people to believe what he says, depend on him, and obey him.

People

Jerub-Baal was a name given to Gideon, which means let Baal contend. It was a challenge for Baal to defend himself against Gideon.

Purah was Gideon's servant who went with him into the Midianite camp.

Oreb and **Zeeb-Oreb** means raven and wolf. They were two Midianite leaders that the Israelites killed.

The Amalekites were a group of nomads who were the Israelites' enemies. Gideon and the Israelites defeated the Amalekites.

Places

The Spring of Harod was the place where the Israelites camped before their battle with the Midianites.

The Hill of Moreh was a hill that was located north of the Spring of Harod. The Midianites camped in the valley of the Hill of Moreh. The battle between the Israelites and Midianites took place nearby.

Terms

To change the guard is a phrase that describes when the guards took turns to sleep and to guard the camp.

The middle watch is a phrase that refers to how the Israelites divided the night into three sections. The middle watch was from about 20h00 to 2h00 (10 P.M. to 2 A.M). The Israelites attacked the Midianites after they went to bed.

📖 STORYTELLING

Each week you will need the following items.

1. A carrier like a small travel bag

2. A storage container for each week's story items (It can be a bag, basket, or box.)

For today's story, you will also need the following items.

3. A glass or a cup of water from which you might drink

4. A round cracker, a round bread loaf, anything round, or a piece of bread

5. A jar, a piece of pottery, or a bottle, or a flashlight

Before class

1. Read Judges 7:1-25; 8:28.

2. Gather today's story items. You may substitute a picture for any unavailable items.

3. Transfer all previous lesson items from the travel bag to the storage container. Place this container beside the storytelling area.

4. Place today's story items inside the travel bag. Place the travel bag in the storytelling area.

Optional activity: follow the leader

Tell the children to stand in a straight line, one behind the other. Choose a child to be the leader. Tell the children that they must watch the leader and mimic everything that he or she does.

The leader leads the group around the room. He or she uses different hand gestures, sounds, or motions for the children to imitate. For example, the leader walks with baby steps, large steps, or skips. End the game at the story telling area.

Lesson review

Ask a volunteer to select an item from the storage container and explain what it represented in the previous lesson.

Story time

Read these instructions before you begin.

1. Focus on the main points as you tell the story in your own words. Remove an item from the bag as you illustrate each point. If you are comfortable, include more details. If needed, you may use the suggested script.

2. As you tell the story, display each item in order. Place the item where the children can see it.

3. After you tell the story, place all the items inside the bag again.

4. To review the story, ask a volunteer to remove an item from the bag and then tell what it represents. Repeat this process with all the items until the children are able to retell the story completely.

5. Review the "Memory motion" described below. Demonstrate this motion any time you mention what it represents.

Main points in order

Say, **Today we continue to explore the book of Judges. Each week I pack our travel bag with the tools that we need for our journey. Today we begin with...** Unpack the items as you tell the story.

1. Hold up the glass or cup of water. Say, **Gideon began with 32,000 men. God told him to reduce his army so Israel would know the victory was the Lord's. Twenty-two thousand men left because they felt afraid. God wanted Gideon to reduce his army even more. Gideon followed God's plan to decide** who would stay to fight. He watched the men drink water from a stream, and then chose the three hundred men who drank from their cupped hands.

2. A round cracker, a bread loaf, anything round, or a piece of bread - Say, **God told Gideon to spy on the Midianites. Gideon and his servant overheard a man tell about his dream in which a round loaf of barley bread rolled into the camp. It hit their tent with a strong force and the tent collapsed. The Midianite thought that this meant that Israel would defeat them. When Gideon heard this, he worshipped God.**

3. Memory motion: Blow your trumpet - Show the children how to close their fists and place one on top of the other. Then hold their fists together as they raise them to their mouths and pretend to blow a horn. Or, invite the children to think of another appropriate motion. Say, **As I tell the story, do this motion when you hear what it represents. God defeated the Midianites in an unexpected way. He used trumpets, torches and jars.**

4. A jar, a container, a bottle, or a flashlight - Say, **God told Gideon to give each soldier an empty jar with a torch inside and a trumpet. The Israelites blew the trumpets and then smashed the jars to reveal the light inside and shouted. The Lord used this to confuse the Midianites, who began to fight each other.**

Say, **Now it is your turn to tell the story.** Return the items to the bag. Invite the children to take turns. Choose a volunteer to choose an item from the bag without looking and then explain what it represents. Or, they may choose to review one of the memory motions and explain what it represents. After the children remove all the items and explain them, ask a volunteer to place them in the correct story order.

BIBLICAL LESSON

Tips for the teacher

As you lead the Bible study, emphasize these ideas.

- Remember that smaller children do not understand abstract ideas very well. Emphasize how a normal army would use weapons like swords. However, Gideon's army used a different kind of weapon.

- Do not rush the story. When you ask the questions, allow time for the children to discover an answer. Encourage the children to search their thoughts and opinions. For older children, ask questions that begin with the word "why." For example, ask, "Why do you think God would make the Israelite army so small?"

- The Midianites were marauders who rode camels through the desert region between the Dead Sea and the Red Sea. They were relatives of Abraham through his wife Keturah's son, Midian.

Read the Scripture

Say, **God wanted to prevent the soldiers from thinking that they could win the battle in their own strength. He reduced their army to only 300 men. Now they were outnumbered. There was no doubt that if they won, the credit for their victory belonged to God.**

Read Judges 7:1-25 and 8:28 aloud. You may choose to use the items and the motions to emphasize the main points.

Discussion questions

Discuss the story and ask the children the following questions.

1. **Why did God reduce the number of Gideon's soldiers?**

2. **What encouraged Gideon and helped him believe that Israel could win the battle?** (Judges 7:13-15)

3. **What kinds of weapons did the Israelite army use to defeat the Midianites? Why did they use those particular weapons?** (Judges 7:16)

4. **Imagine if you were a soldier in Gideon's army. How would you feel as you prepared for battle with only 300 men? What would you think about your weapons?**

5. **Who was responsible for the victory over the Midianites?**

Final thoughts

This is the thought that you want the children to remember.

Say, **God is so much more wonderful and creative than we can imagine. When we think we know what to expect from God, he does something extraordinary. The Israelites defeated Midian with trumpets, jars, and torches. That is not the usual way to win a battle. But, we have a God who does unusual things in unusual ways. Our God is able to win battles with a tiny army who carries musical instruments. God will amaze us if we simply trust him, obey him, and wait.**

MEMORY VERSE PRACTICE

See the "Memory Verse Activities" for suggestions to help the children learn the memory verse.

ADDITIONAL ACTIVITIES

Play a game or do an activity in the CBQM section that relates to this lesson (p. 103ff

PRACTICE FOR BIBLE QUIZ

Practice for Bible Quizzing with games and activities OR questions and answers.

A MESSAGE OF HOPE

Judges 13:1-35

MEMORY VERSE

The Lord delights in those who fear him, who put their hope in his unfailing love.

Psalm 147:11

TRUTHS ABOUT GOD

*This lesson will teach the following truths about God. The asterisk * indicates the primary truth that you should teach the children.*

* God brings hope in times of deep trouble.

* God is our hope when everything seems hopeless.

* God reveals his will to us.

LESSON FOCUS AND SUMMARY

In this study, the children will learn that God keeps his promises, even though it may take a long time. God will never abandon us.

1. God's people sinned again, so God allowed the Philistines to oppress them for 40 years.

2. An angel of the Lord promised Samson's mother that she would bear a son. He would be a Nazirite who would help free the Israelites from the Philistines.

3. Manoah and his wife believed and obeyed God, and Samson was born.

4. When Samson grew up, God's Spirit began to work in him.

BIBLICAL BACKGROUND

The first verse of Judges 13 begins with, "Again the Israelites did evil in the eyes of the Lord" (13:1). Once again, the Israelites' disobedience led to their defeat. Because they failed to keep their promises to God, they suffered under the oppression of the Philistines. Those powerful people ruled over the Israelites for 40 years. Yet God did not abandon Israel.

Sometimes, God plans the deliverance of his people far in advance. That was the case with Samson. During this time of deep trouble for the Israelites, a man named Manoah and his wife saw an angel of the Lord. In the Bible, whenever an angel visited someone, it meant that something significant was about to happen. The angel promised them that a son would be born to them. Because they were unable to have a child, this was wonderful news. However, this baby boy would be extra special. The angel said that they must raise him as a Nazirite. A Nazarite was someone who was especially dedicated to God.

Initially, Manoah did not recognize that the special messenger was an angel of the Lord. When he realised this, he was frightened. Manoah believed that he had seen God and therefore, he would die. Together, Manoah and his wife bowed to the ground and worshipped God. What the angel of the Lord promised finally happened and Samson was born. As he grew up, the Lord blessed him and began to strengthen him for the task to deliver God's people from the oppressive strength of the Philistines.

⧉ DID YOU KNOW?

Both Samuel and John the Baptist were Nazirites from birth, like Samson. A Nazirite was someone who made a vow that lasted his entire life. A Nazirite promised not to drink alcohol, not to cut his hair, and not to touch a dead body. Do not confuse the word Nazirite with the word Nazarene, which means someone from the town of Nazareth or a follower of Jesus who was from Nazareth.

⧉ VOCABULARY

Faith words

Hope means to be certain that God will keep his promises. Hope exists because of trust in God and faith in him.

People

The Philistines were the people who lived on the coast of the Mediterranean Sea and in five major cities. They fought with the Israelites many times.

Manoah and his wife were Israelites who lived in the land of Dan during the time of the judges. Manoah's wife was unable to bear children.

The Danites were the Israelite people from the tribe of Dan. They lived in a location that was slightly east of the Philistines. The Philistines fought the Danites for land.

Samson was the son of Manoah and his wife, the son that the angel had promised. He was a Nazirite.

Places

Mahaneh Dan was a city west of the Dead Sea near Philistia.

Terms

A burnt offering was a gift of an animal that a person burned when they worshipped God.

A Nazirite was a person who made a promise not to cut his hair, not to drink alcohol, and not to touch a dead body. The promise lasted his entire life. A Nazirite was devoted to God because of this promise.

⧉ STORYTELLING

Each week you will need the following items.

1. A carrier like a small travel bag

2. A storage container for each week's story items (It can be a bag, basket, or box.)

For today's story, you will also need the following items.

3. A baby doll

4. A pair of scissors

5. A rock

Before class

1. Read Judges 13:1-35.

2. Gather today's story items. You may substitute a picture for any unavailable items.

3. Transfer all previous lesson items from the travel bag to the storage container. Place this container beside the storytelling area.

4. Place today's story items inside the travel bag. Place the travel bag in the storytelling area.

Optional activity: follow the leader

Tell the children to stand in a straight line, one behind the other. Choose a child to be the leader. Tell the children that they must watch the leader and mimic everything that he or she does. The leader leads the group around the room. He or she uses different hand gestures, sounds, or motions for the children to imitate. For example, the leader walks with baby steps, large steps, or skips. End the game at the storytelling area.

Lesson review

Ask a volunteer to select an item from the storage container and explain what it represented in the previous lesson.

Story time

Read these instructions before you begin.

1. Focus on the main points as you tell the story in your own words. Remove an item from the bag as you illustrate each point. If you are comfortable, include more details. If needed, you may use the suggested script.

2. As you tell the story, display each item in order. Place the item where the children can see it.

3. After you tell the story, place all the items inside the bag again.

4. To review the story, ask a volunteer to remove an item from the bag and then tell what it represents. Repeat this process with all the items until the children are able to retell the story completely.

5. Review the "Memory motion" described below. Demonstrate this motion any time you mention what it represents.

Main points in order

Say, **Today we continue to explore the book of Judges. Each week I pack our travel bag with the tools that we need. Today we begin with...** Unpack the items as you tell the story.

1. Hold up the baby doll. Say, **Because the Israelites turned away from God again, God allowed the Philistines to rule over them for forty years. An angel of the Lord appeared to Manoah's wife, who could not bear children. He said that she would have a son who would save the Israelites from the oppression of the Philistines.**

2. A pair of scissors - Say, **The angel said that the boy would be dedicated to the Lord in a special way. The mother must never cut the boy's hair because he would be a Nazirite. He must follow this rule for his entire life.**

3. A rock – Say, **Manoah sacrificed a goat and some grain on a rock as an offering to the Lord. As they watched the fire on the altar, they saw the angel go up to heaven in the flame. Then they knew he was an angel of the Lord.**

4. Memory motion: the Spirit of the Lord on Samson – Show the children how to pretend to rock a baby in their arms as they blow like the wind to represent the spirit of the Lord that moved in Samson as he grew. Or, invite the children to think of another appropriate motion. Say, **As I tell the story, do this motion when you hear what it represents. The woman gave birth to a son and named him Samson. He grew and the Lord blessed him. The spirit of the Lord stirred in him.**

Say, **Now it is your turn to tell the story.** Return the items to the bag. Invite the children to take turns. Choose a volunteer to choose an item from the bag without looking and then explain what it represents. Or, they may choose to review one of the memory motions and explain what it represents. After the children remove all the items and explain them, ask a volunteer to place them in the correct story order.

📖 BIBLICAL LESSON

Tips for the teacher

As you lead the Bible study, emphasize these ideas.

- Explain how close the Danites lived to the Philistines, and why that was important to the story. The Philistines were more powerful and were prejudiced against the Israelites. The two groups mingled a lot as they lived their lives.

- This is the first time the Israelites did not cry out to the Lord for deliverance. They grew comfortable with their corrupt lifestyle. The Israelites needed a leader who would avoid the corruption of the Philistines and would model faithful obedience.

- Explain to the students what a Nazirite was and why it was important for Samson's parents to understand the rules that the Nazirites promised to live by.

Read the Scripture

Say, **Israel continued to fail to fulfill their promises to God. But, God never abandoned his people. This time he brought hope through a baby boy named Samson.**

Read Judges 13:1-35 aloud. You may choose to use the items and the motions to emphasize the main points.

Discussion questions

Discuss the story and ask the children the following questions. Remember that there might not be a right or wrong answer.

1. **How is the start of this story similar to the start of the other stories we read in Judges?**

2. **What types of things did Samson's parents not allow him to do because he was a Nazirite? Do you think it was too much for God to ask?**

3. **Do your parents provide rules for you? What types of things are you not allowed to do that other children are allowed to do?**

4. **Why did Manoah think he and his wife would die?** (13:19-23)

5. **What makes this story about Samson and his parents a hopeful story?** (13:24)

Final thoughts

This is what you want the children to remember.

Say, **God hears his people's cry for help and he answers them and provides for them. He cares about people and wants to bring them hope and joy. For example, Manoah and his wife were unable to have children. They lived in a land where many Israelites lived the same lifestyle as the people who served other gods. The Philistines fiercely oppressed Israel. Things seemed hopeless, but God provided help. Samson's birth brought hope and joy to his parents. Later, Samson became a judge for Israel and helped save them from the Philistines. How does God bring hope to you when you feel hopeless or experience hopeless situations?**

☑ MEMORY VERSE PRACTICE

See the "Memory Verse Activities" for suggestions to help the children learn the memory verse.

🧩 ADDITIONAL ACTIVITIES

Play a game or do an activity in the CBQM section that relates to this lesson (p. 103ff

PRACTICE FOR BIBLE QUIZ

Practice for Bible Quizzing with games and activities OR questions and answers.

SAMSON'S LAST STAND

Judges 16:1-31

MEMORY VERSE

Hear my voice when I call, Lord; be merciful to me and answer me.

Psalm 27:7

TRUTHS ABOUT GOD

*This lesson will teach the following truths about God. The asterisk * indicates the primary truth that you should teach the children.*

* Sin brings consequences, but God continues to extend his grace to us.

- God does not always protect us from the consequences of our sins.

- God's grace is greater than our sins.

LESSON FOCUS AND SUMMARY

In this study, the children will learn that God remains faithful to help us when we turn to him, even if we were unfaithful in the past.

1. Samson fought the Philistines for 20 years, but he often disobeyed God.

2. Samson fell in love with a Philistine woman named Delilah who discovered the secret source of his strength.

3. When God's Spirit left Samson, the Philistines made him their prisoner.

4. God gave strength to Samson one last time and let him die with the Philistines. He killed more Philistines on that day than he had killed previously throughout his lifetime.

BIBLICAL BACKGROUND

Samson's parents raised him as a Nazirite, consecrated to the service of God. The Nazirites vowed never to cut their hair, never to drink alcohol, and never to touch a dead body. Unfortunately, Samson did not value his vow of faithfulness to God very much. Yet, in spite of Samson's unfaithful choices, God remained faithful. He gave Samson enormous power to help the Israelites in their time of need. The Philistines continued to rule the land, but for 20 years, Samson led Israel. This time, unlike at other times in the Book of Judges, there were no cries from the people for deliverance.

The story of Samson is tragic. Despite his gifts of physical strength and leadership, Samson's terrible mistakes led to his downfall. His biggest failure happened when he shared the secret of his strength with Delilah, who cut his hair and violated his Nazirite vow. We read the terrible words, "But [Samson] did not know that the Lord had left him" (16:20). Samson was once strong and in control of every situation. Now, his recklessness destroyed him.

When Samson had nothing left, he turned to God one last time. The Philistines captured him, blinded him, and humiliated him. He became mere entertainment for them. At the feast, he stood between the columns that supported the building. As he stood there surrounded by his enemies, he prayed, "Sovereign Lord, please remember me; please, God, give me my strength" (16:28). God answered his prayer and

Samson destroyed the Philistines as the building collapsed on them and him in one last act of self-sacrifice.

DID YOU KNOW?

Even though the Philistines ruled the land, the Israelites recognized Samson as their leader. He was larger than life, and his anger was the source of many stories. Once, when he wanted revenge on the Philistines, he caught 300 foxes, tied their tails together, and attached torches to them. Then he freed them and they ran through the Philistine fields and burned their crops (Judges 15:3-5).

VOCABULARY

Faith words

Grace describes God's love, mercy, forgiveness, and power that work in our lives. God freely gives us his grace because he loves us, not because we deserve it.

People

Delilah was a Philistine woman from the Valley of Sorek whom Samson loved. She convinced him to tell her the secret of his strength.

Places

Gaza was an important town. It was located near the coast of the Mediterranean Sea, about forty miles from Zorah.

The Valley of Sorek was an area located between Zorah and Timnah on the border of Judah and Philistia.

Terms

1,100 shekels of silver was a large amount of money. It would have amounted to a year's wage for 110 years!

Dagon was the Philistine god of plants and grain.

A loom was a large wooden tool used to weave fabric.

To gouge out someone's eyes was a harsh but typical treatment of prisoners. The Philistines removed Samson's eyes in this way to injure and humiliate him.

To set someone to grinding was a phrase that described the work that animals and women usually did when they ground grain for flour. The Philistines forced Samson to do this work so that he felt embarrassed and humiliated.

STORYTELLING

Each week you will need the following items.

1. A carrier like a small travel bag

2. A storage container for each week's story items (It can be a bag, basket, or box.)

For today's story, you will also need the following items.

3. A valentine, a heart shape, or something to represent romantic love

4. A piece of string, or a rope

5. A pair of scissors

Before class

1. Read Judges 16:1-31.

2. Gather today's story items. You may substitute a picture for any unavailable items.

3. Transfer all previous lesson items from the travel bag to the storage container. Place this container beside the storytelling area.

4. Place today's story items inside the travel bag. Place the travel bag in the storytelling area.

Optional activity: follow the leader

Tell the children to stand in a straight line, one behind the other. Choose a child to be the leader. Tell the children that they must watch the leader and mimic everything that he or she does. The leader leads the group around the room. He or she uses different hand gestures, sounds, or motions for the children to imitate. For example, the leader walks with baby steps, large steps, or skips. End the game at the storytelling area.

Lesson review

Ask a volunteer to select an item from the storage container and explain what it represented in the previous lesson.

Story time

Read these instructions before you begin.

1. Focus on the main points as you tell the story in your own words. Remove an item from the bag as you illustrate each point. If you are comfortable, include more details. If needed, you may use the suggested script.

2. As you tell the story, display each item in order. Place the item where the children can see it.

3. After you tell the story, place all the items inside the bag again.

4. To review the story, ask a volunteer to remove an item from the bag and then tell what it represents. Repeat this process with all the items until the children are able to retell the story completely.

5. Review the "Memory motion" described below. Demonstrate this motion any time you mention what it represents.

Main points in order

Say, **Today we finish this part of our expedition with the conclusion of the second of the three books in our study. I packed our travel bag with the tools that we will need to complete our journey with Judges. Today we begin with...** Unpack the items as you tell the story.

1. Memory motion: Strong muscles - Show the children how to close their fists and flex their arm muscles. This represents Samson's amazing, God-given strength. Demonstrate this motion multiple times. Or, invite the children to think of another appropriate motion. Say, **As I tell the story, do this motion when you hear what it represents. Samson led Israel and fought the Philistines for twenty years. God gave him wonderful gifts of tremendous strength and strong leadership abilities. Sadly, he often disobeyed God and he eventually dishonored his Nazirite vow.**

2. Hold up the valentine, the heart shape, or something that represents love. Say, **Samson fell in love with a Philistine woman named Delilah. The rulers of the Philistines offered to pay her money if she would find out the secret of Samson's strength.**

3. A piece of string or rope - Say, **Three times Samson lied to Delilah when she asked him the secret of his strength. Each time the Philistines came to seize him, Samson would easily break the ropes or other materials that Delilah used to bind him.**

4. A pair of scissors – Say, **Samson eventually told Delilah the true secret of his strength. As a Nazirite, he has vowed never to cut his hair. If she shaved his head, then he would lose his strength. While Samson slept, Delilah asked someone to cut Samson's braided hair. When this happened, the Lord's spirit left him and he became weak. The Philistines captured him, gouged out his eyes and made him grind grain in the prison. But, time passed and as his hair began to grow, his strength returned.**

Say, **Now it is your turn to tell the story.** Return the items to the bag. Invite the children to take turns. Choose a volunteer to choose an item from the bag without looking and then explain what it means/ represents. Or, they may choose to review one of the memory motions and explain what it represents. After the children remove all the items and explain them, ask a volunteer to place them in the correct story order.

⛪ BIBLICAL LESSON

Tips for the teacher

As you lead the Bible study, emphasize these ideas.

- Focus on the fact that God extends grace to those who do not deserve it. It is not only for good people.

- Point out that although God offered grace to Samson, Samson's sin resulted in unavoidable consequences.

Read the Scripture

Say, **Although God blessed Samson with extraordinary strength and a position of leadership, Samson often forgot the source of his strength and his important job. Samson made a promise to God but forgot how important it was to be faithful and to fulfill his promise. Often he did not resist temptation, and as a result, he experienced terrible consequences. But, God loved Samson and did not abandon him. When Samson asked for help, God provided it.**

Read Judges 16:1-31 aloud. You may choose to use the items and the motions to emphasize the main points.

Discussion questions

Discuss the story and ask the children the following questions. Remember that there might not be a right or wrong answer.

1. **Why did the Philistine rulers ask Delilah to find out the secret to Samson's strength? Would you betray someone you loved for a high price?** (16:5)

2. **How did Delilah get Samson to tell her the true answer? Do you ever do what she did to get what you want?** (16:15-17)

3. **Why do you think Samson did not know that the Lord had left him?**

4. **Why did the Philistines take away Samson's eyesight?**

5. **How is Samson's death scene an example of God's grace?**

Final thoughts

This is the thought that you want the children to remember.

Say, **Samson's decisions resulted in both physical and spiritual consequences. When Delilah cut Samson's hair and God's Spirit left him, Samson did not even notice. That is because he had already made decisions that had separated him from God. At the end of the passage, Samson was a prisoner and had suffered the loss of his eyesight. But, God gave him one last opportunity to participate in the mission to which God had called him. This is an example of the grace that God gives to each of us. None of us always acts or thinks perfectly. We have all sinned, and sin deserves punishment. But God eagerly offers us grace through forgiveness and the opportunity to experience a relationship with him.** If you feel prompted by the Holy Spirit, lead the children in a prayer for salvation. If needed, you may use the resource, "Leading a Child to Christ."

☑ MEMORY VERSE PRACTICE

See the "Memory Verse Activities" for suggestions to help the children learn the memory verse.

🧩 ADDITIONAL ACTIVITIES

Play a game or do an activity in the CBQM section that relates to this lesson (p. 103ff

❓ PRACTICE FOR BIBLE QUIZ

Practice for Bible Quizzing with games and activities OR questions and answers.

A BIG DECISION

Ruth 1:1-22

MEMORY VERSE

But Ruth replied, "Don't urge me to leave you or to turn back from you. Where you go I will go, and where you stay I will stay. Your people will be my people and your God my God."

Ruth 1:16

TRUTHS ABOUT GOD

*This lesson will teach the following truths about God. The asterisk * indicates the primary truth that you should teach the children.*

* Our choice to follow God changes the direction of our lives.

• God is at work, even when we cannot see it.

• God comes to the aid of his people.

LESSON FOCUS AND SUMMARY

In this study, the children will learn that God provides for those who choose to follow him and trust him.

1. Elimelek, Naomi, and their sons moved to Moab. Later, Naomi's husband and sons died.

2. When Naomi decided to return to Judah, she urged her daughters-in-law to remarry.

3. Orpah went back home, but Ruth determined to go with Naomi and serve her God.

4. Naomi and Ruth returned to Bethlehem at the onset of the harvest season.

BIBLICAL BACKGROUND

Ruth is a love story, although it is not what we might expect. This is a story about the love and devotion of a daughter-in-law for her mother-in-law.

The events happened a long time ago, but the lessons we learn are able to help us today. We do not know the time of these events, although they probably happened during the period of the judges.

The story begins with a famine in Bethlehem that forced Naomi and her family to relocate to Moab. After several years, her two sons married Moabite women. However, tragedy struck when her husband and two sons died, and left three widows: Naomi and her two daughters-in-law, Ruth and Orpah. In biblical times, there were not many opportunities for a woman to work to support herself. Therefore, a widow with no children faced poverty and even starvation unless she remarried.

At this time, things were better in Bethlehem, so Naomi decided to return. She wanted Ruth and Orpah to go back to their families in Moab. Orpah agreed, but Ruth held tightly to Naomi. Naomi is probably the person who taught her about faith in the one, true God. Ruth knew that it was better to go with Naomi and count on God's help than for each of them to endure difficulties alone. She owned no possessions, only her faith in God and her love for Naomi, her widowed mother-in-law.

"Where you go I will go," Ruth declares (1:16). So together, Ruth and Naomi returned to Bethlehem, arriving just as the harvest began. One of the lessons we learn from our story today is that God is dependable. He provides care on our journey of faith.

DID YOU KNOW?

The word "Bethlehem" means "House of Bread," which is an ironic name since our story starts at a time when the city experienced a famine. Bethlehem is most famous for three births:

- Rachel died there when she gave birth to Benjamin, the last of Jacob's 12 sons.

- Obed, the son of Ruth and Boaz, was born there (Ruth 4:13). Obed was the grandfather of David. It was also in Bethlehem that Samuel anointed David as the future king (1 Samuel 16:1).

- Jesus was born in Bethlehem, and he is known as the "Bread of Life" (John 6:35).

VOCABULARY

Faith words

A commitment is a promise or agreement to do something or to give yourself fully to a person or a cause.

People

Elimelek was a wealthy man from the tribe of Judah. He was from Bethlehem and was married to Naomi.

Naomi was Elimelek's wife. Her name meant "my joy." She trusted God even when her life was hard.

Mahlon and **Kilion** were Naomi's sons. They both died in Moab.

Orpah was Naomi's daughter-in-law, the wife of Kilion.

Ruth was Naomi's daughter-in-law, the wife of Mahlon. Ruth went with Naomi to Bethlehem.

Places

Judah is the land that the tribe of Judah received as their inheritance. It is located in southern Israel, west of the Dead Sea.

Moab is the land that is located south of Judah on the east side of the Dead Sea.

Bethlehem is a town that is located in northern Judah and is located five miles south of Jerusalem.

Terms

Mara is a Hebrew word that means bitter.

STORYTELLING

Each week you will need the following items.

1. A carrier like a small travel bag

2. A storage container for each week's story items (It can be a bag, basket, or box.)

For today's story, you will also need the following items.

3. An empty bowl or plate

4. A red heart, a valentine card or something red

5. A black or white cloth

6. A plate with a piece of food on it

Before class

1. Read Ruth 1:1-22.

2. Gather today's story items. You may substitute a picture for any unavailable items.

3. Transfer all previous lesson items from the travel bag to the storage container. Place this container beside the storytelling area.

4. Place today's story items inside the travel bag. Place the travel bag in the storytelling area.

Optional activity: follow the leader

Tell the children to stand in a straight line, one behind the other. Choose a child to be the leader. Tell the children that they must watch the leader and mimic everything that he or she does. The leader leads the group around the room. He or she uses different hand gestures, sounds, or motions for the children to imitate. For example, the leader walks with baby steps, large steps, or skips. End the game at the storytelling area.

Lesson review

Ask a volunteer to select an item from the storage container and explain what it represented in the previous lesson.

Story time

Read these instructions before you begin.

1. Focus on the main points as you tell the story in your own words. Remove an item from the bag as you illustrate each point. If you are comfortable, include more details. If needed, you may use the suggested script.

2. As you tell the story, display each item in order. Place the item where the children can see it.

3. After you tell the story, place all the items inside the bag again.

4. To review the story, ask a volunteer to remove an item from the bag and then tell what it represents. Repeat this process with all the items until the children are able to retell the story completely.

5. Review the "Memory motion" described below. Demonstrate this motion any time you mention what it represents.

Main points in order

Say, **Today we begin to explore the book of Ruth. I packed our travel bag with the tools that we will need for our journey. Today we begin with...** Unpack the items as you tell the story.

1. Hold up the empty bowl or plate. Say, **Naomi was married to Elimelek, and they had two sons. Their family moved from Bethlehem to Moab because of a famine. While they were in Bethlehem, Elimelek died.**

2. A red heart - Say, **After the death of their father, Naomi's sons married Moabite women named Ruth and Orpah.**

3. A black or white cloth – **Say, After about ten years, Naomi's sons died. Now Naomi, Orpah and Ruth were childless widows. In that culture, without a husband to support her, a widow depended on others to help her survive. The three widows were in a very difficult situation and they could starve.**

4. The bowl or plate with food – **Naomi heard that God provided food for his people in Bethlehem. Therefore, she decided to return there.**

5. Memory motion: Time for a journey - Show the children how to wave goodbye and walk in place to represent the journey from Bethlehem to Moab. Or, invite the children to think of another appropriate motion. Say, **As I tell the story, do this motion when you hear what it represents. Naomi's daughters-in-law began the trip with her. Even though they wanted to stay with her, Naomi asked Ruth and Orpah to go back to their own homes and to remarry. Orpah went back home, but Ruth decided to follow Naomi.**

Say, **Now it is your turn to tell the story.** Return the items to the bag. Invite the children to take turns. Choose a volunteer to choose an item from the bag without looking and then explain what it means/ represents. Or, they may choose to review one of the memory motions and explain what it represents. After the children remove all the items and explain them, ask a volunteer to place them in the correct story order.

✝ BIBLICAL LESSON

Tips for the teacher

As you lead the Bible study, emphasize these ideas.

- Teach the children about the plight of women in ancient days. A husband was almost the only way an adult woman could survive. Very few women worked at a job for payment.

- Explain the differences between Moab and Judah (different cultures, gods, rivalry between the two nations). Moab oppressed the Israelites in the time of the Judges. For Elimelek to move his family to Moab means that the famine was extremely severe.

- Explain how desperate Naomi's situation was (She was in a foreign land without a husband or sons to care for her).

Read the Scripture

Say, **This story happened in the time of the Judges when "everyone did as they saw fit" (Judges 21:25). But, in these rebellious times, there were some like Naomi and her family who followed God.**

Read Ruth 1:1-22 aloud. You may choose to use items and motions to emphasize the main points.

Discussion questions

Discuss the story and ask the children the following questions. Remember that there might not be a right or wrong answer.

1. **What hardships did Naomi experience? How would you handle those hardships?**

2. **Why did Naomi urge Ruth and Orpah to stay in Moab? How might it have been easier for Ruth to allow Naomi to return to Judah alone?**

3. **Why do you think that Ruth felt so strongly that she should stay with Naomi? How would you describe Ruth?**

4. **Ruth chose to go to a land where she was a stranger. Have you ever felt like a stranger? What happened?**

5. **What season began in Bethlehem when Naomi and Ruth arrived? How did this affect the two women?**

Final thoughts

This is what you want the children to remember.

Say, **The choice Ruth made to follow Naomi was not an easy one, but it honored God. When she decided to go with Naomi, Ruth left her home, her family, her friends, her culture, and her religion. It was possible that the people in Bethlehem would disrespect her and treat her poorly because she was from Moab. Still, Ruth said to Naomi, "Your people will be my people and your God my God"** (Ruth 1:16b).

Ruth made an intentional choice to follow God and remain faithful to Naomi. The result was that an entirely new life was possible for her. God offers everyone the same choice, either to follow God or to refuse him. God wants us to choose to trust and follow him. He sent Jesus to be our Savior, and he enables us to make this choice if we will do it. Will you accept Jesus as your Savior? If so, your life will forever change.

You may feel that the Holy Spirit prompts you to lead the children to pray for salvation. If so, you may refer to the "Leading a Child to Christ" resource for guidance as needed.

☑ MEMORY VERSE PRACTICE

See the "Memory Verse Activities" for suggestions to help the children learn the memory verse.

🧩 ADDITIONAL ACTIVITIES

Play a game or do an activity in the CBQM section that relates to this lesson (p. 103ff

PRACTICE FOR BIBLE QUIZ

Practice for Bible Quizzing with games and activities OR questions and answers.

BOAZ TO THE RESCUE

Ruth 2:1-23

MEMORY VERSE

Share with the Lord's people who are in need. Practice hospitality.

Romans 12:13

TRUTHS ABOUT GOD

*This lesson will teach the following truths about God. The asterisk * indicates the primary truth that you should teach the children.*

* God provides for those in need through the obedience of his people.

• God knows our needs.

• God often works through people to meet our needs.

LESSON FOCUS AND SUMMARY

In this study, the children will learn that God provides for our needs. He sometimes meets our needs through faithful people.

1. Ruth went to the fields to gather grain for Naomi and herself.

2. Boaz, a relative of Naomi's husband, noticed Ruth and talked with her.

3. Boaz took special care of Ruth, gave her food, and made sure she gathered plenty of grain.

4. Naomi encouraged Ruth to return to Boaz's fields because she would be safe there.

BIBLICAL BACKGROUND

The Law of Moses included strict rules that applied to the treatment of poor people. Those laws recognized that widows and orphans relied on the kindness of others. When Ruth and Naomi arrived in Bethlehem, for example, Ruth gleaned in Boaz's fields. This means that she picked up grain that the harvesters left. The law required that the field owners allow this practice to provide for the poor (see Leviticus 19:9-10).

God rewarded Ruth's faithfulness to Naomi. The people noticed Naomi and Ruth, the Moabite, when they arrived in Bethlehem. So Boaz, a relative of Naomi's husband, knew about her when they first met each other. Often, rumours and gossip are ugly and negative. However in this case, everyone talked about how good Ruth was. Normally, someone like Boaz would be especially suspicious of Ruth because she was a foreigner and a Moabite. However, the facts about Ruth were different. She had a good reputation because of how well she cared for Naomi, one of their own. Because of her faithfulness, Boaz was kind to Ruth.

People notice when someone is generous and faithful over a long period. A good reputation does not guarantee success, but it often creates opportunities for more good things to happen. Ruth got permission from Boaz to glean in his fields. Because of her good reputation, he also allowed her to harvest grain with his regular workers. When she brought the news home, Naomi exclaimed, "The Lord bless him!" (2:20). The Lord provided for Ruth and Naomi through obedient people like Boaz.

DID YOU KNOW?

The process to harvest a field took a very long time. First, the workers cut the stalks of grain. Then they tied up the stalks and carried them to the threshing floor where they took the kernels out of the shells. Then they separated the grain from the dirt around it. A harvest required seven steps to go from a stalk of grain to a bag of grain.

VOCABULARY

Faith words

Compassion means concern for others that motivates us to help.

People

Boaz was most likely an older man from the same clan as Elimelek. He was wealthy enough to have fields and workers.

A foreigner is someone from a different country. In the Old Testament, a foreigner was someone who was not a part of Israel.

An overseer was a person in charge of a group of workers.

A guardian-redeemer was a wealthy person with the ability to redeem or buy back what a relative lost. Boaz was Naomi's guardian-redeemer.

Terms

Sheaves are large bundles of grain still on their stalks.

To glean means to gather leftover grain or other crops. The Law of Moses required field owners to leave some grain for the poor to glean.

A refuge was a place of shelter or protection from danger.

STORYTELLING

Each week you will need the following items.

1. A carrier like a small travel bag

2. A storage container for each week's story items (It can be a bag, basket, or box.)

For today's story, you will also need the following items.

3. A small bag or container of grain

4. Some coins

5. A piece of bread or food

6. A larger bag or container of grain

Before class

1. Read Ruth 2:1-23.

2. Gather today's story items. You may substitute a picture for any unavailable items.

3. Transfer all previous lesson items from the travel bag to the storage container. Place this container beside the storytelling area.

4. Place today's story items inside the travel bag. Place the travel bag in the storytelling area.

Optional activity: follow the leader

Tell the children to stand in a straight line, one behind the other. Choose a child to be the leader. Tell the children that they must watch the leader and mimic everything that he or she does. The leader leads the group around the room. He or she uses different hand gestures, sounds, or motions for the children to imitate. For example, the leader walks with baby steps, large steps, or skips. End the game at the storytelling area.

Lesson review

Ask a volunteer to select an item from the storage container and explain what it represented in the previous lesson.

Story time

Read these instructions before you begin.

1. Focus on the main points as you tell the story in your own words. Remove an item from the bag as you illustrate each point. If you are comfortable, include more details. If needed, you may use the suggested script.

2. As you tell the story, display each item. Place the item where the children can see it.

3. After you tell the story, place all the items inside the bag again.

4. To review the story, ask a volunteer to remove an item from the bag and then tell what it represents. Repeat this process with all the items until the children are able to retell the story completely.

5. Review the "Memory motion" described below. Demonstrate this motion any time you mention what it represents.

Main points in order

Say, **Today we continue to explore the book of Ruth. Each week I pack our travel bag with the tools that we need for our journey. Today we begin with...** Unpack as you tell the story.

1. Hold up the small bag or container of grain - Say, **There were not many ways for a widow to earn money or get enough to eat. Therefore, Ruth went to the fields to gather grain for herself and Naomi. She followed behind the workers and gathered the grain that they dropped. The Israelites' law required the farmers to leave some grain for the needy. This was how God provided for their needs.**

2. Hold up the coins. Say, **Boaz was a wealthy man and Naomi's relative through her**

husband, Elimelek. Boaz came out to the fields where Ruth gleaned grain and greeted his workers with a blessing. This demonstrated that he was a kind and godly man. He asked his workers about Ruth and talked with her.

3. A piece of bread or food– Say, **Boaz discovered that Ruth was kind to Naomi and that she had left her home in Moab to help Naomi. He gave Ruth special care and allowed her to eat with his workers. She ate all that she wanted and there was food left to share with Naomi. Boaz allowed Ruth to gather as much grain as she wanted.**

4. A large bag or container of grain – **That evening, Ruth returned to Naomi with the grain she had gathered. She also gave Naomi the food that she did not eat. Boaz's kindness toward Ruth was more than the law required.**

5. Memory motion – Shield and protection – Show the children how to close their fits and cross their arms in front of their chest to form a shield in the form of an "X" and not a cross. Or, invite the children to think of another appropriate motion. Say, **When Naomi learned that Ruth worked in Boaz's field, she was very excited because he was one of their guardian-redeemers. She told Ruth to continue to work there because he would care for her and keep her safe.**

Say, **Now it is your turn to tell the story.** Return the items to the bag. Invite the children to take turns. Choose a volunteer to choose an item from the bag without looking and then explain what it means/ represents. Or, they may choose to review one of the memory motions and explain what it represents. After the children remove all the items and explain them, ask a volunteer to place them in the correct story order.

BIBLICAL LESSON

Tips for the teacher

As you lead the Bible study, emphasize these ideas.

- Discuss the role of a guardian-redeemer (or whatever phrase is used in the biblical translation you use). The Law of Moses allowed the guardian-redeemer to provide for their relatives who were poor, who lost their property, their income, or their freedom when a husband died. God provided this way for families to stay bound to one another. A guardian-redeemer was the closest male relative of a dead man who could volunteer to marry the dead man's widow. The law provided this because in Israelite culture, the widow did not receive anything that her husband owned when he died. Instead, the son of the nearest male relative received the inheritance unless a guardian redeemer volunteered to marry the woman. Then the inheritance of property would stay with the widow, her family and her new husband. In this way, families could keep their property and provide for those in need. A guardian-redeemer shared out of their abundance and compassion.

Read the Scripture

Say, **Ruth was a widow who lived with another widow, Naomi. Neither woman could provide for herself. In addition to this circumstance, Ruth was a foreigner. But, Ruth did not feel pity for herself or wait on something good to simply happen to her. She decided to do what she could. She was not afraid to try something new or work hard. She went to work in the fields and God provided for her in a way that she never imagined.**

Read Ruth 2:1-23 aloud. You may choose to use the items and the motions to emphasize the main points.

Discussion questions

Discuss the story and ask the children the following questions. Remember that there might not be a right or wrong answer.

1. Read Deuteronomy 24:19. **Why did God make this law? Whom did this law help?**

2. **Why was Boaz impressed by Ruth? How did he show kindness to her?**

3. **Find all the times in chapter 2 that refer to Ruth as a foreigner. How do you think she felt because she was a foreigner?**

4. **Why did Naomi encourage Ruth to return to Boaz's fields?**

5. **Ruth 2:1 says that Boaz was "a man of standing." After you read chapter two, what do you think this phrase means?**

Final thoughts

This is the thought that you want the children to remember.

Say, **When we first met Ruth, she was a widow with no money. Her future did not appear very good. What changed? Yes, Ruth cared about Naomi and wanted to help her. But, she also made a choice to follow Yahweh, the one true God, the God of the Israelites. That decision changed her life. She became God's friend. When she surrounded herself with God's people, they were able to help meet her needs.**

God often works in this same way today. Sometimes he uses miracles to help his people. But, God often includes his people in his plan. That means he invites us to participate in his work. God invites you to join him as he meets the needs of people around you. Will you accept the opportunity and obediently respond to him?

You may feel that the Holy Spirit prompts you to lead the children to pray for salvation. If so, you may refer to the "Leading a Child to Christ" resource for guidance as needed.

✓ MEMORY VERSE PRACTICE

See the "Memory Verse Activities" for suggestions to help the children learn the memory verse.

ADDITIONAL ACTIVITIES

Play a game or do an activity in the CBQM section that relates to this lesson (p. 103ff

PRACTICE FOR BIBLE QUIZ

Practice for Bible Quizzing with games and activities OR questions and answers.

HAPPILY EVER AFTER

Ruth 3:1-12; 4:1-17

MEMORY VERSE

For the Lord is good and his love endures forever; his faithfulness continues through all generations.

Psalm 100:5

TRUTHS ABOUT GOD

*This lesson will teach the following truths about God. The asterisk * indicates the primary truth that you should teach the children.*

* What God does at any moment is bigger than we can see at the time.

- God is sovereign and he accomplishes his purposes.

- God blesses us in ways that are greater than we are able to imagine.

LESSON FOCUS AND SUMMARY

In this study, the children will learn that God faithfully works in our lives to accomplish his plan in a way that we cannot see or imagine.

1. Naomi decided to secure Ruth's future and instructed her to ask Boaz for protection.

2. Boaz redeemed Naomi's property and married Ruth.

3. Naomi once again had a family.

4. The Lord blessed Ruth and Boaz with a child whose descendant David was Jesus' ancestor.

BIBLICAL BACKGROUND

Naomi felt a responsibility to find a husband for Ruth. She wanted to find a man from among the relatives of her deceased husband, Elimelek. Boaz was the most likely man because Ruth already gleaned in his fields. Naomi planned an opportunity for Boaz to notice Ruth. It was also an opportunity for Ruth to appeal to Boaz for his protection.

Boaz felt affection for Ruth and accepted the responsibility to marry her. But, he was aware of another relative to whom he needed to speak first. This man was a closer relative to Naomi than Boaz. Therefore, he was the "guardian-redeemer" who would have the first opportunity to marry Ruth and redeem Naomi's property. When this relative declined, Boaz arranged to marry Ruth in the presence of the city elders. Boaz was wise to follow the Israelite law to ensure that his marriage to Ruth was legal. This protected Naomi and Elimelek's property, which remained in the family.

It probably seems strange to us that Boaz believed he must ask someone else before he married Ruth. However, marriage in Ruth's time was rarely about love. It was like a family business arrangement that had to follow the law's requirements.

Ruth, a Moabite, not an Israelite, would become the great-grandmother of King David, which means she was also an ancestor of Jesus. This dramatic story of tragedy, hope for the future, and faith in God is a great source of spiritual enrichment.

DID YOU KNOW?

The Levirate law (Deuteronomy 25:5-6) says that if a man died before his wife bore a child, his oldest brother should marry the widow. The first son from that marriage would legally become the "heir" of the deceased brother. If the oldest brother wanted to avoid this obligation, he could allow the widow to remove one of his shoes. This freed her to marry someone else.

VOCABULARY

Faith words

To redeem means to rescue someone from hardship or slavery and set that person free.

People

Obed was Ruth's son, who became the father of Jesse.

Jesse was the son of Obed, who became the father of King David.

David was one of the most famous kings of Israel. People recognize him for his musical abilities, his love for God, and because he was an ancestor of Jesus.

Places

A city gate was similar to the modern-day courtroom. This is where legal transactions took place in the presence of the elders of the city. They were witnesses.

Terms

A threshing floor is the place where harvesters separated the grain from the grain stalks. The threshing floor was sometimes a rock, or a large area of flat ground.

"Spread the corner of your garment over me" is a phrase that is a request for marriage. The corner of the garment symbolized Boaz's protection over Ruth.

To remove someone's sandal meant that a legal transaction was completed. Today we would sign a contract.

STORYTELLING

Each week you will need the following items.

1. A carrier like a small travel bag

2. A storage container for each week's story items (It can be a bag, basket, or box.)

For today's story, you will also need the following items.

3. A blanket

4. A map

5. A sandal

6. A baby doll

Before class

1. Read Ruth 3:1-12 and 4:1-17.

2. Gather today's story items. You may substitute a picture for any unavailable items.

3. Transfer all previous lesson items from the travel bag to the storage container. Place this container beside the storytelling area.

4. Place today's story items inside the travel bag. Place the travel bag in the storytelling area.

Optional activity: follow the leader

Tell the children to stand in a straight line, one behind the other. Choose a child to be the leader. Tell the children that they must watch the leader and mimic everything that he or she does. The leader leads the group around the room. He or she uses different hand gestures, sounds, or motions for the children to imitate. For example, the leader walks with baby steps, large steps, or skips. End the game at the storytelling area.

Lesson review

Ask a volunteer to select an item from the storage container and explain what it represented in the previous lesson.

Story time

Read these instructions before you begin.

1. Focus on the main points as you tell the story in your own words. Remove an item from the bag as you illustrate each point. If you are comfortable, include more details. If needed, you may use the suggested script.

2. As you tell the story, display each item in order. Place the item where the children can see it.

3. After you tell the story, place all the items inside the bag again.

4. To review the story, ask a volunteer to remove an item from the bag and then tell what it represents. Repeat this process with all the items until the children are able to retell the story completely.

5. Review the "Memory motion" described below. Demonstrate this motion any time you mention what it represents.

Main points in order

Say, **Today we complete our expedition with the conclusion of Ruth, the last of the three books in our study. I packed our travel bag with the tools that we need to complete our journey. Today we begin with...** Unpack the items as you tell the story.

1. Hold up the blanket. Say, **Naomi wanted Ruth to marry Boaz. If this happened, then Ruth would not worry about her future because Boaz would take care of her. Naomi told Ruth to meet Boaz on the threshing floor that night. Naomi knew that Boaz would sleep there to protect his grain from thieves. Ruth went to meet Boaz as Naomi had instructed. When he was asleep, Ruth uncovered his feet, lay down and waited for** **Boaz to tell her what to do. Boaz promised to help her.**

2. A map – Say, **Boaz knew there was a closer relative to Elimelek who was also a guardian-redeemer. Boaz met with him and gave him the chance to buy Naomi's land. If the relative chose to redeem her land, then he would also be required to marry Ruth.**

3. The sandal – Say, **The man chose not to buy Naomi's land because he did not want to marry Ruth. Instead, he told Boaz to buy it. To demonstrate that he was serious about this agreement, he took off his sandal and gave it to Boaz. Boaz bought the land and married Ruth. This demonstrated his kindness and compassion.**

4. Memory motion: Kindness hug – demonstrate how to wrap your arms around yourself in a hug. Or, invite the children to think of another appropriate motion. Say, **As I tell the story, do this motion when you hear what it represents. When Boaz married Ruth, Naomi finally gained a family to care for her again.**

5. The baby doll – Say, **God blessed Ruth and Boaz with a son named Obed. Obed's grandson, David, became King David, who was Jesus' ancestor. Because of Boaz's kindness to Ruth and Naomi, he and his family became a part of the Lord's larger plan to bring our savior Jesus into the world.**

Say, **Now it is your turn to tell the story.** Return the items to the bag. Invite the children to take turns. Choose a volunteer to choose an item from the bag without looking and then explain what it means/ represents. Or, they may choose to review one of the memory motions and explain what it represents. After the children remove all the items and explain them, ask a volunteer to place them in the correct story order.

📖 BIBLICAL LESSON

Tips for the teacher

As you lead the Bible study, emphasize these ideas.

- Naomi's advice seems strange, but she told Ruth to follow the customs and laws of Israel. A servant often slept at the foot of his master and shared a portion of his blanket. This showed that Ruth wanted Boaz to be her guardian-redeemer. He could either find someone to marry her or he could marry her himself. It was like a family business arrangement and not necessarily romantic.

- Read Matthew 1:1-6 and explain to the children how the story of Ruth connects with Jesus' birth.

Read the Scripture

Say, **As widows, Ruth and Naomi's future would include a difficult life. But, when Naomi realized that Boaz was the kind owner of the fields where Ruth gleaned the grain, it renewed her hope.**

Read Ruth 3:1-12; 4:1-17 aloud. You may choose to use the items and the motions to emphasize the main points.

Discussion questions

Discuss the story and ask the children the following questions.

1. **Ruth told Naomi, "I will do whatever you say" (3:5). What does Ruth's response say about their relationship?**

2. **Why did the closest kinsman-redeemer to Naomi decide not to buy her property or marry Ruth? Why did Boaz buy the property and marry Ruth?**

3. **After Ruth and Boaz had a baby, why do you think the women said, "Naomi has a son"? (4:17)**

4. **How was the birth of Obed important for the future of Israel?**

5. **In what ways does this story have a "happily ever after" conclusion?**

Final thoughts

This is the thought that you want the children to remember.

Say, **God's perspective is so much bigger than ours.**

What is the reason for everything that happens? Only God knows. Ruth did not know God's complete plan for her life. But, she chose to follow him. She had no idea that, because of her unselfish choices, God would use her in huge ways. Ruth became part of the family line of King David and eventually Jesus, our Savior. Her choice contributed to God's biggest blessing for the whole world! We must follow Ruth's example. To live for God blesses our lives, but it also allows us to participate in God's plan in unimaginable ways!

✓ MEMORY VERSE PRACTICE

See the "Memory Verse Activities" for suggestions to help the children learn the memory verse.

🧩 ADDITIONAL ACTIVITIES

Play a game or do an activity in the CBQM section that relates to this lesson (p. 103ff

PRACTICE FOR BIBLE QUIZ

Practice for Bible Quizzing with games and activities OR questions and answers.

MEMORY VERSE ACTIVITIES

MISSING WORDS

You will need a chalkboard, white board or paper for this activity. You will also need chalk, marker, and eraser.

Write the memory verse on a chalkboard or marker board. Ask the children to recite the verse. Choose a volunteer to erase one word. Lead the children as they recite the verse again (include the missing word). Continue this until all the words disappear. If a chalkboard or marker board is not available, write each word of the verse on a separate piece of paper, and ask the children to remove one word at a time.

BIBLE WAVE

Ask the children to sit in a straight line. Tell the first child to stand, to say the first word of the verse, to wave both hands excitedly in the air, and to sit down. Ask the second child to stand, to say the second word of the verse, to wave both hands excitedly in the air, and to sit down. Continue until the verse is complete. If a child forgets a word or says the wrong word, let the other children tell the correct word. Encourage the children to say the verse quickly so that their motions look like an ocean wave.

BIBLE PASS

You will need a Bible and a source of music for this activity.

Have the children sit in a circle. Give one child the Bible. When the music starts, tell the children to pass the Bible around the circle. When the music stops, the child holding the Bible says the Bible verse. Strategically stop the music so each child has an opportunity to say the verse.

BIBLE VERSE RACE

Before the lesson, write each word or phrase of the Bible verse and the reference on a piece of paper. Make two sets.

Divide the class into two teams. Scramble the cards so that the words are out of order. Place a set of word cards on the floor in front of each team. At your signal, the first child on each team will find the first word of the verse and run to a goal line. He or she places the card on the floor and races back to the second player. The second child finds the second word of the verse and races with it to the goal line, placing it in order next to the first word. Continue until one team completes the verse in perfect order. Allow time for the second team to complete its verse. Then have both teams recite the verse together.

BIBLE VERSE LINE

Before the lesson, write each word or phrase of a Bible verse on a separate piece of paper.

Distribute the words to different children, and scatter them throughout the room. Choose one child to arrange the words in order by tagging each individual child holding the words. Then have the class read the verse together.

HIDE AND SEEK

Before the lesson, write each word or phrase of a Bible verse on a separate piece of paper. Then hide the pieces of paper around the room before the children arrive.

Have the children search the room for the pieces of paper and bring them back to the front. Have the children arrange the words in order, and then ask the class to recite the verse together.

STAND UP VERSES

Arrange the children in a circle, and have everyone sit down. Ask one child to stand and say the first word of the verse and then sit down. The next child stands and says the second word and then sits down. Continue until the children complete the verse. Play the game several times, encouraging the children to finish faster than the previous time.

CHAMPION & CHALLENGER

Choose two children who think that they know the memory verse. Stand them back to back in front of the group. One child will start by saying the first word of the verse. Then, the other child will say the second word. Continue back and forth until one child makes a mistake. The other child is the "champion." Ask the whole class to say the memory verse. Then, select a new "challenger," and repeat the game. Soon, both children will be able to complete the memory verse without error.

BLINDFOLD CHALLENGE

You will need a blindfold for this activity. Ask the children to stand and arrange themselves in a large circle.

Select one child to stand in the center of the circle. Place a blindfold on this child. Ask the children in the circle to join hands and walk around the circle as they repeat the phrase, "God's Word helps me each day" a few times. This will prevent the child in the middle from remembering where each child in the circle stood. Stop the children and ask the child in the middle to point to a child in the circle. The child will recite the verse in a disguised voice (high pitch voice, squeaky voice, low voice, etc.). The child in the center then tries to guess who said the verse. If the child fails to guess correctly, he or she will point to another child who will say the verse. Continue until the child in the center guesses the correct child or the child guesses wrong three times. Then choose another child to go into the center.

MEMORY VERSE TOSS

You will need a small ball for this activity. Ask the children to stand and arrange them in a large circle.

Tell the children that whoever catches the ball has to say the next word in the memory verse. Toss the ball to one child to start. He or she recites the first word and then tosses the ball to another child until the entire verse is recited correctly. Repeat the game and encourage the children to complete the verse faster each time.

WORD IN ACTION

Before the lesson, write a different action on separate pieces of paper or index cards, such as "turn in a circle," "lie on the floor," "pat your head," "stand one foot," "skip," "stand in a corner," "whisper," and so on.

Ask each child to choose one of the index cards and to do the activity listed on it while he or she recites the memory verse.

THE REPEATER

Before the lesson, write one or two words of the verse on a small piece of paper. Make more than one set if you want to work in groups, one set per group.

Instruct students to sit in a circle, and distribute the papers around the circle in the correct verse order. The student with the first word of the verse says the first word. Then the next student says the first word and the new word. The third student says the first, second, and third words. Repeat this process, adding a new word each time. After you complete the verse, have students pass their card to the person on their left and begin the game again.

SPIDER WEB REVIEW

You will need a ball of yarn for this activity.

Instruct the children to stand in a circle. Toss the ball of yarn to one child and ask him or her to say the first word of the verse. The child will wrap the yarn around his or her hand and toss the ball of yarn to another child across the circle. This child will say the second word of the verse and wrap the yarn around his finger. Continue playing and saying words of the verse until every child has a turn. The back and forth motion of the yarn will produce a spider web.

BALLOON POP

You will need balloons, a permanent marker, and tape.

Blow up the balloons. Write one word of the Bible verse on each balloon. Attach the balloons to the wall in correct order. Let the children read the verse together. Select one child to pop one balloon. Have the children recite the verse again, and remember to say the missing word. Select another child to pop a balloon. Let the children say the verse again. Continue until all the balloons are gone, and the children can recite the verse from memory.

HAPPY FACES MEMORY GAME

Write each word or phrase of a Bible verse on a paper plate or a circular piece of paper.

Distribute the plates to the children, and ask them to draw a happy face on the blank side of the plate (circle). Attach the plates to the wall so the children can see the words of the verse. Read the verse together. Select one child to turn over one of the plates so the happy face shows. Then have the children read the verse. Select another child to turn over another plate. Say the verse again. Continue until all of the plates show happy faces, and children can recite the verse from memory.

BIBLE VERSE UNSCRAMBLE

Write each word or phrase of a Bible verse on a piece of paper or index card.

Distribute the word cards in mixed order. Let the children arrange themselves in a circle in the correct order according to the portion of the verse they received. Have the children say the verse together. Then ask one child to turn the card around, so the other children cannot see his or her word. Have the children say the verse again. Continue in this manner until all the cards are turned around and no words are visible.

This could also be played as a race between two or more teams to see which one is the first to arrange themselves with the words of the verse in the correct order.

CHILDREN'S BIBLE
QUIZZING MINISTRY

What is Children's Bible Quizzing Ministry (CBQM) Activity based quizzing?

The Church of the Nazarene has always set aside a special space for children. Jesus Christ himself did it when he strongly told his disciples not to separate the children because theirs is the kingdom of heaven. "Starting children off on the way they should go" (Proverbs 22: 6) is a pressing mandate that the Lord gives us, especially in our convoluted societies in which our children are dying physically and spiritually. Children's Bible Quizzing Ministry - Activities, known by its acronym as CBQM, was derived from the need to deepen and energize the Bible study for children. It is considered a powerful and effective tool for evangelism and children's discipleship in local churches .

Starting from the playful principle (learning by playing), CBQM - Activities consists of a series of games divided into the categories of memorization, reflection, arts and crafts, acting and music. (This is different than the traditional style of Children's Bible Quizzing using questions and answers.) Each of the games is related to, or has been adapted to, the subject of study. Each local church forms a team with 10 members between 7 and 11 years old. (They can be under 7 years old, but it is recommended that they be children who already know how to read and write.) This team will be prepared by a coach throughout the year. The head of the district Children's Ministries plans a demonstration (competition) in which each team demonstrates what they have learned from the Bible through the games that they participate in. The team that demonstrates greater preparation, by accumulating points, will represent their district in a national demonstration. However, it should be clear that the goal is to learn the Word of God, not to compete.

We trust that this attractive and experiential teaching will allow children to treasure the Word of God in their hearts and that "they will not depart from the right path" even if they leave childhood behind.

Mission:
To prepare children as disciples of Jesus by studying and treasuring God's Word in their hearts.

Vision:
To be an effective means of evangelism and a dynamic tool of discipleship.

Values:
We are moved by Christian values such as love, fellowship, and commitment. This ministry also promotes teamwork, collaboration, respect, among many others among children.

What Resources Do I Need?
✓ NIV Bible
✓ CBQM Manual (You can visit the Discipleship Ministries page for this and other resources: www.SdmiResources.MesoamericaRegion.org
✓ Teaching materials (paper, paint, glue, scissors, pens, crayons, colored paper, etc.)

Joshua Judges Ruth

How do I form a team in my local church?

The **local SDMI President** must get the materials that are available for CBQM (physical copy or download electronic copies), and select a brother / sister who is helpful, dynamic and who loves working with children to work as a team coach.

Coach - his/her function is to prepare the team, motivating them to study the Word, giving or coordinating the Bible lessons, leading the learning activities and games, accompanying the team to all the quiz demonstrations organized by the district, etc.

Team – the team will consist of a maximum of 10 children from 7 to 11 years of age. (They may be younger, but they should be able to read and write.) If a child reaches 12 years between the months of July-December, they can still participate.

How Do We Prepare The Children?

A teaching and study time must be established with the team. The study must consider the theme assigned for the bible quizzing.

To study the subject better, it can be divided into chapters or specific events, for this use the coach's guide which will guide you in this process. Start with teaching about the events, and discuss with them by using questions and having them answer from memory about situations, characters, places and names. Explain facts that motivate the curiosity of the team in terms of customs, meaning of objects or rites and other interesting features that complement and clarify the text and context read. Create lists of words, names, places, objects, animals. Find out in which other books of the Bible the main characters are mentioned. Have the children memorize the key verses exactly. Help the children memorize events and sequences of the stories, in a non-textual way, so they can relate it as completely as possible. It is necessary to help them remember important data. Guide them to discover individually and as a team the teaching of God for their lives and perform the games that are related to the lesson studied.

THIS STUDY GUIDE CAN HELP WITH THE FOLLOWING THEMES:

- Where did this character(s) come from?
- Who are they related to?
- Where does the story unfold?
- How does God work in their lives?
- What is the reason why this story is found in the Bible?
- How does this passage relate to Christ and therefore to salvation?
- Take each story and bring it to the current time. How would you do it?
- What values are found in the story?
- What places are mentioned? Find them on a map.
- What are the characters like?
- What characteristics do they have?
- What things stand out in the culture and do you need to investigate (animals, crafts, rites or customs)?

Joshua Judges Ruth

IN ADDITION:

- Invite Sunday School teachers and / or people with theological studies to teach lessons about the topic and answer questions.

- Encourage people of the church to support the team.

- Practice each game only after having studied and clarified the subject considerably.

- Remember that it is important to establish the skills in which the child performs best.

Who are the officials in a Demonstration?

Moderator – He or she must be an impartial person. They can be a guest from another district or from a local church that is not participating in the demonstration.

- This is the person who chooses the games and prepares the material for them.
- Directs the competition.
- Reads the instructions for each category or game.
- Chooses the team of judges.

Judges - They must be impartial. They can be invited from another district or from a church that is not participating.

A judge will be assigned to each participating team. That is, if there are 5 teams participating, there must be 5 judges. They must:

- Ensure that the rules of each game are kept.
- Oversee the participant(s) from that team during each game.
- Let the moderator know if any rules are broken.

Time Judge – They must keep time for each game, giving the signal for the start and the end of the time allotted for the game.

ANNUAL STUDY CYCLE

- JOSHUA, JUDGES & RUTH: 2021-2022
- 1 & 2 SAMUEL: 2022–2023
- MATTHEW: 2023-2024
- ACTS: 2024-2025
- GENESIS: 2025-2026
- EXODUS: 2026-2027

NOTES

If you have worked with CBQM - Activities before, you will notice some changes. For example, we have changed the word "trainer" to "coach" because we think it is more appropriate.

Some games have been modified, others have been removed and new games directly related to the subject of study have been added.

Remember that a competition is a demonstration, because each team demonstrates how much they have learned from the Word of God. We must ensure that competitiveness is healthy and creates bonds of friendship between the participating teams.

LIST OF VERSES TO MEMORIZE

Keep this Book of the Law always on your lips; meditate on it day and night, so that you may be careful to do everything written in it. Then you will be prosperous and successful. Joshua 1:8	Have I not commanded you? Be strong and courageous. Do not be afraid; do not be discouraged, for the Lord your God will be with you wherever you go. Joshua 1:9	When we heard of it, our hearts melted in fear and everyone's courage failed because of you, for the Lord your God is God in heaven above and on the earth below. Joshua 2:11
Joshua told the people, "Consecrate yourselves, for tomorrow the Lord will do amazing things among you." Joshua 3:5	And the Lord said to Joshua, "Today I will begin to exalt you in the eyes of all Israel, so they may know that I am with you as I was with Moses." Joshua 3:7	The priests who carried the ark of the covenant of the Lord stopped in the middle of the Jordan and stood on dry ground, while all Israel passed by until the whole nation had completed the crossing on dry ground. Joshua 3:17
He said to the Israelites, "In the future when your descendants ask their parents, 'What do these stones mean?' tell them, 'Israel crossed the Jordan on dry ground.'" Joshua 4:21-22	When the trumpets sounded, the army shouted, and at the sound of the trumpet, when the men gave a loud shout, the wall collapsed; Joshua 6:20a	So the Lord was with Joshua, and his fame spread throughout the land. Joshua 6:27
Achan replied, "It is true! I have sinned against the Lord, the God of Israel. This is what I have done:" Joshua 7:20	Joshua said to the Lord in the presence of Israel: "Sun, stand still over Gibeon, and you, moon, over the Valley of Aijalon." 13 So the sun stood still, and the moon stopped, till the nation avenged itself on its enemies, Joshua 10:12b-13a	Not one of all the Lord's good promises to Israel failed; every one was fulfilled. Joshua 21:45
So be very careful to love the Lord your God. Joshua 23:11	"Now fear the Lord and serve him with all faithfulness. Throw away the gods your ancestors worshiped beyond the Euphrates River and in Egypt, and serve the Lord." Joshua 24:14	But if serving the Lord seems undesirable to you, then choose for yourselves this day whom you will serve, whether the gods your ancestors served beyond the Euphrates, or the gods of the Amorites, in whose land you are living. But as for me and my household, we will serve the Lord. Joshua 24:15

Joshua Judges Ruth

And the people said to Joshua, "We will serve the Lord our God and obey him." Joshua 24:24	When the angel of the Lord appeared to Gideon, he said, "The Lord is with you, mighty warrior." Judges 6:12	When I and all who are with me blow our trumpets, then from all around the camp blow yours and shout, "For the Lord and for Gideon." Judges 7:18
The woman gave birth to a boy and named him Samson. He grew and the Lord blessed him, Judges 13:24	Then Samson prayed to the Lord, "Sovereign Lord, remember me. Please, God, strengthen me just once more" Judges 16:28a,b	Then Samson reached toward the two central pillars on which the temple stood. Bracing himself against them, his right hand on the one and his left hand on the other, Samson said, "Let me die with the Philistines!" Judges 16:29-30a
But Ruth replied, "Don't urge me to leave you or to turn back from you. Where you go I will go, and where you stay I will stay. Your people will be my people and your God my God." Ruth 1:16	So Boaz took Ruth and she became his wife. When he made love to her, the Lord enabled her to conceive, and she gave birth to a son. Ruth 4:13	The women living there said, "Naomi has a son!" And they named him Obed. He was the father of Jesse, the father of David. Ruth 4:17

GO TO PAGE 94 FOR MEMORY VERSE
MEMORIZATION ACTIVITIES

Joshua Judges Ruth

Team Name

Instructions:
1. In advance and with the help of the coach, each team must choose a name.
2. The name must be related to the subject of study.
3. It must have biblical support which will be explained by one or more participants.
4. At this time, the team members must also be presented.
5. Judges should consider the following aspects:
    - The relationship to the subject of study
    - Creativity of the name
    - Biblical reference
    - Creativity of presentation
    - Mention of the team members

Foul:
Points are deducted from a team if anyone is talking while another team is presenting.

Points
100 points

Time
Less than 5 minutes

Participants
The whole team

Mode
One team at a time

Distinctive

Instructions:
1. In advance and with the help of the coach and parents, each team must carry/wear something that distinguishes them. It can be a shirt, cap, sports uniform, etc. It can include the name of the team, the member's name and a logo.
2. The judges evaluate according to the following scale:
    - Uniformity (all the same)
    - Badge Creativity
    - Presentation creativity

Foul:
Points are deducted from a team if anyone is talking while another team is presenting.

Points
50 points

Time
Less than 5 minutes

Participants
The whole team

Mode
One team at a time

Team Cheer

Instructions:

1. In advance and with the help of the coach, each team must prepare a team cheer.
2. It should be based on the subject of study and the name of the team.
3. It may not contain offensive ideas or words towards other teams.
4. The judges evaluate according to the following scale:
   - Relevance to the subject of study
   - Cheer creativity
   - Creativity in Presentation
   - Mention of team name

Foul:

Points are deducted from a team if anyone is talking while another team is presenting.

Points

50 points

Time

Less than 5 minutes

Participants

The whole team

Mode

One team at a time

Mascot

Instructions:

1. In advance and with the help of the coach, each team must have a mascot.
2. Preferably it should be an animal that is related to the subject of study.
3. It must contain a biblical teaching.
4. The judges evaluate according to the following scale:
   - Relevance to the subject of study
   - Costume Creativity
   - Creativity of Presentation
   - Biblical teaching

Foul:

Points are deducted from a team if anyone is talking while another team is presenting.

Points

100 points

Time

Less than 5 minutes

Participants

The whole team

Mode

One team at a time

Joshua Judges Ruth

Team banner

Instructions:

1. In advance and with the help of the coach, each team must have a team banner.
2. It must be related to the name of the team.
3. It must be drawn and painted by the team participants and will serve to decorate their space at a demonstration.
4. It must be related to the subject of study and biblical support which will be explained by one or more participants.
5. The judges evaluate according to the following scale:
   - Relevance to the subject of study
   - Drawing creativity
   - Order and cleanliness
   - Biblical teaching
   - Creativity in the presentation

Foul:

Points are deducted from a team if anyone is talking while another team is presenting.

Points

100 points

Time

Less than 5 minutes

Participants

The whole team

Mode

One team at a time

Joshua Judges Ruth

MEMORIZATION CATEGORY

Memorization and reasoning are fundamental for learning, and repetition is one of the keys to memorization. The objective of this category is to help children memorize and understand the Bible in a dynamic and attractive way.

SOME MEMORIZATION TECHNIQUES:
- Connect and link
- Associate objects with places
- Create stories
- Link words with numbers to remember sequences
- Draw mental maps
- Acronyms, using the first letter of each word
- Repeat the keywords
- Use all the senses

For a local, district, zone, national demonstration, etc. the moderator will choose:

3 Memorization Games

The teams will know which specific games will be played ONLY on the day of the demonstration.

Joshua Judges Ruth

Advance

Instructions:

1. The moderator draws the order in which the teams participate and they are placed in front of their three rings (hula hoops).

2. The first participant must say a verse from the list of memory verses (their choice). They must say it exactly; if it is correct, the moderator indicates it and the participant advances into the first ring.

3. The next participant must recite another verse (their choice); the difficulty is that they cannot recite a verse that has already been quoted by another participant; in case this happens, the child will not be able to advance.

If during the first 30 seconds the child does not begin to say his verse, he loses the opportunity and does not advance.

10 points are awarded for each verse correctly quoted, up to 30 points per team

Consultations:
Are not permitted.

Foul:
If someone from the audience says a part of the passage or reference out loud, or if the child consults with their coach or team, their participation in this game is disqualified and canceled.

Suggestion:
If there are many teams participating, it can be reduced to 2 rings per team.

Example:

Points
10 points for correct passage

Time
30 seconds to start

Participants
1 per team

Mode
One team at a time alternating

Materials
- Three hoops (hula hoops) per team.
- The judge must have the list of the memory passages.

Maria of team "Joshua" quoted two passages, advancing 2 rings, earning 20 points. James of team "Strong and Courageous" quoted 3 passages, advancing 3 rings, earning 30 points. Jamie from team "Jordan" quoted 1 passage, advancing 1 ring, earning 10 points for her team.

Joshua Judges Ruth

Answer and Advance

Instructions:

1. The moderator draws the order of participation, and then attaches on the board or wall a drawing to connect the dots, which must have 15 dots to connect. (see example).
2. The first team to participate stands three meters away from the drawing, one participant behind the other, the moderator allows them to choose an envelope with questions and gives them the markers.
3. The moderator reads the first question, immediately after which the five minutes start counting down. Each participant has 30 seconds to give their answer. If it is correct, they connect two dots with black color. If it is incorrect, they must connect the two dots with red color. Then the participant runs back to their team to hand the markers to the next person in line and the moderator reads the next question.
4. If the participant doesn't respond with the answer within 30 seconds, the judge indicates it, and the participant must draw a red line, and the moderator will say the answer.
5. The time does not stop nor can the questions be repeated.

Consultations:

Are not permitted

Foul:

- If one of the participants goes twice in a row, the judge indicates it and cancels a question.
- If one of the participants draws two lines of the drawing, the judge indicates it and cancels a question.
- If someone in the audience says an answer out loud, the judge indicates it and a red line must be drawn.
- Take into account that time does not stop at any time.

Example:

Following you will find an example of a set of questions and a drawing.

Points

5 points for each correct answer

Time

5 minutes

Participants

2 per team

Mode

One team at a time

Materials

- A drawing with 15 points to connect for each team.
- Closed envelopes with sets of 15 questions (different for each team).
- A black marker (correct), and a red marker (incorrect).

Joshua Judges Ruth

Answer and Advance Set of questions

1. To whom did the Lord speak after Moses' death?
   To Joshua, (1:1)

2. What did the Lord say to Joshua after Moses' death?
   Get ready to cross the Jordan River (1:2)

3. What did the Lord say to Joshua when he became Israel's leader?
   I will be with you; I will never leave you nor forsake you (1:5)

4. Who would lead the people to inherit the land that Jehovah swore to his fathers?
   Joshua. (1:6)

5. What did the Lord say Joshua had to be?
   Strong and courageous (1:6-7)

6. When was Joshua supposed to meditate on the Book of the Law?
   Day and night (1:8)

7. What things was Joshua not to do?
   Be afraid or discouraged (1:9)

8. According to Joshua 1:14, what were the fighting men, ready for battle, to do?
   They would help their fellow Israelites until the Lord gives them rest.

9. How were they to obey Joshua?
   In all things, as they did with Moses. (1:17)

10. Who sent two spies to Jericho?
    Joshua (2:1)

11. Where did the spies stay?
    In the house of a prostitute named Rahab (2:1)

12. What did Rahab tell the king of Jericho about the spies?
    Yes, the men came to me, but I did not know where they had come from. (2:4)

13. Where did Rahab hide the spies?
    On the roof under the stalks of flax (2:6)

14. What happened when the pursuers left?
    The gate was shut. (2:7)

15. According to Joshua 2:9, what did Rahab tell the spies?
    I know that the Lord has given you this land. (2:9)

Answer and Advance drawing

Joshua Judges Ruth

Bible Verse Bingo

Instructions:

1. The moderator places the Bingo cards face down on a table or floor in front of each team, and hands each team the marker or highlighter.
2. The moderator gives the indication to turn over their cards and begins reading the biblical verses one by one, giving a few seconds after each verse. The moderator will only read the verses without saying the references.
3. Participants should listen carefully to the reading of each verse to identify the reference on the card and mark each one they recognize. The team that manages to do three in a row (horizontal, vertical or diagonal) yells "BINGO", and everyone stops.
4. If there is a tie between teams, 30 points are awarded to each one. If at the end of reading the verses, no team manages to do three in a row, no one gets any points.

Consultations:
Are not permitted.

Foul:
If the team interrupts or asks questions during the reading of the verses, the judges will deduct 2 points. If the audience says part of the verse or quote out loud, their team is disqualified and their participation in this game is canceled.

Verses to play:
- Only memory verses from the book of Joshua will be used.

Example of the Bingo Cards:

Points
30 points

Time
The duration of the reading of the verses

Participants
2 per team

Mode
Simultaneous

Materials
- Bingo cards, one per team.
- One person per team can be the marker (make a dot or other mark) or use a highlighter.
- List of memoriy verses

BIBLE BINGO

24:15	6:20a	3:17
1:9	7:20	21:45
6:27	2:11	10:13

BIBLE BINGO

2:11	7:20	24:15
3:7	24:14	1:9
1:8	3:5	6:20a

BIBLE BINGO

3:5	24:15	24:14
21:45	1:8	4:21-22
7:20	6:27	6:20a

BIBLE BINGO

4:21-22	2:11	6:20a
24:15	1:8	10:13
6:27	24:14	21:45

Joshua Judges Ruth

Crossword Puzzle

Instructions:

1. Each team is given a crossword puzzle of 6 or 8 questions. Each team is given five minutes to answer. Teams must submit their crossword puzzle in the allotted time.
2. At the end of the five minutes, 10 points are awarded for each correct answer.

Consultations:

Consultation is only allowed among the 3 participants of the team.

Foul:

If team members consult with the coach or other children of the team who are not participating, the judge will inform the moderator and the moderator will disqualify the crossword of that team, thereby eliminating their participation in this game only.

Example:

Three crosswords based on one of the books of the study (Joshua, Judges, and Ruth) are proposed.

Suggestion:

Since the category is memorization, it is suggested that the proposed crosswords be used in the competition.

Points
10 points for each correct answer

Time
5 minutes

Participants
3 per team

Mode
Simultaneousus

Materials
- A paper with the same crossword puzzle for each team.
- One pen per team

Answers:

CROSSWORD 1	CROSSWORD 2	CROSSWORD 3
Horizontal	**Horizontal**	**Horizontal**
Refuge, Golan, Kedesh, Bezer, Lord, Shechem	Milk, Tent Peg, Mount Tabor, Nine hundred, Sword	Obed, Grandmother, Ruth, Right, Town Gate
Vertical	**Vertical**	**Vertical**
Murderers, Ramoth, Accident, Home.	Heber, Barak, Deborah, Blanket, Sisera.	Arms, Sandal, Perez, Israel, Elimelek.

Crossword #1 - Joshua

Based on: Joshua Designates the Cities of Refuge, Chapter 20

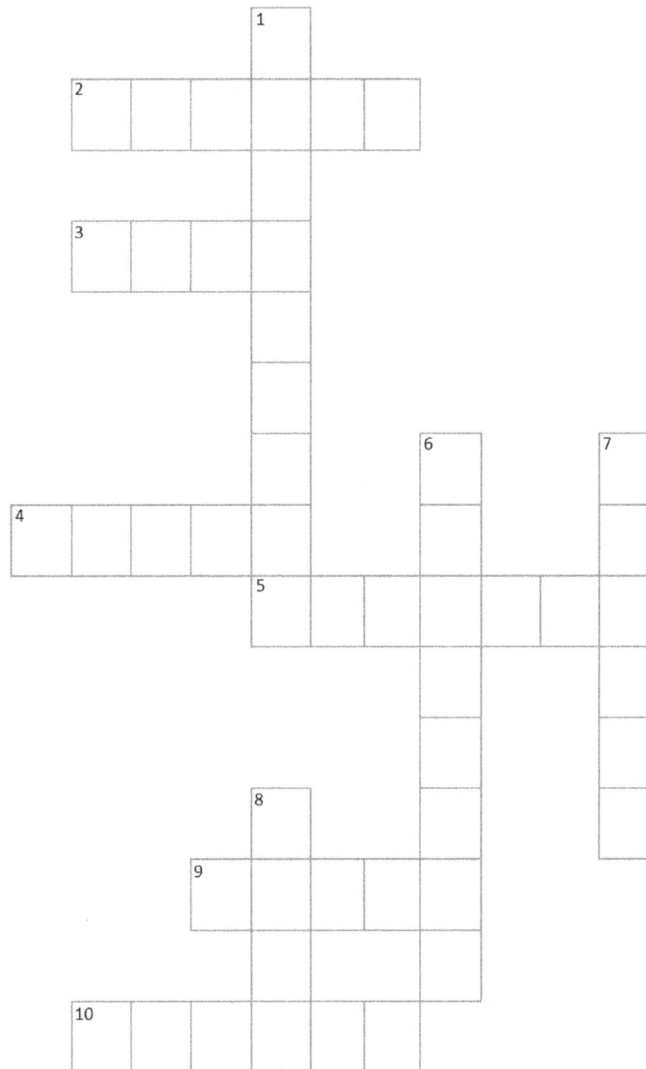

Across

2. Joshua had to tell Israel to designate cities of _____.
3. Who spoke to Joshua?
4. What city did they designate in the plateau in the tribe of Reuben?
5. What city did they designate in the hill country of Ephraim?
9. Which city did they designate from the tribe of Manasseh?
10. Which city did they designate in Galilee?

Down

1. Who would be welcomed in the cities of refuge?
6. These cities would welcome only those who killed someone by _____?
7. Which city did they designate from the tribe of Gad?
8. When the high priest died, where could the murderer go?

Joshua Judges Ruth

Crossword puzzle #2 - Judges

Based on: Deborah and Barak Defeat Sisera, Chapter 4

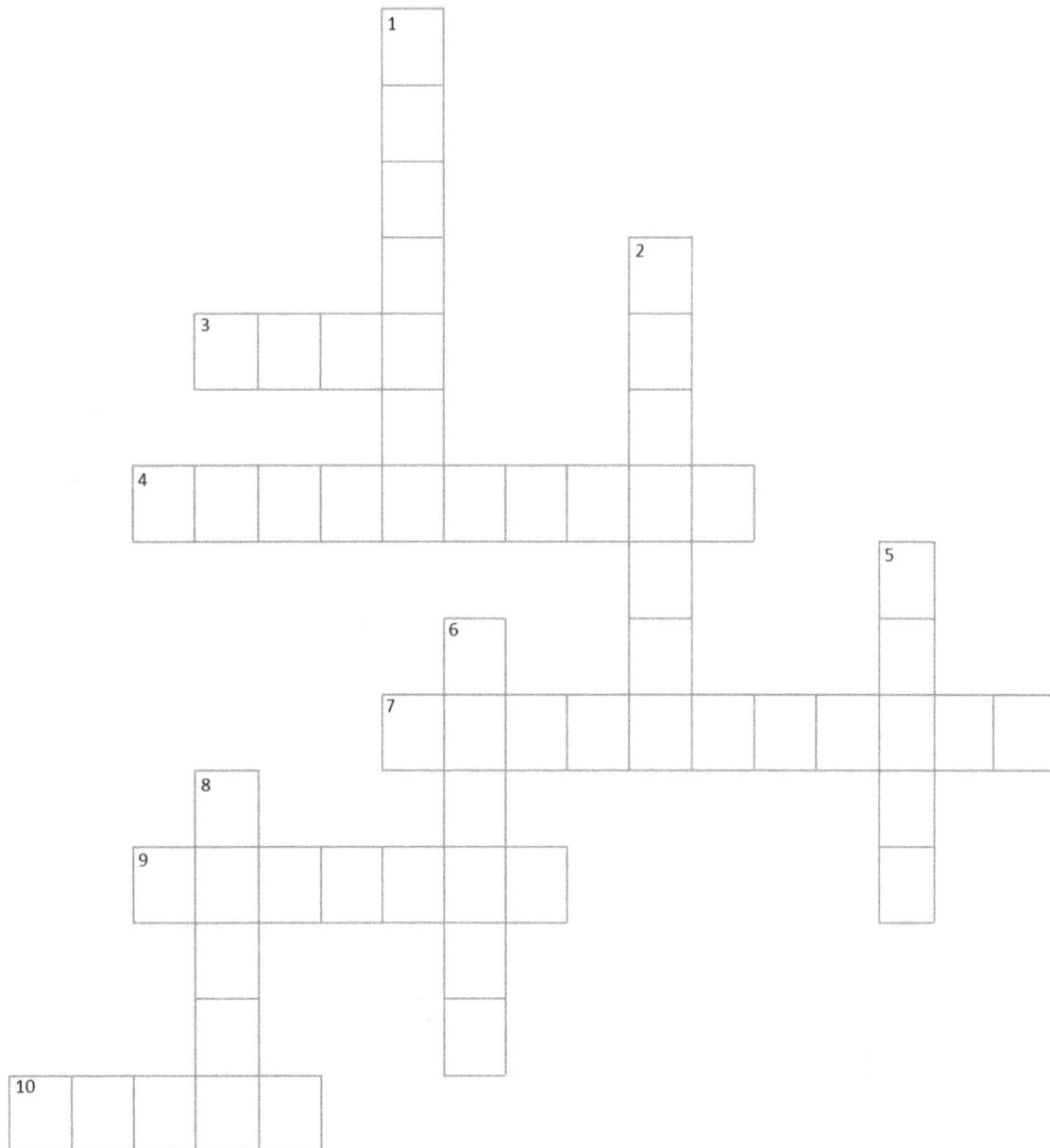

Across

3. What did Jael give Sisera to drink?

4. Where was Barak to gather his people?

7. How many iron chariots did Sisera gather?

9. What did Jael take in her hands?

8. The whole army of Sisera fell by the _____.

Down

1. Sisera took refuge in Jael's house and she covered him with a _____.

2. Who led Israel at that time?

5. Who did Deborah send for?

6. What was the name of the captain of the army of Jabin, King of Canaan?

8. Whose wife was Jael?

116

Joshua Judges Ruth

Crossword Puzzle #3 - Ruth

Based on: Boaz Marries Ruth, Chapter 4

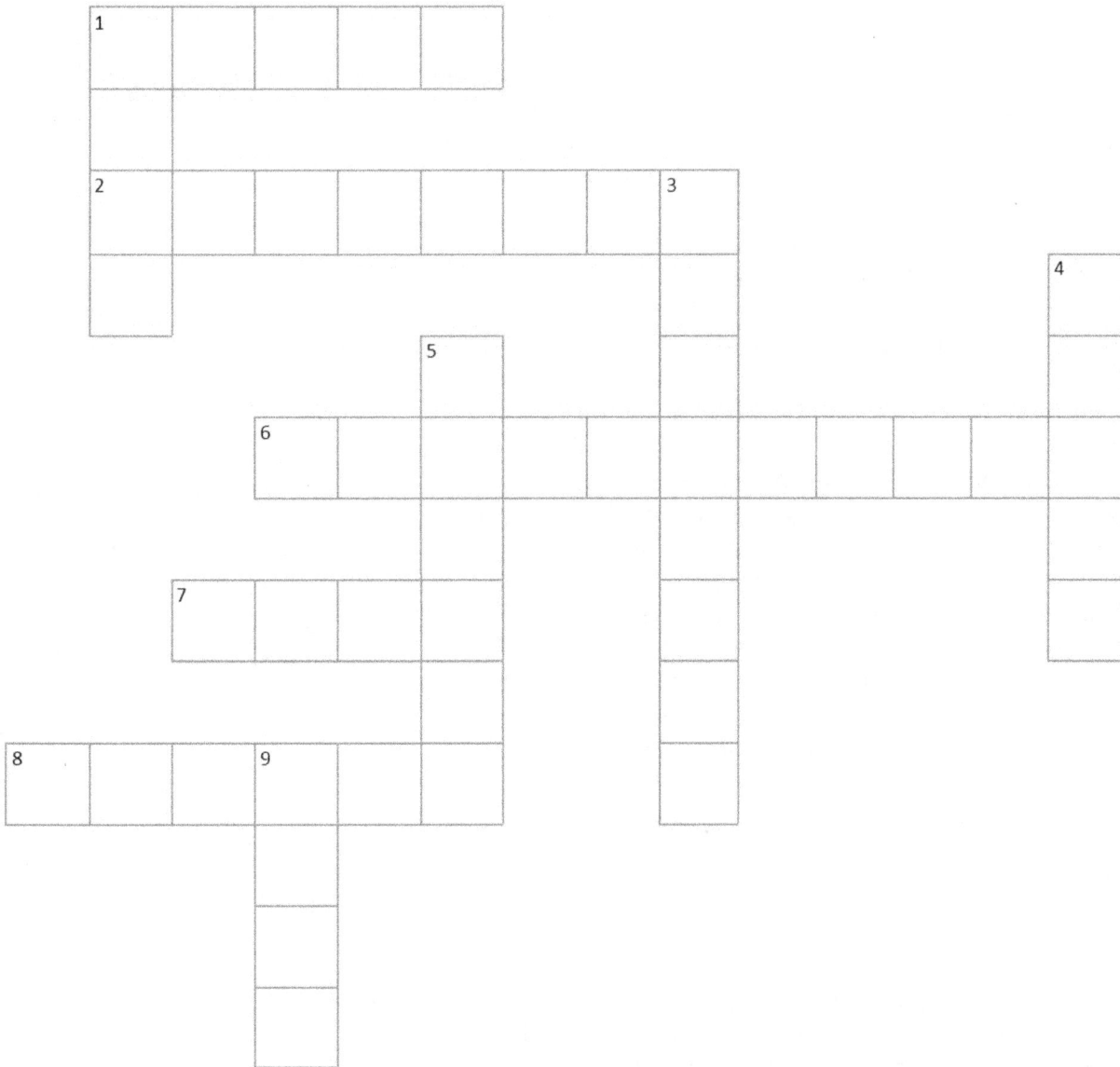

Across

1. The relative told Boaz to redeem him, using his _____.

2. Where did Boaz go up and sit?

6. Naomi was Obed's _____?

7. What name did the neighbors give to the son of Boaz and Ruth?

8. The people and the elders said that Boaz would become famous in _____.

Down

1. Who did Boaz take as his wife?

3. Boaz bought from Naomi all that belonged to _.

4. Boaz and Obed were descendants in the family line of _____.

5. What did the relative take off as confirmation of the business?

9. Naomi put Ruth and Boaz's son in her _____.

117

Joshua Judges Ruth

Discover the Verse

Instructions:

1. The moderator chooses the order of participation at random.
2. The moderator must prepare as many memory verses as teams that will be participating. The verses must be different for each team, taken from the list of memory verses. The length of the verses chosen should be similar. Cards are presented with one letter of the verse on each card; the cards are to be the size of a quarter piece of letter size paper (4.25 x 5.5 inches) and the letter written proportionally to the size of the card. The cards are to be taped or hung on a board or wall with the letter facing the wall so that the participants can't see the letter. You can number the back side of the cards to locate the letters faster.
3. The participant stands two meters away from the verse and has the opportunity to choose four letters and/or numbers. The moderator will then flip over all the cards that have the chosen letters/numbers. (Similar to the American game show "Wheel of Fortune.")
4. The participant has 1 minute to discover the verse. If they are correct, the judge indicates it and 40 points are scored. If they do not discover it or do not say it during the first minute, then they don't accumulate any points.

Consultations:

Are not permitted.

Foul:

If the participant consults with his team, or someone in the audience says a letter aloud, attention is called to the foul. If the foul is committed again, the judge will cancel the participant's participation in this game.

If the team or a member of the audience says any part of the verse, the participation of the team in this game is canceled.

Example: The sample text is: And the people said to Joshua, "We will serve the LORD our God and obey him."
Joshua 24:24

Points
50 points

Time
1 minute

Participants
1 per team

Mode
One team at a time alternating

Materials
- Bible memory verses written one letter per card on cards the size of ¼ letter size paper. Different verse for each team.

A	N	D		T	H	E		P	E	O	P	L	E		S	A	I	D		T	O	
1	2	3		4	5	6		7	8	9	10	11	12		13	14	15	16		17	18	

J	O	S	H	U	A	,		"	W	E		W	I	L	L		S	E	R	V	E
19	20	21	22	23	24			25	26		27	28	29	30		31	32	33	34	35

T	H	E		L	O	R	D		O	U	R		G	O	D		A	N	D	
36	37	38		39	40	41	42		43	44	45		46	47	48		49	50	51	

O	B	E	Y		H	I	M	.	"		J	O	S	H	U	A		2	4	:	2	4
52	53	54	55		56	57	58				59	60	61	62	63	64		65	66		67	68

The moderator can use this key to make flipping cards easier, however, one of these must be created for each verse.

A	1, 14, 24, 49, 64,		K	----------------		U	23, 44, 63
B	53		L	11, 29, 30, 39		V	34
C	----------------		M	58		W	25, 27
D	3, 16, 42, 48, 51		N	2, 50		X	----------------
E	6, 8, 12, 26, 32, 35, 38, 54		O	9, 18, 20, 40, 43, 47, 52, 60		Y	55
F	----------------		P	7		Z	_____
G	46		Q	_____		2	65, 67
H	5, 22, 37, 56, 62		R	33, 41, 45		4	66, 68
I	15, 28, 57		S	13, 21, 31, 61			
J	19, 59		T	4, 17, 36			

Tell Me the Person

Instructions:

This is a guessing game which is based on people from the book being studied. Each riddle must have three to four clues about a character in the book being studied.

1. The moderator must have two questions in an envelope for each participating team, with a participation number on the outside. The envelopes are then chosen by the teams.
2. Each participant must answer their question without consulting with his/her teammate. The participant has one minute to give the answer. If the answer is correct, the moderator says "**CORRECT**" and the judges award 20 points to the team (for each correct answer). If the answer is not correct or is not answered in the given time, the participant loses their chance and the moderator gives the correct answer. (No points are awarded to the team.)
3. The moderator continues with a participant from the other team, and alternates between each of the teams until each of the 2 participants from each team have been given the opportunity to answer a question.

Consultations:
Are not permitted.

Foul:
If a judge observes that a participant consults with his/her team or someone else present, the moderator will cancel the question and ask a different question. If the participant has already been caught doing this before, the moderator will cancel the question and the team loses its opportunity.

Example:

Points
25 points for each correct answer

Time
1 minute

Participants
2 per team

Mode
One team at a time alternating

Materials
- Envelopes with the clues, two per team and some extras.

Tell Me the Person EXAMPLES OF RIDDLES:

I am the son of Nun and successor of Moses. Jehovah told me that I had to be strong and courageous, because I would lead the people to inherit the land that God had promised to His people. Who I am? **Answer/ JOSHUA (Joshua 1:1-6)**	I live in Jericho, I hid two spies in my house, I made them swear that they would save my life and that of my family. who I am? **A/ RAHAB (Joshua 2:1-13)**	I came before Joshua with a drawn sword and asked him to remove the shoes from his feet. Who I am? **A/ THE COMMANDER OF THE ARMY OF THE LORD (Joshua 5:13-15)**
I am the son of Karmi from the tribe of Judah, I sinned against Jehovah by taking devoted things and hiding them in my tent. Who I am? **A/ ACHAN (Joshua 7)**	I am the son of Jephunneh the Kenizzite. I was 40 years old when Moses sent me to explore Kadesh Barnea and I obeyed by following the Lord. Moses said that they would give me the land that my foot had walked on. Who I am? **A/ CALEB (Joshua 14:6-9)**	I am a prophetess, married to Lappidoth. I governed the people of Israel. I sent for Barak and together we defeated Sisera. Who I am? **A/ DEBORAH (Judges 4)**
I am the son of Joash the Abiezrite. I was threshing wheat when the angel of the Lord appeared to me and told me that he would save Israel from the Midianites. Who I am? **A/ GIDEON (Judges 6)**	My father is Manoah. No razor was to touch my head because I am a Nazarite of God from my mother's womb, Who I am? **A/ SAMSON (Judges 13)**	I am from the valley of Sorek, Samson fell in love with me, because of me the Philistines cut his hair, gouged out his eyes and tied him up with chains and put him in prison. Who I am? **A/ DELILAH (Judges 16)**
We are Ephrathites from Bethlehem in Judah. We came to the fields of Moab, our sons took Moabite wives for themselves. Who are we? **A/ ELIMELEK, NAOMI, MAHLON AND KILION (RutH 1:1-4)**	I bought from Naomi all that belonged to Elimelek and his sons, and I also took Ruth the Moabite to be my wife. Who I am? **A/ BOAZ (Ruth 4)**	I am the son of Boaz and Ruth. Naomi took me in her arms and cared for me. I became the father of Jesse and grandfather of David Who I am? **A/ OBED (Ruth 4)**

Joshua Judges Ruth

The Dice

INSTRUCTIONS:

The moderator prepares a dice on which actions will be written on each side: SING A SONG, SAY A VERSE, CHARACTERISTICS OF A BIBLE CHARACTOR.

1. Each team draws a participation number. The moderator starts with number 1.
2. Number 1 participant is called forward, rolls the dice, and then has 30 seconds to do the activity that comes up on the top or the dice. If the participant can do the action, the judge gives 20 points to the team. If the participant doesn't do the action or remains silent during the 30 seconds, the judge will not award a score.
3. Next, the moderator will call up the next participant to roll the dice, and so forth until each team has participated.

Consultations:

Not permitted.

Foul:

If the boy or girl consults with his coach or team, or the audience helps them, the judge will indicate it and the moderator will give them another opportunity to throw the dice. If the same thing happens again, the person's participation in this game is canceled.

Example of a Dice:

Points

20 points

Time

1 minute

Participants

1 per team

Mode

One team at a time

Materials

- 1 large dice, (follow the example below)

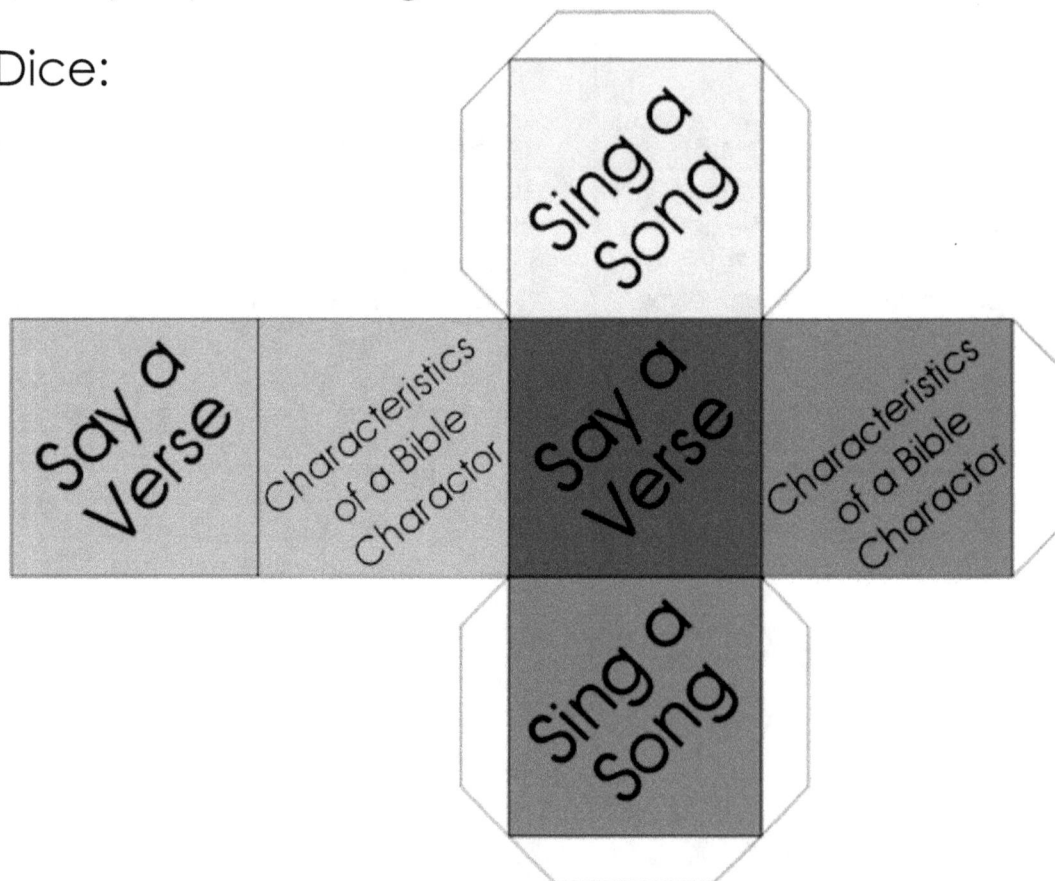

Memory

Instructions:

1. The moderator randomly chooses the order in which the teams participate.
2. The cards are placed on the floor or on a table face down and scrambled.
3. When given the starting signal, the participants of the first team turn over all the cards and have a maximum of 5 minutes to match up the 8 verses with their biblical references.
4. When all the pairs are connected, or at the end of the time period, the judge reviews the pairs and awards 10 points per correct pair.
5. The cards are scrambled and put back on the floor or table for the next team.
6. The judge must also record the time in which each team connects the 8 pairs. A bonus of 10 points is given to the team that completes all the pairs in the shortest time.
7. The verses must be taken from the list of memory verses.

Consultations:

The participants cannot consult with their coach or with other members of their team; only among themselves.

Foul:

If someone from the audience says a verse or reference, the judge will subtract 10 points from the team.

Points

10 points for each correct pair
10 bonus points for the team that matches all the pairs in the least amount of time

Time

5 minutes

Participants

2 per team

Mode

One team at a time

Materials

- 16 cards (8 with the biblical texts and 8 with the respective biblical reference) for each team. The texts must be taken from the list of verses to be memorized.

Example:

| "Have I not commanded you? Be strong and courageous. Do not be afraid; do not be discouraged, for the LORD your God will be with you wherever you go." | JOSHUA 1:9 |

| When the angel of the LORD appeared to Gideon, he said, "The LORD is with you, mighty warrior." | JUDGES 6:12 |

;tructions:

...aw a line in any direction, even diagonally, to join the letters and find   minute

...e game is started immediately. No team may see the puzzle

nsultatio   a few e)

...yone present says the word aloud, the judge will indicate it. This

Barak, Angel, Naomi, Jabin, Caleb   horns

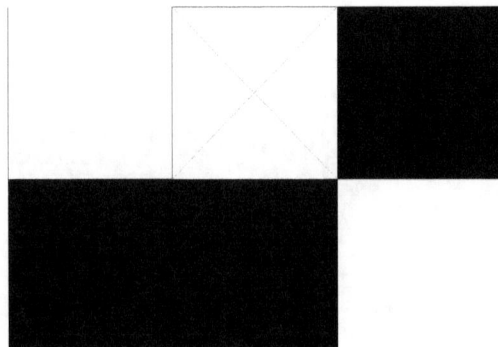

Joshua Judges Ruth

The Key Letter

Instructions:

The moderator will give a sealed envelope that will contain a category (characters, places, objects, animals, miscellaneous) and a base vowel to each participating team. The teams will participate Simultaneoususly by writing a list of words related to the selected category containing the specific base letter they received in their envelope.

1. Each team will choose an envelope containing a category and base letter from the moderator.
2. The 3 participants will form a line three meters away from the board. When the moderator gives the signal, the first participant of each team goes to the board and writes a qualifying word, then returns to their team and hands the marker/chalk to the next participant of his team.
3. That second participant then goes to the board and writes the second word and so on until the time limit of one minute is over.

NOTE:
The participant can run or walk to and from the board.

Consultations:
Are not permitted.

Foul:
If the judge observes that the participants of a team are speaking among themselves, the value of a word is deducted. If someone from the audience says a word in a loud voice, a judge will indicate it and the value of a word is deducted from all teams.

Example:

Points
5 points for each correct word

Time
1 minute

Participants
3 per team

Mode
Simultaneousus

Materials
- Sealed envelopes that contain a category (characters, places, objects, animals, miscellaneous) and a base vowel for each participating team
- Chalk boards, white boards, or large pieces of paper - enough for all teams to write on at the same time.
- A marker/chalk for each team

```
            PERSON "E"
                    E
        M   O   S   E   S
    E   L   I   M   E   L   E   K
        C   A   L   E   B
            D   E   L   I   L   A   H
        G   I   D   E   O   N
        S   I   S   E   R   A
```

```
            PLACE "A"
                    A
        G   O   L   A   N
    G   I   L   E   A   D
    B   A   S   H   A   N
            H   A   Z   O   R
            A   M   M   O   N
    T   I   M   N   A   H
```

Joshua Judges Ruth

Alphabet Soup

Instructions:

Each team will receive the same puzzle at the same time.

Each team must discover the words that appear horizontally, vertically, diagonally, top to bottom, left to right or vice versa.

1. The moderator places the puzzles face down on the table or floor in front of each team. The puzzles must have in the title a topic related to the search, for example: Moses' Birth, The Plagues, etc.

2. When the start signal is given, each team must turn over the puzzle and find the words. Words must be circled and written down on the side of the puzzle.

3. When a team finishes, they must take their completed puzzle to one of the judges for review (the time is recorded). (The other teams continue working on their puzzles.) If the judge observes that the team has found all of the correct words, he/she will inform the moderator. The competition stops and one of the participants reads the list aloud and that team wins 50 points.

4. If the word puzzle is incorrect on some word(s), the judge will simply say "Incorrect" and the team will continue to search for words

The maximum time for this competition is 7 minutes. If no team finishes during the set time, the competition is scored according to the correct answers (5 points per correct answer).

Consultations:

Consultation on the puzzle will only be between the two participants of the team.

Foul:

If a participant consults with someone other than their other participating teammate, the judge will indicate it and give them a 30-second penalty.

Points
5 points for
each correct word

Time
7 minutes

Participants
2 per team

Mode
Simultaneousus

Materials
- A marker or pencil per team.
- Word-search puzzles with ten words to discover – sufficient number for each participating team to receive one copy.

Answers:		
ALPHABET SOUP 1	**ALPHABET SOUP 2**	**ALPHABET SOUP 3**
Joshua, Jordan, ark, river, water, twelve, tribe, stopped, priests, covenant.	Gideon, Midianites, Lord, water, tongues, knees, threehundred, trumpets, camp, sword.	Ruth, Boaz, grain, field, harvesters, Bethlehem, sheaves, Moabite, bread, vinegar.

Joshua Judges Ruth

ALPHABET SOUP 1

Based on Joshua 3, the crossing of the Jordan River

A	M	U	P	E	J	C	X	S	T	O	P	P	E	D	T	Q	D	X	C
F	E	C	N	Q	O	R	I	F	K	B	S	L	G	Y	K	T	J	L	O
S	B	Y	A	W	R	Z	D	C	A	R	K	I	S	H	P	A	U	G	V
M	W	H	K	V	D	U	M	I	L	H	P	T	W	E	L	V	E	K	E
J	O	S	H	U	A	X	B	P	T	R	S	J	M	D	E	N	O	I	N
N	Y	Q	G	H	N	R	J	E	R	T	E	V	C	W	R	K	B	T	A
R	T	D	O	L	W	Q	U	C	I	O	K	D	F	H	I	S	D	P	N
N	M	W	A	T	E	R	Y	Q	B	X	I	S	L	R	V	G	W	V	T
X	A	B	K	E	M	Z	F	C	E	S	M	Z	J	T	E	U	L	F	X
G	V	L	D	Z	P	R	I	E	S	T	S	P	C	T	R	R	E	Q	B

1.	6.
2.	7.
3.	8.
4.	9.
5.	10.

Joshua Judges Ruth

ALPHABET SOUP 2
Based on Judges 7, Gideon defeats the Midianites

A	M	U	P	E	J	C	X	N	L	I	M	N	O	E	D	Q	D	X	H
F	E	C	A	M	P	R	I	F	O	B	S	L	G	Y	K	K	J	L	O
S	B	Y	A	W	B	Z	D	E	R	R	K	I	S	H	N	O	U	G	J
M	W	H	K	V	D	U	M	I	D	I	A	N	I	T	E	S	E	V	D
U	O	G	K	U	P	X	B	P	T	R	S	J	M	D	E	N	O	I	S
T	Y	Q	G	H	N	B	J	E	Z	T	E	V	C	W	S	K	B	T	J
O	T	H	R	E	E	H	U	N	D	R	E	D	F	H	X	S	D	P	D
N	M	N	E	H	E	E	C	Q	U	X	I	S	L	R	T	G	W	V	T
G	I	D	E	O	N	Z	F	C	W	S	M	W	A	T	E	R	L	F	X
U	A	B	R	E	M	B	I	H	L	T	S	O	C	T	S	R	E	Q	B
E	Q	B	J	G	T	D	N	F	X	P	T	R	U	M	P	E	T	S	D
S	K	W	E	O	Z	A	V	U	R	I	B	D	M	F	Y	C	S	G	A

1.		6.	
2.		7.	
3.		8.	
4.		9.	
5.		10.	

Joshua Judges Ruth

ALPHABET SOUP 3

Based on Ruth 2, Ruth picks grain in Boaz's field

A	H	U	P	E	B	R	E	A	D	I	M	T	K	E	D	Q	D	X	H
B	A	Z	L	B	E	U	Y	D	P	B	S	H	E	A	V	E	S	L	N
S	R	Y	A	O	H	Z	D	E	R	V	T	I	S	E	R	T	M	G	M
M	V	H	K	A	K	R	M	I	F	I	E	L	D	T	L	S	E	V	O
B	E	E	O	Z	Y	N	B	J	T	N	W	J	M	D	V	G	O	I	A
N	S	Q	G	H	J	R	J	E	Z	E	E	V	C	W	S	R	B	T	B
T	T	R	H	G	A	U	N	M	C	G	P	A	F	H	P	A	D	P	I
B	E	T	H	L	E	H	E	M	E	A	H	S	L	R	I	I	W	V	T
L	R	R	K	E	M	Z	F	C	W	R	M	W	B	T	K	N	S	F	E
G	S	F	R	D	N	R	U	T	H	T	S	P	C	T	B	R	E	Q	B

1.		6.	
2.		7.	
3.		8.	
4.		9.	
5.		10.	

Joshua Judges Ruth

Finish The Story

Instructions:

The moderator will have a list of biblical passages to read, one for each participating team. The biblical passages must be different, but they must have the same number of verses.

1. The moderator draws the order of participation.

2. The 3 participants of the first team will sit in the three chairs. The moderator begins by reading the biblical passage to the first team. As soon as one of the three participants of the team recognizes the passage, they must interrupt the moderator by rising from their place to continue the story. The time begins the moment the moderator starts reading and stops when the participant gets up. The judges record this time. The moderator instructs the participant to finish the story. The participant has 1 minute to do so.

3. When the participant finishes the story, the moderator announces if the rest of the story is correct or not, and the time obtained. If the story is not correct, the moderator announces "INCORRECT." If 2 or 3 participants of the team get up at the same time, they must immediately decide which participant will continue.

4. The moderator then repeats the process with a different passage for the next team.

5. The winning team is the one who correctly finishes the story and has the shortest time elapsed during the reading of the moderator. The time judge must make sure that the participant does not exceed the 1-minute time limit to complete the story.

Consultations:

Quiet consultation between the 3 participants of the team is allowed.

Foul:

If one of the participants gets up from his place to finish the story, but forgets the rest of the story, he is given 15 seconds to start his response. If he remains silent or sits down again, the judge indicates "INCORRECT" to the moderator, ending the participation of that team in this game.

Stories:

- The 12 stones taken from the Jordan, Joshua 4
- The taking of Jericho, Joshua 6
- Deborah and Barak defeat Sisera, Judges 4
- Gideon defeats the Midianites, Judges 7
- Samson defeats the Philistines at Lehi, Judges 15
- Ruth and Naomi, Ruth 1
- Ruth picks ears of corn in Boaz's field, Ruth 2

Points

50 points

Time

1 minute

Participants

3 per team

Mode

One team at a time

Materials

- One biblical passage for each team. Each passage must be different, but the same number of verses.
- Three chairs

REFLECTION CATEGORY

The coach facilitates the lesson considering the objective or purpose of the teaching, and dialogues with the children of the team allowing them to formulate their questions. The objective of this category is to motivate the boys and girls to reflect on the Bible reading in terms of the spiritual teachings it contains, and the context (historical, cultural, idiomatic, etc.) in which it is developed.

Let children know that learning is the result of personal effort.

SOME REFLECTION TECHNIQUES:

- Dialogue
- Directed Questions
- Active listening and intense participation
- Focus on the essentials
- Harmonize theory and practice

For a local, district, zone, national demonstration, etc. the moderator will choose:

2 reflection games

The teams will find out which games will be played only on the day of the demonstrations.

Joshua Judges Ruth

Chest Of Memories

Instructions:

The moderator will place the objects inside the chest/trunk/box beforehand.

1. Each team will choose a participation number.

2. Starting with team 1, the moderator will invite the first participant to put his hand into the chest and take out an object without looking. The participant then will have 2 minutes to explain what that object represents from the Bible verses being studied.

3. If the participant relates his story well, the judge will give him 10 points, and then continue on to the second participant of the same team. The same directions apply to the second participant, as well as to additional teams. Each participant can earn 10 points, for a maximum of 20 points per team.

NOTE:

An object that has been taken out of the chest is not put back in after the participant is finished with it.

Consultations:

Are not permitted.

Foul:

If a participant consults with his partner or anyone else, the judge will deduct 10 points from the team.

Example:

Book	Joshua 1:8, 8:31, 34	Fire	Joshua and Judges chap. 6
Camp	Joshua 1:11, 8:13 Judges 7	Sandals	Joshua chap. 9, Ruth 4:7
Gate	Joshua 8:29, 20:4 Judges 16	bread	judges chap. 6
scarlet cord	Joshua 2:18, 21	Dog	Judges 7:5
ark of the covenant	Joshua chap. 3, 4	Trumpets	Judges 7:16
stones	Joshua chap. 4, 7	Jars	Judges 7:16
grain	Joshua 5:11, Ruth chap. two	Razor	Judges 13:5
Sword	Joshua 5:13, Judges 4 and 7	Tent peg	Judges 4:21
horns	Joshua chap. 6	Barley	Ruth chap. 2 and 3

Joshua Judges Ruth

How Do You Imagine It?

Instructions:

1. The moderator has the participants choose a random envelope.
2. The moderator opens the envelope of the first participant and reads the place, and the child has a minute to give the name of the event that happened in that place and a description of what he imagines that place was like.
3. The judge evaluates both the name of the event and the description of the place according to the study book. If both are correct, the team receives 30 points.
4. If the participant only says what event happened in the place, 10 points are recorded. If the participant does not respond during the minute, the points are not recorded and the moderator gives the answer.

Consultations:

Are not permitted.

Foul:

If the child consults with the coach or with other members of his team or if someone in the audience says something out loud, the judge indicates it and that person's participation in this game is forfeited.

Points
30 points

Time
1 minute

Participants
1 per team

Mode
One team at a time

Materials

- One envelope per team with a place name where an important event happened.

Places:

PLACE	EVENT	DESCRIPTION
Jericho	It was the city to which Joshua sent 2 spies. A woman named Rahab lived there. The Lord delivered Jericho to Joshua in a very spectacular way.	Allow the children to use their imagination to describe what these places were like.
Valley of Sorek	In this place Samson met Delilah and was tricked by her.	
Country of Moab	It is the place where a man from Bethlehem went to dwell with his wife and children. They were Elimelek, Ruth, Mahlon, and Kilion. They married the Moabite women Ruth and Orpah.	

Bible Word Bingo

(This is similar to the popular game BINGO, using words instead of numbers, and one must fill up the whole card, not just a row.)

The moderator will prepare ½ or ¼ page sized game cards with 9 squares drawn on them for each participant (see next page for an example). Each square will have 1 word in it. All of the words will be different words taken from the scripture passage to be read by the moderator. 8 out of the 9 words will be different than all of the other words on all of the other game cards that all of the other participants have. However, the 9th word in each group will contain the same word – it will be the last word of the biblical passage. (Look at the example on the next page.) You can see that every word on every game card is different except the key word, which is one of the last words of the passage, which is "covenant."

1. When it is time to start, each participant will place their game card and small game pieces in front of themselves on the table, and familiarize themselves with the words on their game card.

2. The moderator will begin to read the chosen biblical passage. (The passage must be no shorter than ten verses and cannot last for more than 3 minutes.) While the moderator reads, the participants must listen carefully to the reading. When the moderator reads a word that is written on a participant's game card, that participant will place one of their game pieces on their game card. (Similar to the game BINGO.)

3. Whoever correctly fills her/his game card first and yells out "FINISHED" will receive 30 points for their team.

NOTE: If there is a tie between teams, 30 points will be awarded to each team. If there is a tie between 2 participants of the same team, only 30 points are given. If at the end of the passage reading, no participant has completely filled their card, nobody gets points.

CONSULTATIONS:
Not permitted.

FOUL:
If a team interrupts or asks questions during the reading, the judge will take away 2 points from that team.

SUGGESTED BIBLE PASSAGES
- Joshua's Farewell to the Leaders, Joshua 23:1-16
- Birth of Samson, Judges 13:1-25
- Ruth picks up grain in Boaz's field, Ruth 2

Points
30 points

Time
However long the moderator takes in reading the biblical passage.

Participants
2 per team

Mode
Simultaneousus

Materials
- Selected Bible passage
- 2 Game cards for each team
- 9 small objects for each participant that will be used as game pieces or markers (beans, corn, buttons, bottle caps, plastic disks, etc.)

Joshua Judges Ruth

Example of game cards:

Below is an example of the game cards based on the biblical passage "**Joshua's Farewell to the Leaders.**" In this case, the key word is "Covenant."

Joshua	old	promises
Sea	obey	Moses
man	survivors	covenant

snares	thorns	inheritance
great	Written	right
soul	eyes	covenant

Officials	Lord	Tribes
earth	Book	gods
intermarry	whips	covenant

Judges	Nations	Jordan
land	Law	strong
powerful	Israel	covenant

Joshua Judges Ruth

Statements

Instructions:

1. The moderator places the game cards on the table or floor, face down, in front of each team participants.
2. When given the start signal, the participants will turn over their game card and will have 1 minutes to link the places or characters with the statements and write them in the spaces provided.
3. At the end of Time, the teams give their game cards to the judge. 5 points are awarded per correct box.

Consultations:
Only between the two participants from the team.

Foul:
If the participants try to see the responses of another team, the judge points it out and their participation in this game is forfeited.

Example:

Deborah	Barak	Sisera	Jael

I am the captain of the Army of Jabin, king of Canaan. I live in Harosheth Haggoyim. *Sisera*	Wife of Lappidoth, prophetess and leader of Israel, I hold court under a palm tree.	I am the son of Abinoam, from Kedesh in Naphtali. Deborah sent for me
I went with Zebulun and Naphtali and 10,000 men to Kedesh, and Deborah went with me.	I gathered all of my 900 iron-fitted chariots, but we fell by the sword, and I fled on foot	I said to Barak, "Go! This is the day the LORD has given Sisera into your hands."
I pursued all the chariots and the army of Sisera until they fell by the sword	I am the wife of Heber the Kenite. Sisera entered my tent and I told him "Come right in. Don't be afraid."	I took a tent peg and a hammer and drove through Sisera's temple.

Joshua Judges Ruth

Two Edged Sword

Instructions:

1. The moderator has each participant choose a random envelope with 3 questions inside and a participation number on the outside.
2. The moderator reads the questions from the envelope to the participant of the first team. The child must answer if it is false or true. To do this, they will have 1 minute after the moderator begins reading the first question.
3. If the participant does not answer correctly, the moderator will say the correct answer and read the next question.
4. The judge will give 10 points for each correct answer.

Note:

It must be taken into account that time does not stop once the moderator has begun reading the first question.

Consultations:

Are not permitted.

Foul:

If the participant consults with his team or a member of the audience says one of the answers aloud, the judge indicates it and their participation in this game is forfeited.

Points

10 points for each correct answer

Time

1 minute

Participants

1 per team

Mode

One team at a time alternating

Materials

- Envelopes with three different questions for each team.

Example:

Envelope 1

1. The inhabitants of Gibeon pretended to be a delegation and that they were coming from a very distant land and told Joshua to make an alliance. TRUE OR FALSE
   A/ TRUE (Joshua 9:4-6)

2. The supposed delegation said that they had taken the hot bread from their homes and showed them that it was already old and moldy to make it appear that they had come from far away. TRUE OR FALSE
   A/ TRUE (Joshua 9:12)

3. It was 5 days after they made the alliance with Israel when they realized that the delegation were their neighbors and lived among them. TRUE OR FALSE
   A/ FALSE (9:16)

Order Of Events

Instructions:

1. The moderator will put five scenes of a story into a sealed envelope with a participation number on the outside. He will prepare as many stories as there are teams to participate. The story must be different for each team.
2. When the moderator gives the start signal, each participant will have 2 minutes to put their story scenes into the correct order according to how the biblical event happened. At the end of the time (2 minutes), the moderator will give each participant 1 minute to tell the story, going in order of the participation number on the outside of their envelopes.
3. 50 points will be given for putting the story scenes into the correct order, and 10 points for telling the story correctly, for a maximum total of 60 points per team.

Note:

It is best to have the story scenes on 5 separate pieces of paper or cards so that the participants can move them around to put them into the correct order instead of just having all of the scenes on the same piece of paper.

Consultations:

Are not permitted.

Foul:

Consultation with the coach or anyone else is prohibited, and will result in disqualification of the team for this game.

Example:

The example is based on "The sin of Achan" Joshua chapter 7 (Images taken from HermanaMargarita.com)

Points

60 points (50 for correct order and 10 for telling the story)

Time

3 minutes (2 to put in order and 1 to tell the story)

Participants

1 per team

Mode

Simultaneousus for putting in order and one at a time to tell the story.

Materials

- Stories of Joshua, Judges or Ruth divided into 5 scenes.

139

Joshua Judges Ruth

Joshua Judges Ruth

Joshua Judges Ruth

Follow the Footprints

Instructions:

1. All teams will choose an envelope from the moderator and then line up at the START in front of the giant footprints on the floor.
2. The moderator will receive the envelope from team #1 and ask a question from the questions inside to the participant from team #1. The participant has 30 seconds to give the answer. If in 30 seconds they correctly answer the question, they put their color card on the first footprint. If they don't give the correct answer or remain silent, the moderator will say the correct answer and they won't be able to advance.
3. Then the moderator will receive the envelope from the second team and ask that team's participant the first question from that list, and so forth through the teams.
4. Once all teams have been asked question 1, the moderator begins again with team #1 by asking their question #2 and so forth. When a team answers correctly, they advance their colored card marker along the footprints. When a team answers incorrectly, they don't move their colored card marker.
5. The game is over after 12 questions have been asked to each participant. Teams that answer all 12 questions correctly will reach footprint #12 and receive 60 points. All other teams will receive 5 points for each correct answer they give.

Consultations:
Are not permitted.

Foul:
If someone from the audience says the answer aloud, 10 points will be deducted from the team that committed this infraction.

Example:

Points
5 points for each correct answer

Time
30 seconds to give the answer

Participants
1 per team

Mode
One team at a time alternating

Materials
- The moderator will prepare a questionnaire with 12 different questions for each team and put it in a sealed numbered envelope.
- 12 FOOTPRINTS made of any material
- 2 signs, one that says "START," the other "FINISH,"
- a different colored card for each team.

Isabel from Team "Jordan" correctly answered 9 questions, earning 45 points for her team.

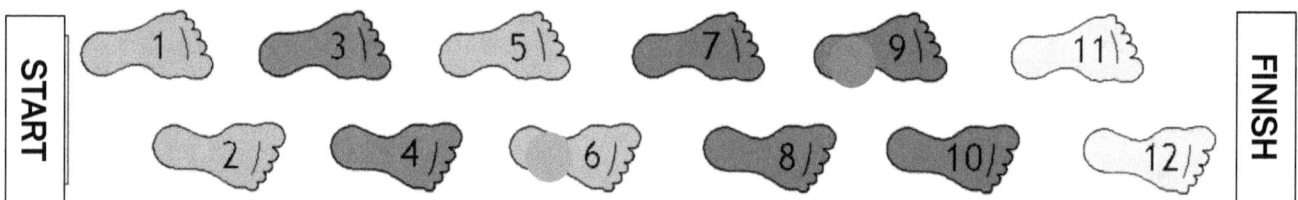

START 1 3 5 7 9 11 FINISH
       2 4 6 8 10 12

Raymond from Team "Gideon" correctly answered 6 questions, earning 30 points for his team.

Joshua Judges Ruth

What Does This Teach Us?

Instructions:

1. The moderator draws the order of participation, allowing each participant to choose an envelope at random.
2. The moderator reads the verse and the three values to the participant of the first team and the boy or girl has 1 minute to explain what value this bible verse teaches us. If it is correct, the moderator indicates it and the judge adds 20 points to their team. If the answer is not correct or is not answered in the required time, they lose their opportunity and the moderator gives the correct answer. No points are awarded for the team.
3. Then continue with the participant from the next team until every team has had a turn.

Consultations:

Not permitted

Foul:

If anyone in the audience says the answer out loud, 10 points will be deducted from their team.

List of values:

Generosity, respect, gratitude, friendship, responsibility, peace, solidarity, tolerance, honesty, justice, freedom, strength, loyalty, integrity, forgiveness, kindness, humility, perseverance, love, unity, trust, provision, protection, equality.

Points

20 points

Time

1 minute

Participants

1 per team

Mode

One team at a time alternating

Materials

Put the following in a sealed numbered envelope for each team.

- 1 Bible verse (different for each team)
- A piece of paper with 3 values for the verse (1 value must be related to the verse and 2 not.)

Example:

"Joshua said to the priests, 'Take up the ark of the covenant and pass on ahead of the people.' So they took it up and went ahead of them." (Joshua 3:6)	Trust Gratitude **Obedience**
"Watch the field where the men are harvesting, and follow along after the women. I have told the men not to lay a hand on you. And whenever you are thirsty, go and get a drink from the water jars the men have filled." (Ruth 2:9)	Peace Unity **Provision**

ARTS & CRAFTS CATEGORY

Arts and Crafts can also be used as teaching tools, helping the children with their personal creativity development, as well as a form of recreation. They are used in the early stages of learning because they help with the development of gross and fine motor skills.

This category will help the children represent biblical knowledge through different arts and crafts expressions.

IDEAS:

- Ask your local SDMI president to supply you with teaching materials, paper of different colors and textures, scissors, glue, yarn, glitter, straws, finger paint, paints, brushes, etc.

- Do activities that allow children to develop their creativity.

For a local, district, zone, national demonstration, etc. the moderator will choose:

1 Arts and Crafts game

The teams will know the game that will be played only on the day of the demonstration.

Flags

Instructions:

1. Each team will receive an envelope and materials to create their flag. When the moderator gives the signal, each team will have 5 minutes to create a flag that somehow illustrates the place or character that they received in their envelope.

2. At the end of 5 minutes, all teams will stop working. Then one participant from each team will have 1 minute to explain their flag. This will be done according to their participation number.

The judges will award points based on the following criteria:

- Quality of workmanship and creativity: 5-10 points
- Explanation: 5-10 points
- Good use of the materials: 5-10 points

Consultations:
Only among the participants of the team.

Foul:
If during the explanation, a different participant or a member of the audience speaks, 10 points will be deducted from the team that commits this infraction.

SUGGESTION OF PLACES:

- The Jordan River, Joshua 3
- Jericho, Joshua 6
- Golan, Joshua 20 and 21
- Bokim, Judges 2
- Hill Country of Ephraim, Judges 4
- Oak of Ophrah, Judges 6
- Boaz's field, Ruth 2

Points
30 points

Time
5 minutes to make the flag and 1 minute to explain it

Participants
2 per team

Mode
Simultaneousus - all teams participate at one time making their flags, and one team at a time explaining them

Materials

- The moderator will prepare 1 card per team, on which is written the name of a place or Bible character from the biblical passages being studied. Each card must be different. These cards are placed in sealed envelopes with a participation number on the outside.

- Sheets of paper, colored paper, wooden or plastic sticks of 60 cm. White glue, scissors, markers.

Collage

Instructions:

1. The moderator will have each team choose an envelope with a theme and participation number.

2. Each team will be given materials and a place to make their collage.

3. The moderator will start the game with a whistle – all teams will participate at the same time. Each team will have 5 minutes to make a collage to illustrate the theme that they received in their envelope. Team members may talk with one another, but not with anyone else.

4. After 5 minutes, all teams will stop working on their collages. Each team will appoint a representative from among the three, who will have 1 minute to explain their collage. Teams will present in the order of their participation number.

THE JUDGES WILL AWARD POINTS BASED ON THE FOLLOWING CRITERIA:

- Creativity and good use of colors: 5-10 points
- Use of materials: 5-10 points
- Explanation: 5-10 points

Consultations:

Talking only among the 3 participants of the team.

Foul:

5 points will be deducted from the team that is talking to each other during the explanation of the collages by any of the participating teams.

Suggested Themes:

- The 12 stones taken from the Jordan, Joshua 4
- The defeat of Jericho, Joshua 6
- Achan's sin, Joshua 7
- Death of Sisera, Judges 4
- Call of Gideon to lead, Judges 6
- Samson's death, Judges 16
- Ruth picks up grain in Boaz's field, Ruth 2
- Birth of Obed, Ruth 4

Points

30 points

Time

5 minutes to make the collage
1 minute to explain it.

Participants

3 per team

Mode

Simultaneousus - all teams participate at one time to make their collages, and then 1 team at a time will explain their collage.

Materials

The moderator will prepare 1 theme for each team in sealed envelopes, with the participation number on the outside.

Cardboard or letter-sized paper, scissors, white glue, paper of different colors and textures, such as tissue paper, newspaper, etc.

Joshua Judges Ruth

Answer And Draw

Instructions:

1. The moderator will give each team an envelope containing the base drawing, as well as a theme story and 5 different questions about that story. The envelopes will be numbered on the outside.
2. When it is time for the first team to start, the team will hand their envelope to the moderator, who will tape the base picture to a board or wall that the team can easily reach to draw on.
3. The team will form a line in front of the base drawing with the 5 participants. The moderator will announce their theme story, and then ask the first participant a question from the envelope. When the moderator finishes the first question, the time of 1 minute is started per participant. If the participant answers the question correctly, he will start drawing on the base picture, illustrating the theme story that they have been given. He draws until his minute is up. If the participant answers incorrectly, he does not proceed to draw on the picture, his turn is over, and the moderator continues by asking the next team participant a question. If that participant answers the question correctly, he goes and continues the same drawing that the first person started, and so forth. After all 5 participants of the team have had the opportunity to answer a question and draw, the moderator will ask a team representative to explain the picture they drew (1 minute time limit).
4. After the first team finishes, the moderator moves on to the second team, and so forth.

The judges award points based on these criteria:
- Clarity of the drawing: 5-10 points
- Drawing is relevant to the subject of study: 5-10 points
- The picture is drawn realistically: 5-10 points

Consultations:
Not permitted.

Foul:
If another participant answers the question asked to their teammates or if someone else answers out loud, the participation of this team is canceled for this game only.

Suggested Themes:
- Joshua sends spies to Jericho, Joshua 2
- Deborah and Barak defeat Sisera, Judges 4
- Call of Gideon to lead, Judges 6
- Samson defeats the Philistines at Lehi, Judges 15
- Ruth picks up grain in Boaz's field, Ruth 2

Points

30 points

Time

3 minutes

Participants

5 per team

Mode

One team at a time

Materials

- The moderator will present a base drawing, such as a prison, city, mountains, sea, etc., on a sheet of paper for each team to draw on. The drawing must be different for each team.
- Colored markers for the team drawing.

Joshua Judges Ruth

Emotion-Art

Instructions:

This game was designed with the understanding that the coach of each team should be teaching the children about emotions and how to manage them.

1. The moderator chooses numbers for the order of the teams.

2. Each participant is given a paper with two silhouettes of faces (male/female) and a marker.

3. The moderator will say the name of a character(s) and an event in which the character(s) felt some emotion. For example: "Paul in the Shipwreck."

4. Each participant must draw the facial expressions that correspond to the emotion that the character felt, in this case, the drawing would be done on the male silhouette. They will have 1 minute to do this. (In case you talk about several characters such as guards, church, etc., they can use both silhouettes).

5. After the minute of drawing, according to the order that was drawn, each participant will give an explanation to the judges about the emotion and why they think the character felt it.

For this game, the following evaluation scale will be used:
- Clarity and quality of the drawing: 5-10 points
- Explanation: 5-10 points

Consultations:
Are not permitted.

Foul:
If a participant tries to see or replicate what another team is doing, the judge indicates it and their participation in this game is canceled.

Suggested Themes:
- The Israelites seeing the Jordan River stop flowing, Joshua 3
- Samson seeing his hair cut off, Judges 16
- Ruth and Orpah when Naomi asked them to return home, Ruth 1

Points

20 points

Time

1 minute to draw,
1 minute to explain

Participants

1 per team

Mode

Simultaneousus - all teams participate at one time drawing, and one at a time explaining

Materials

- Papers with silhouettes of faces (man / woman) (2 silhouettes per team)
- Markers

annoyed	confused	deceived	disgusted
embarrassed	joyful	frustrated	angry
happy	innocent	irritated	lonely
nervous	peaceful	proud	sad
afraid	shocked	sick	joking
amazed	suspicious	tired	worried

Joshua Judges Ruth

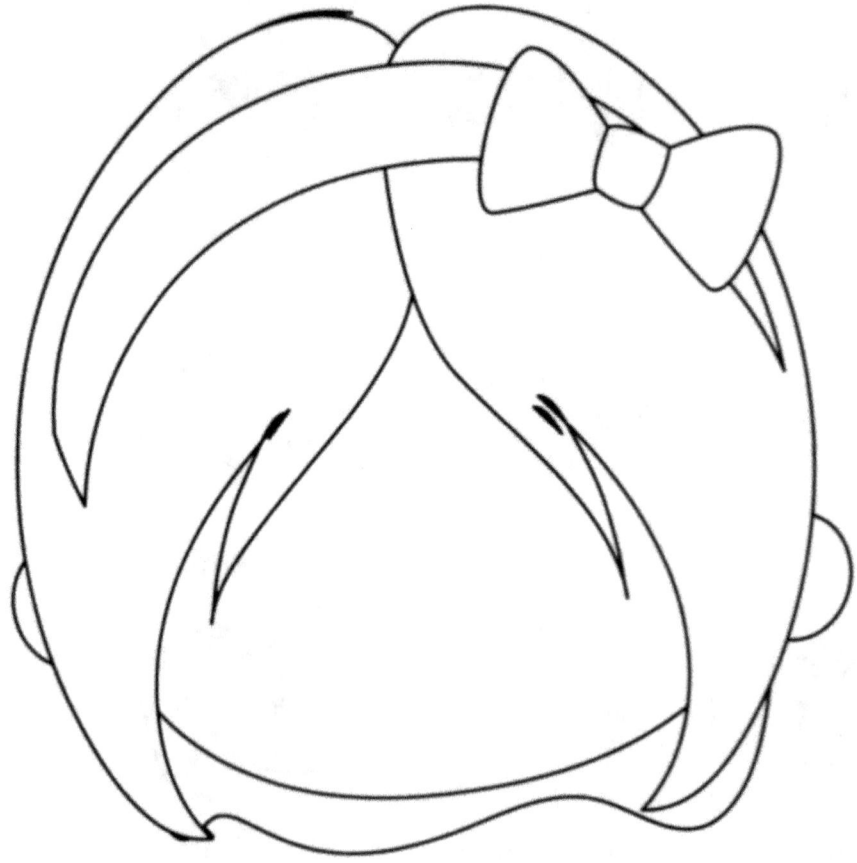

150

Joshua Judges Ruth

3D characters

Instructions:

1. The moderator distributes a sealed envelope with the character template pieces, and participation number on the outside, to each team.
2. The moderator arranges the same construction materials for each team on a table or on the floor.
3. Each team will have 5 minutes to make their character.
4. After 5 minutes, according to their participation number, each team will creatively present their character, explaining who their character was, what their role was in the exodus story, some events they participated in, biblical quotes, etc.
5. The following evaluation scale should be taken into account when scoring:
   - Neatness and quality of workmanship: 5-10 points
   - Presentated details about the character: 5-10 points
   - Presentation creativity: 5-10 points

Consultations:
Only allowed between the two team members.

Foul:
5 points are deducted from the team that is talking to each other when another team is presenting.

Observations:
The moderator can adapt the templates, and will have to make sure to give all the pieces to the team. (Fold on dotted lines and glue at black dots.) (Templates taken from Bible MiniWorld - Jesus - The Easter Story - pages 22-29)

Characters:
- Joshua
- Rahab
- Deborah
- Gideon
- Samson
- Ruth
- Boaz

Points
30 points

Time
5 minutes to develop the character
1 minute for presentation

Participants
2 per team

Mode
Simultaneous for building, one team at a time for the presentation

Materials
- Character templates
- Markers, scissors, glue, etc.

Joshua Judges Ruth

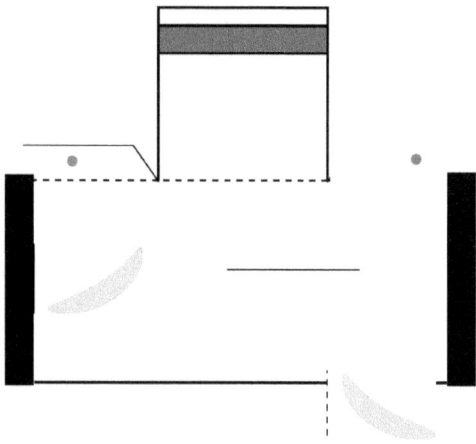

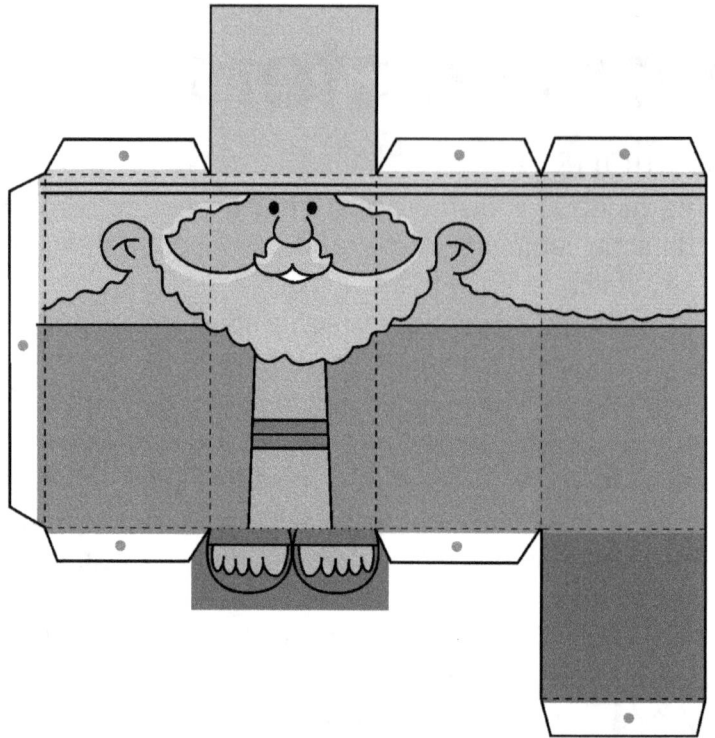

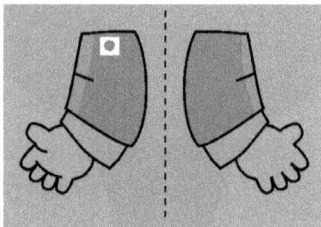

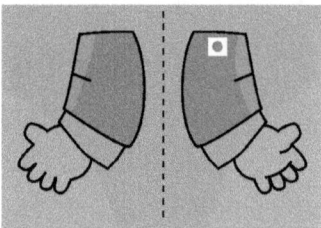

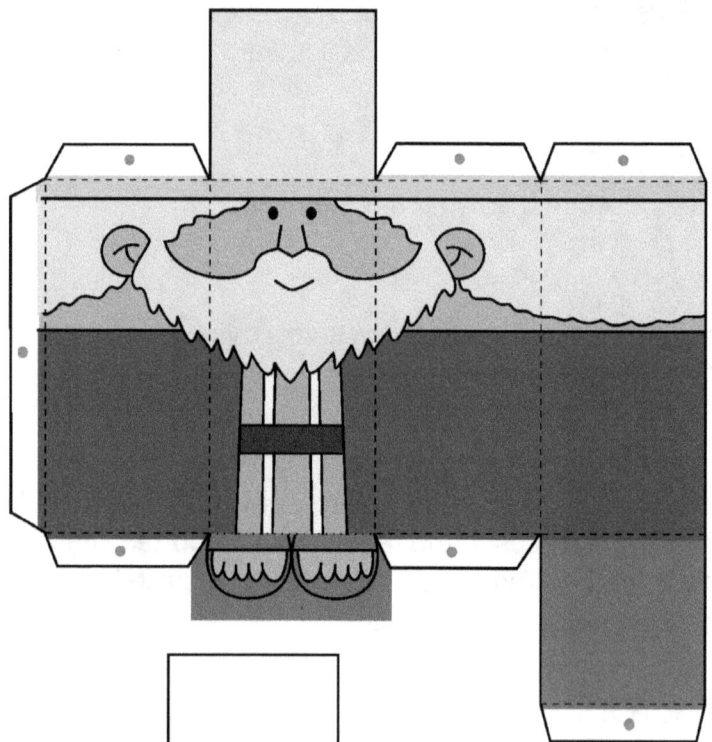

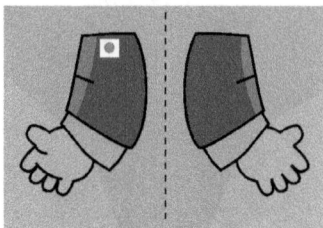

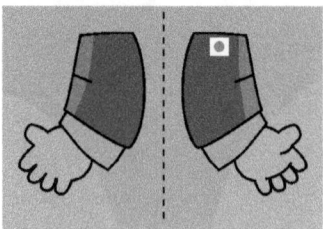

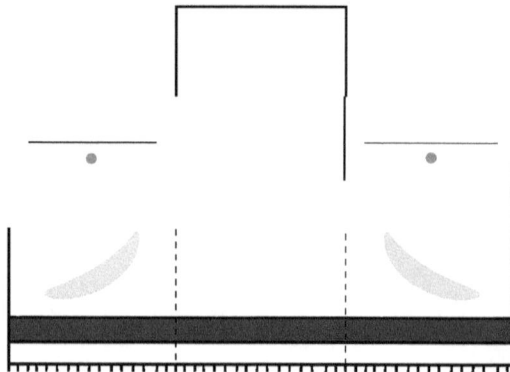

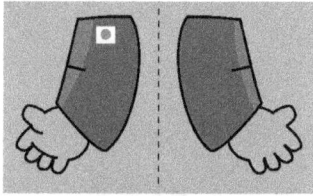
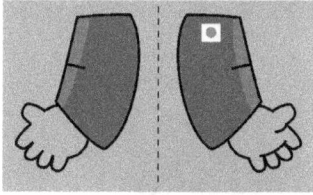

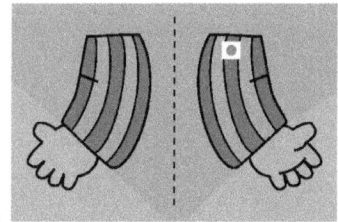
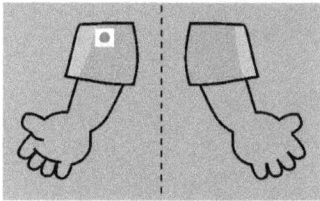
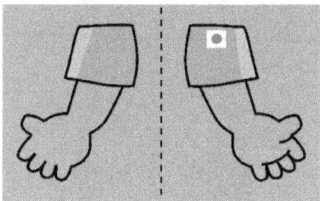
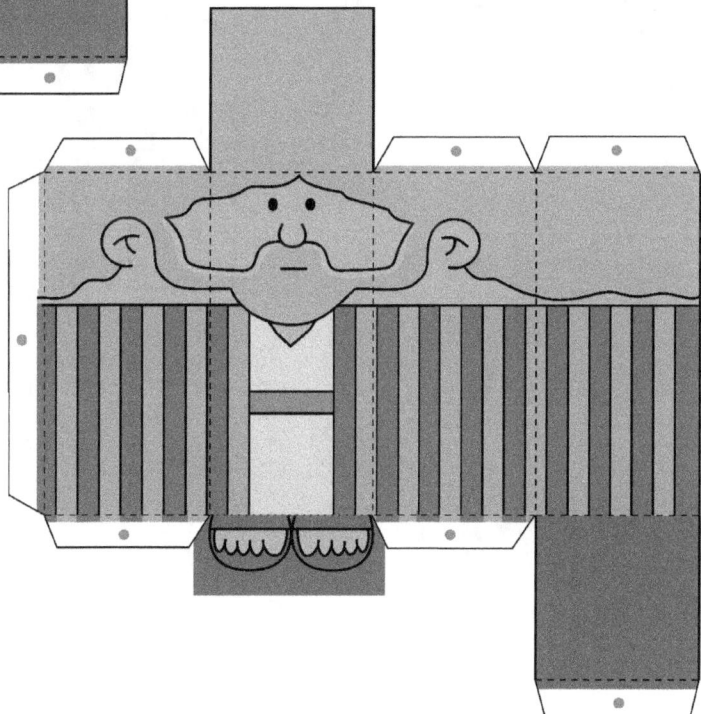
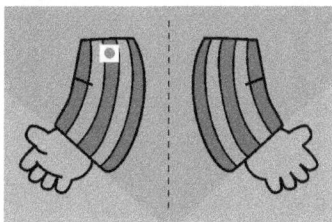

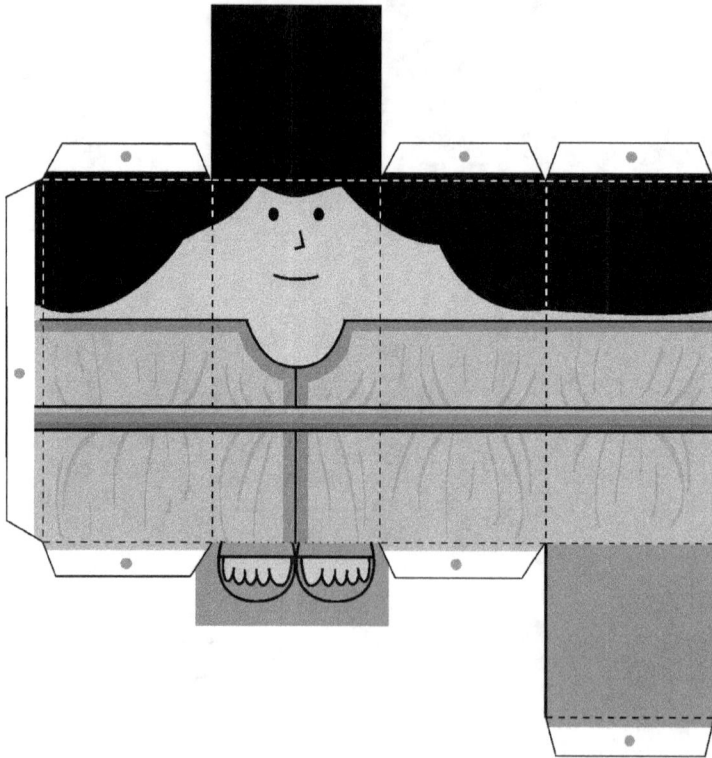

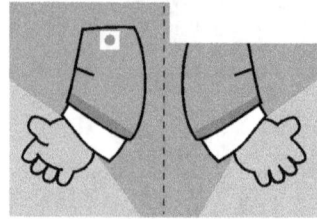

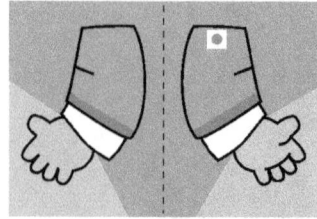

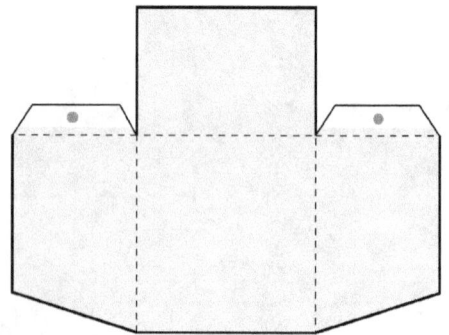

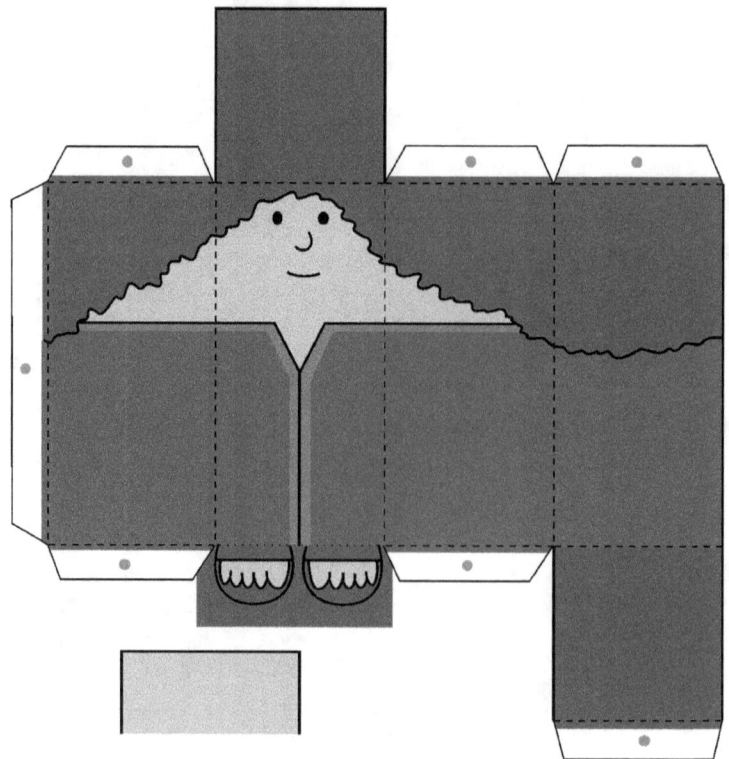

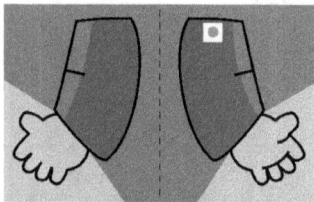

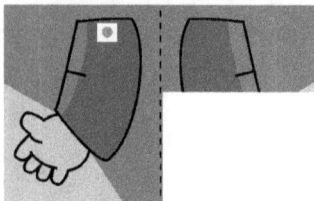

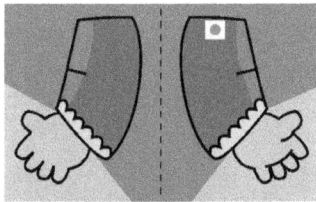

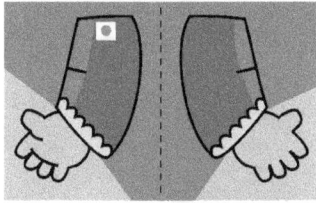

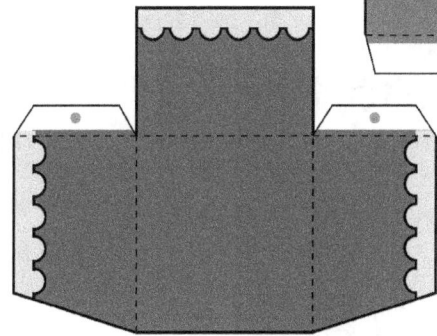

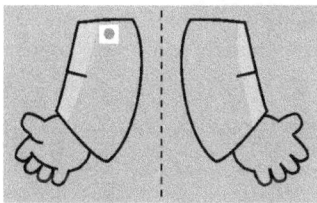

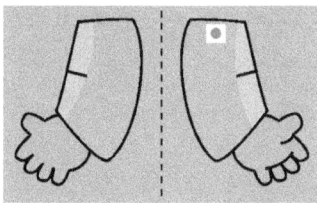

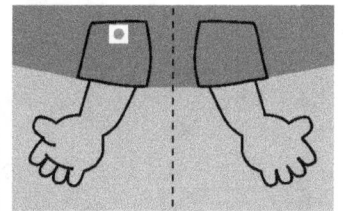

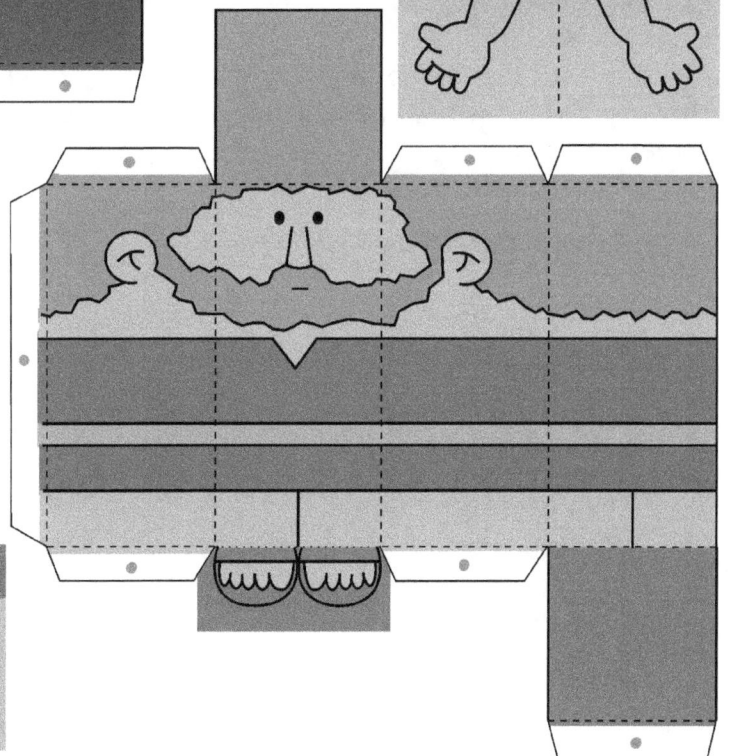

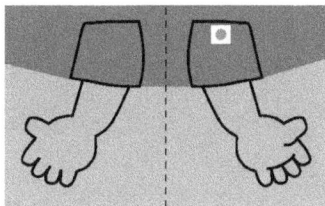

Puppets

Instructions:

1. The moderator will ask the two participants of each team to sit on the floor or at a table, along with their envelope and supplies.

2. When the moderator blows his whistle, each team will create a puppet that represents their Bible character. At the end of 5 minutes, all the teams must stop working. Then in order of participation number, 1 member from each team will have 1 minute to use their puppet to explain who they are.

The judges will award points based on the follow criteria:
- Creativity and workmanship of the puppet: 5-10 points
- Creativity in the presentation: 5-10 points
- Good use of the materials: 5-10 points

Consultations:

Consultations permitted only between the 2 members of the team.

Foul:

5 points will be deducted from teams that talk during the explanation of their character or while other teams are presenting.

Note:

At the end of the activity, an exhibition can be made to appreciate the work the children did and to reward their creativity.

Suggested Characters:
- Joshua
- Rahab
- Caleb
- Deborah
- Barak
- Gideon
- Samson
- Ruth
- Naomi
- Boaz

Points
30 points

Time
5 minutes to make the puppet, 1 minute for the presentation

Participants
2 per team

Mode
Simultaneousus - all teams participate at one time making the puppets, and one team at a time for the presentations

Materials
- The moderator will prepare an envelope for each team with the name of the Bible character the team needs to portray and a participation number on the outside. This Bible character must be different for each team.
- Paper bag, white glue, paper of different textures and colors wool or yarn, markers, scissors for each team.

ACTING CATEGORY

The game consists in representing a character in an integral way. For this it is necessary that the actor, the child, knows the character and can express it with his body expressions and voice.

In this category, the objective is to develop in the child the ability to express with his body a spiritual message that involves the study of the Word of God.

SOME IDEAS:

- Create an atmosphere of respect and a positive spirit in the children so that they do not mock or laugh when one of their classmates participates in this category.

- Perform activities that allow the children to gain self-confidence and lose shyness.

For a local, district, zone, national demonstration, etc. the moderator will choose:

1 performance game

The teams will know the game that will be done only on the day of the demonstration.

Acrostic

Instructions:

1. The moderator will give a sealed envelope with a character name, and a participation number on the outside, to each team.
2. The moderator will give a poster board and markers to each team.
3. Each team will have 5 minutes to write their acrostic, using the character name and writing a characteristic or activity for each letter (see example below).
4. After 5 minutes, according to their participation number, each team will make a creative presentation of their acrostic.
5. The following evaluation scale will be taken into account:
   - Gestures: 5-10 points
   - Coordination between the 2 team members: 5-10 points
   - Intonation: 5-10 points
   - Creativity: 5-10 points
   - Content related to the study topic: 5-10 points

Consultations:

Only allowed between the two team members.

Foul:

5 points will be deducted from the team that is talking to each other when another team is presenting.

Characters:

- Joshua
- Rahab
- Deborah
- Gideon
- Samson
- Naomi

Example

Jericho

Obedient

Spy

FaitHful

HUmble

LeAder

Points

50 points maximum

Time

1 minute

Participants

2 per team

Mode

All teams will create their acrostic at the same time. Then one team will present their acrostic at a time.

Materials

- 1 Character for each team
- 1 Posterboard and markers for each team

Joshua Judges Ruth

Poetry

Instructions:

1. Each team will receive a participation number. The moderator starts with the first team, giving one minute for the 2 participants to present their poem together.

The judges will award points based on the following criteria:

- Gestures   5-10 points
- Coordination between the 2 members of the team   5-10 points
- Intonation   5-10 points
- Lyrics   5-10 points
- Content related to the study theme   5-10 points

Note: The poem must have 3 stanzas and the presentation must be no longer than 1 minute. It must have been written by the team, and have unpublished lyrics.

Consultations:

Are not permitted.

Foul:

5 points will be deducted from a team that is talking when another team is making its presentation.

Example:

Sheave after sheave she gathered in the field
Ruth the Moabite, full of charm
She loved her mother-in-law Naomi
and to her she promised
Where you die, I will die.

She ate and drank from the maids' supplies
Ruth the Moabite, harvested grain in the fields
Orpah left, but she stayed
And to Naomi she promised
Where you go, I will go.

Redemption was enough for a good man
Ruth the Moabite, went to the threshing floor
Full of grace, she and Naomi were praised
Because a son was born, the grandfather of a King.

Points

50 points

Time

1 minute

Participants

2 per team

Mode

One team at a time

Materials

Joshua Judges Ruth

Charades

Instructions:

1. The moderator will write down a theme/Bible story on note cards, a different one per team, and put them in sealed envelopes with participation numbers on the outside. The envelopes must not be opened until it is time for the team to participate.

2. The participant who chooses the envelope must act out the theme/Bible story so that his 4 remaining teammates can try to guess the theme/Bible story he is trying to communicate through his actions. The team has 2 minutes to give the correct answer.

3. The judge awards 25 points if the team answers correctly. If the team answers incorrectly, the judge indicates it and no score is given to that team. The moderator should say the correct answer out loud if it is not guessed.

Consultations:
Only among the 4 participants who must guess the theme.

Foul:
If anyone in the audience or other members of a team interrupt by saying possible answers, the judge indicates it and the moderator cancels the team's participation in this game only.

Suggested Themes:
- Joshua sends spies to Jericho, Joshua 2
- The crossing of the Jordan River, Joshua 3
- Deborah and Barak defeat Sisera, Judges 4
- Call of Gideon to lead, Judges 6
- Samson defeats the Philistines at Lehi, Judges 15
- Death of Samson, Judges 16
- Ruth picks up grain in Boaz's field, Ruth 2
- Birth of Obed, Ruth 4

Points
25 points

Time
2 minutes

Participants
5 per team

Mode
One team at a time

Materials
- 1 envelope for each team with their theme (different for each team) and a participation number

Drama

1. Each team will choose an envelope.

2. With all teams starting at the same time, the moderator will give the go ahead, and the teams will have 5 minutes to prepare their dramas with the themes that they received in their envelopes. The drama should be presented as if it were happening today in modern times.

3. After the 5 minutes of preparation time, coaches must leave and the teams must present their dramas in the order of their participation numbers. Once team #1 has finished, team #2 will begin, etc....

Note: It's important to take into account that teams must bring their costumes, decorations and other props they wish to use with them to the demonstration.

The judges will award points based on the following criteria:

- Participation of the whole team: 5-10 points

- The ability to represent the story accurately: 5-10 points

- The fluidity of the dialogue: 5-10 points

- Use of available resources (props, decorations, etc.): 5-10 pts

- The drama is faithful to the teaching of the event/theme: 5-10 pts

Consultations:
During the first 5 minutes, they can consult with the coach and among themselves. During the presentation, coaches cannot be consulted.

Foul:
10 points will be deducted from a team if they speak during another team's presentation

Suggested Themes:
- Joshua sends spies to Jericho, Joshua 2
- The crossing of the Jordan River, Joshua 3
- Deborah and Barak defeat Sisera, Judges 4
- Call of Gideon to lead, Judges 6
- Samson defeats the Philistines at Lehi, Judges 15
- Death of Samson, Judges 16
- Ruth picks up grain in Boaz's field, Ruth 2

Points
50 points

Time
5 minutes

Participants
The whole team

Mode
Simultaneousus - all teams participate at one time preparing their dramas, and one team at a time presenting

Materials
- The moderator will write down a biblical event on cards, a different one for each team, and then place them in sealed envelopes with participation numbers on the outside.

Breaking News

Instructions:

- Each team will choose an envelope.

- When the moderator gives the go ahead, the teams will have 3 minutes to prepare their news report about the event they received in their envelope. After the 3 minutes of preparation time, one of the team participants will have 1 minute to present the news report as informatively, creatively and interestingly as possible.

- Once team #1 has finished, team #2 will begin.

The judges will award points based on the following criteria:

- Creativity points   5-10
- Content related to the study theme   5-10 points
- Fluidity of the dialogue   5-10 points

Consultations:
Only permitted among the 4 participants during the first 4 minutes. In addition, they can consult their Bibles.

Foul:
Ten points are deducted from a team that is talking to each other while another team is presenting.

Suggested Themes:
- Rahab hides the spies, Joshua 2
- The waters of the Jordan stand still, Joshua 3
- The walls of Jericho fall, Joshua 6
- Achan and his family sentenced to death, Joshua 8
- Jael kills Sisera with a stake, Judges 4
- Samson and the Philistines die, Judges 16

Points
30 points

Time
4 minutes

Participants
4 per team

Mode
All teams will prepare their newscast at the same time, and then one team at a time will present

Materials

- The moderator will put a biblical event or bible passage on note cards, a different one for each team, and then place them in sealed envelopes with participation numbers on the outside.

- Letter size piece of paper and pencil or pen for each team.

MUSIC CATEGORY

Music is the art of organizing sounds in a sensible and coherent way, with harmony, melody and rhythm. The objective of this category is to teach the child to praise God intelligently, doing so with the knowledge of God's Word, with a biblical foundation and spiritual knowledge.

IDEAS:

- Ask for help from members of the worship ministry.
- Provide small times of praise in your meetings with the team.
- Identify the children with skills on instruments or a good singing voice.
- Allow children to participate in the creation of an unpublished song, thus develop their creativity.

For a local, district, zone, national demonstration, etc. the moderator will choose

1 music game

The teams will know the games that will be played only on the day of the demonstration.

As for the unpublished song, this must be presented in the final demonstration.

Joshua Judges Ruth

Sing The Verse

Instructions:

1. Each team will choose an envelope with their Bible verse and participation number.

2. When the moderator gives the start signal for the first team to start, the team will have 3 minutes to read the verse and then come up with a tune and choreography. The team will then present the "song."

The judges will award points based on the following criteria:

- Intonation and harmony: 5-10 points
- Creativity in the presentation: 5-10 points

Consultations:
The team can consult with their coach during the first 3 minutes.

Foul:
If a team talks while another team is presenting, 10 points will be deducted from the team that commits this infraction.

Suggested Texts:
Choose a text from the Memory Verse list found on pages 102-103.

Points
20 points max.

Time
3 minutes

Participants
The whole team

Mode
One team at a time

Materials
- The moderator will prepare a card for each team with Bible verses from the memory verse list (a different one for each team) and put them in sealed envelopes with participation numbers on the outside.

New Song

Instructions:

Each team must present an unpublished song, which will be sung by the whole team. The team can present it with choreography or spiritual dancing, etc. The song must have:

- Unpublished lyrics (lyrics must be written by the team)
- Lyrics related to the theme of Bible Quizzing.
- The actual tune may be from a published Christian song, but the lyrics must be changed.
- Minimum of two verses, maximum of four.
- Maximum duration of three minutes.

1. The moderator will draw the order of participation.
2. Each team will have a maximum of 3 minutes to present their song, ideally with music, and actions.

The judges will award points based on the following criteria:

- Quality of the Unpublished lyrics: 5-10 points
- Lyrics related to the theme of the Quizzing Study: 5-10 pts
- Music (intonation, harmony): 5-10 points
- Creativity in the presentation: 5-10 points
- Full team participation: 5-10 points

Consultations:
Are not permitted.

Foul:
20 points will be deducted from a team that is talking while another team is presenting.

Points

50 points

Time

3 minutes

Participants

The whole team

Mode

One team at a time

Materials

Joshua Judges Ruth

Musical Roulette

Instructions:

1. The moderator draws the order of participation and places the roulette in front of the spectators.

2. The participants make a line in the order of participation three meters away from the roulette wheel.

3. Each child will rotate the wheel and according to the character that the wheel stops at, he will have a maximum of 1 minute to sing a small musical jingle. (These musical jingles should be prepared in advance with the help of the coach.)

The judges will award points based on the following criteria:
Music (intonation, harmony): 5-10 points

Creativity in the presentation: 5-10 points

Consultations:
Are not permitted

Foul:
Ten points are deducted from a team if it is talking while another team is presenting.

Suggested Characters

- Joshua
- Rahab
- Deborah
- Gideon
- Samson
- Naomi
- Ruth

Points
20 points

Time
1 minute

Participants
1 per team

Mode
One team at a time

Materials
- Roulette of Characters

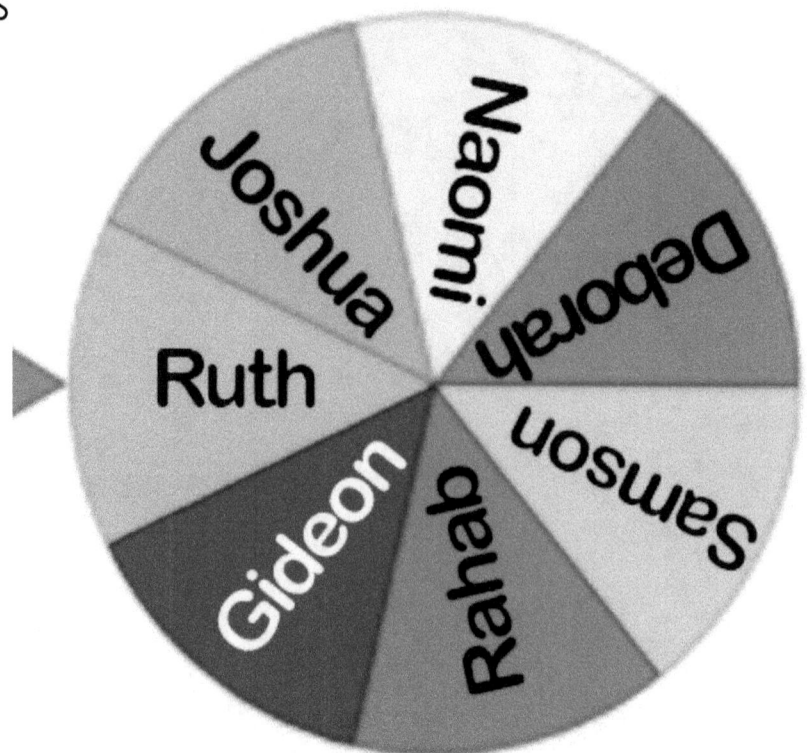

Joshua Judges Ruth

children'squizzing

GUIDE FOR CHILDREN'S BIBLE QUIZZING USING QUESTIONS AND ANSWERS

Children's Bible Quizzing is an optional part of Bible Studies for Children. Each church and each child decides whether to participate in a series of competitive events.

Quizzing events follow the rules outlined in this book. Children do not compete against each other to determine a single winner. Churches do not compete against each other to determine a winner.

The purpose of Quizzing is to help the children to determine what they learned about the Bible, to enjoy the competitive events, and to grow in the ability to display Christian attitudes and Christian behaviors during competitive events.

In Quizzing, each child challenges himself or herself to attain an award level. In this approach, children quiz against a base of knowledge, not against each other. Quizzing uses a multiple-choice approach that allows every child to answer every question. Multiple choice questions offer several answers, and the child chooses the correct one. This approach makes it possible for every child to be a winner.

QUIZZING SUPPLIES

Each child uses a quiz box (see picture) (or similar device) to answer questions during events. The quiz box contains four tab inserts that are numbered 1, 2, 3, and 4. The numbers represent possible answer choices. Participants pull one numbered insert to indicate the correct answer. Children can also use the quiz box to answer multiple-choice review questions in the classroom. The quiz box dimensions are 30 cm wide X 13 cm deep X 28 cm high. Quiz boxes may be purchased from The Foundry (*www.gokidsquiz.com*), or a local team may make their own. For instructions to make quiz boxes, visit *kidzfirstpublications.net*

Each group of children will need a person to score their answers. There is a reproducible score sheet at the end of the book. Use this score sheet to keep track of the answers of each child.

If possible, provide some type of an award for the performance of the children in each Quizzing event. Suggested awards are certificates, stickers, ribbons, trophies, or medals.

Certificate templates are included on pages 58-59.

Please follow these rules. Competitions that do not operate in accordance with the Children's Quizzing Official Competition Rules and Procedures will not qualify for other competition levels.

AGES AND GRADES

Children in grades 1-6 may participate in Children's Quizzing competitions. Seventh graders, regardless of age, participate in Teen Quizzing. (For countries other than the United States, grades 1-6 are generally ages 6-12).

BASIC LEVEL COMPETITION

This competition level is for younger or beginning quizzers. Older quizzers who prefer an easier level of competition may also participate in the Basic Level. The questions for the Basic Level are simpler. There are three answers for each question, and there are fifteen questions in each round. The district or regional Children's

Quizzing director determines the questions and the number of rounds at each Quizzing competition. Most competitions have two or three rounds.

ADVANCED LEVEL COMPETITION

This competition level is for older quizzers or experienced quizzers. Younger quizzers who want a greater challenge may participate in the Advanced Level. The questions for the Advanced Level are more comprehensive. There are four answers for each question, and there are twenty questions in each round. The district or regional Children's Quizzing director determines the questions and the number of rounds at each Quizzing event.

SWITCHING BETWEEN LEVELS

Children may switch between Basic Level and Advanced Level only for invitational Quizzing competitions. This helps the leaders and the children determine the best level for each child.

For the zone/area, the district, and the regional competitions, the local director must register each child for either Basic Level or Advanced Level. The child must compete at the same level for zone/area, district, and regional competitions.

TYPES OF COMPETITION

Invitational Competition

An invitational competition is between two or more churches. Local Children's Quizzing directors, zone/area Children's Quizzing directors, or district Children's Quizzing directors may organize invitational competitions. Individuals who organize an invitational competition have the responsibility to prepare the competition questions.

Zone/Area Competition

Each district may have smaller groupings of churches that are called zones. If one zone has more quizzers than another zone, the district Children's Quizzing director may separate or combine the zones to create areas with a more equitable distribution of quizzers. The term area means combined or divided zones.

The churches located in each zone/area compete in that zone/area. The district Children's Quizzing director organizes the competition. Questions for the zone/area competitions are official questions.

E-mail ChildQuiz@nazarene.org to request these questions from the General Children's Quizzing Office.

District Competition

Children advance from the zone/area competition to the district competition. The district Children's Quizzing director determines the qualifications for the competition and organizes the competition.

Questions for district competitions are official questions. E-mail ChildQuiz@nazarene.org to request these questions from the General Children's Quizzing Office.

Regional Competition

The regional competition is a competition between two or more districts.

When there is a regional Children's Quizzing director, he or she determines the qualifications for the competition and organizes the competition. If there is not a regional director, the participating district directors organize the competition.

Questions for the regional competitions are official questions. To request these questions from the General Children's Quizzing Office, e-mail ChildQuiz@nazarene.org.

WORLD QUIZ COMPETITION

Every four years, the General Children's Quizzing Office in conjunction with Sunday School and Discipleship Ministries International sponsors an international World Quiz. The Global Children's Quizzing Office determines the dates, the locations, the costs, the qualifying dates, and the overall qualifying process for all World Quiz competitions.

E-mail ChildQuiz@nazarene.org for more information.

DISTRICT CHILDREN'S QUIZZING DIRECTOR

The district Children's Quizzing director operates all competitions according to the Children's Quizzing Official Competition Rules and Procedures.

He or she has the authority to introduce additional Quizzing procedures on the district as long as the procedures do not conflict with the Children's Quizzing Official Competition Rules and Procedures. The district Children's Quizzing director contacts the General Children's Quizzing Office, when necessary, to request a specific change in the

Children's Quizzing Official Competition Rules and Procedures for a district. The district Children's Quizzing director makes the decisions and solves the problems within the guidelines of the Children's Quizzing Official Competition Rules and Procedures. The district Children's Quizzing director contacts the General Children's Quizzing Office for an official ruling on a specific situation, if necessary.

REGIONAL CHILDREN'S QUIZZING DIRECTOR

The regional Children's Quizzing director creates a regional Children's Quizzing leadership team that consists of all of the district Children's Quizzing directors on the region. The regional Children's Quizzing director remains in contact with this team to keep the procedures consistent across the region. He or she operates and organizes the regional competitions according to the Children's Quizzing Official Competition Rules and Procedures. The regional Children's Quizzing director contacts the General Children's Quizzing Office to request any changes in the Children's Quizzing Official Competition Rules and Procedures for a specific region. He or she resolves any conflicts that arise with the help of the guidelines of the Children's Quizzing Official Competition Rules and Procedures. The regional Children's Quizzing director contacts the General Children's Quizzing Office for an official ruling on a specific situation, if necessary. He or she contacts the General Children's Quizzing Office to place the regional quiz date on the general church calendar.

In the United States and Canada, the regional Children's Quizzing director is a developing position. Currently that person does not preside over district Children's Quizzing directors on the region.

QUIZMASTER

The quizmaster reads the competition questions at a Quizzing competition. The quizmaster reads the question and the multiple-choice answers two times before the children answer the question. He or she follows the Children's Quizzing Official Competition Rules and Procedures established by the General Children's Quizzing Office and the district Children's Quizzing director/regional coordinator. In the event of a conflict, the final authority is the district/regional Children's Quizzing

director who consults the Children's Quizzing Official Competition Rules and Procedures. The quizmaster may participate in discussions with scorekeepers and the district/regional Children's Quizzing director about a challenge. The quizmaster may call a time-out.

SCOREKEEPER

The scorekeeper scores a group of children's answers. He or she may participate in discussions with scorekeepers and the district/regional Children's Quizzing director about a challenge. All scorekeepers are to use the same method and the same symbols to insure correct tabulation of the scores.

SYNOPSIS OF HOW THE QUESTIONS ARE READ AND ANSWERED

The quizmaster reads the question and all answer choices twice. After the quizmaster reads the second time, he or she will call the children to respond. The quizmaster never reads questions once.

- The quizmaster says, "QUESTION" and then reads the question and all answer choices.

- The quizmaster repeats this sequence.

- The quizmaster says, "ANSWER," which prompts the participants' to respond.

Example: The quizmaster says, **"QUESTION: What did Mary name her baby? Answer number one, Joseph. Answer number two, John. Answer number three, Jesus."** The quizmaster briefly pauses and starts again and says, **"QUESTION: What did Mary name her baby? Answer number one, Joseph. Answer number two, John. Answer number three, Jesus."** The quizmaster briefly pauses and calls for the answer and says, **"ANSWER."** The children then indicate their answer choice by removing the number from their box that corresponds to their answer.

The quizmaster *may* read a question a third time for especially difficult or long questions or if a mistake was made when the question was initially read. However, this practice should be the exception, and the participants should be notified of a third repeat in advance to avoid premature responses after the second question and answer sequence.

After the answers are indicated, the quizmaster pauses and watches for the scorekeepers to record all the scores. When the scores are recorded, the quizmaster instructs the children to return their answer numbers to their boxes.

For bonus questions, the quizmaster instructs the team representatives who will answer the bonus question for each team to stand and all the other children to place their hands in their laps. The quizmaster reads the question two times. The child who is ready to answer the bonus question steps to the scorekeepers and quietly gives their answer. The child speaks carefully and quietly so that they do not reveal their answer to other teams. When everyone completes their answer, the quizmaster asks the scorekeepers to raise their hand to reveal who correctly answered. The quizmaster affirms the correct answer or invites a participant to share the correct answer.

When possible, use PowerPoint or other visual media to project questions onto a screen that is visible to all quizzers.

The projected presentation will only include the questions. All answers will be read.

OFFICIAL COMPETITION QUESTIONS

The district Children's Quizzing director is the only individual on the district who may obtain a copy of the official zone/area and district competition questions.

The regional Children's Quizzing director is the only individual on the region who may obtain a copy of the official regional competition questions. If there is not a regional Children's Quizzing director, one participating district Children's Quizzing director may obtain a copy of the official regional competition questions.

Order forms for annual official questions will be sent by E-mail each year. Contact the General Children's Quizzing Office at ChildQuiz@nazarene.org to update your E-mail address. The official questions will arrive by Email to the people who request them.

COMPETITION METHODS

There are two methods of competition.

Individual method

In the individual method of competition, the children compete as individual children. The score of each child is separate from all other scores. Children from the same church may sit together, but do not add together the individual scores to obtain a church or a team score. There are no bonus questions for individual quizzers.

The individual method is the only method to use for the Basic Level competition.

Combination Method

The combination method combines individual and team Quizzing. In this method, churches may send individual quizzers, the teams, or a combination of these to a competition.

The district Children's Quizzing director determines the number of children needed to form a team. All teams must have the same number of quizzers. The recommended number for a team is four or five children.

The children from the churches that do not have enough quizzers to form a team can compete as individual quizzers.

In the combination method, teams qualify for bonus questions. The bonus points awarded for a correct answer to a bonus question become part of the total score of the team, instead of a score for an individual quizzer. There are bonus questions with the official questions for zone/area, district, and regional competitions. Bonus questions typically involve the recitation of a memory verse.

The district Children's Quizzing director selects either the individual method or the combination method for the Advanced Level of the competition.

TIE SCORES

Ties between individual quizzers or the teams remain as tied scores. All individual children or teams who tie receive the same recognition, the same award, and the same advancement to the next level of competition.

BONUS QUESTIONS

Bonus questions are part of the Advanced Level, but only with teams, not individuals. Teams must qualify for a bonus question. Bonus questions occur after questions 5, 10, 15, and 20.

To qualify for a bonus question, a team may have only as many incorrect answers as there are members on the team. For example, a team of four members may have four or fewer answers that are incorrect. A team of five members may have five or fewer answers that are incorrect.

The bonus points for a correct answer become part of the total score of the team, not of the individual score of a child.

The district Children's Quizzing director determines the way that the children answer bonus questions. In most situations, the child verbally gives the answer to the scorekeeper.

Prior to the reading of the bonus question, the local Children's Quizzing director selects one team member to answer the bonus question. The same child may answer all of the bonus questions in a game, or a different child may answer each bonus question.

TIME-OUTS

The district Children's Quizzing director determines the number of time-outs for each church. Each church receives the same number of time-outs, regardless of the number of individual quizzers or teams from that church. For example, if the district director decides to give one time-out, each church receives one timeout.

The district Children's Quizzing director determines if an automatic time-out will occur during the game and the specific point at which the time-out will occur in each game.

The local Children's Quizzing director is the only individual who may call a time-out for a local church team.

The district Children's Quizzing director or quizmaster may call a time-out at any time.

The district Children's Quizzing director, prior to the start of the competition, determines the maximum length of the time-outs for the competition.

SCORING

There are two methods for scoring. The district Children's Quizzing director selects the method.

Five Points

• Award five points for every correct answer. For example, if a child answers 20 questions correctly in an Advanced Level round, the child earns a total of 100 points.

• Award five points for every correct bonus answer in an Advanced Level team Quizzing round. For example, if every member of a team with four persons answers 20 questions correctly in an Advanced Level round and the team answers four bonus questions correctly, the team earns a total of 420 points. Basic Level points will be lower as there are only 15 questions per round, and it is individual competition only.

One Point

Award one point for each correct answer as follows:

• Award one point for every correct answer. For example, if a child answers 20 questions correctly in an Advanced level round, the child earns a total of 20 points.

• Award one point for every correct bonus answer in an Advanced Level team Quizzing round. For example, if every member of a team with four persons answers 20 questions correctly in an Advanced Level round and the team answers four bonus questions correctly, the team earns a total of 84 points.

Basic Level points will be lower as there are only 15 questions per round, and it is individual competition only.

CHALLENGES

Challenges are to be an exception and are not common during a competition.

Request a challenge only when the answer marked as correct in the questions is actually incorrect according to the Bible reference given for that question. Challenges issued for any other reason are invalid.

A quizzer, a Children's Quizzing director, or any other competition participant may not request a challenge because they dislike the wording of a question or answer or think a question is too difficult or confusing.

The local Children's Quizzing director is the only person who may issue a challenge to a competition question. If an individual other than the local Children's Quizzing director attempts to issue a challenge, the challenge is automatically ruled as "invalid."

Individuals who issue invalid challenges disrupt competition and cause the children to lose their concentration. Individuals who consistently issue invalid challenges or create some problems by arguing about a challenge ruling will lose their privilege of challenging the questions for the remainder of the competition.

The district Children's Quizzing director, or the quizmaster in the absence of the district Children's Quizzing director, has the authority to remove the privilege of challenging questions from any or all individuals who abuse the privilege.

The district Children's Quizzing director determines how to challenge a competition question prior to the start of the competition.

• Will the challenge be written or verbal?

• When can a person challenge (during a game or at the end of a game)?

The district Children's Quizzing director should explain the procedure for the challenges to local Children's Quizzing directors at the beginning of the quiz year.

The quizmaster and district Children's Quizzing director follow these steps to rule the challenge.

• Determine if the challenge is valid or invalid. To do this, listen to the reason for the challenge. If the reason is valid, the answer given as the correct answer is incorrect according to the Bible reference, follow the challenge procedures outlined by the district.

• If the reason for the challenge is invalid, announce that the challenge is invalid, and the competition continues.

If more than one person challenges the same question, the quizmaster or district Children's Quizzing director selects one local quiz director to explain the reason for a challenge. After a question has one challenge, another person may not challenge the same question.

If a challenge is valid, the district Children's Quizzing director, or quizmaster in the director's absence, determines how to handle the challenged question. Select one of the following options.

Option A: Eliminate the question, and do not replace it. The result is that a game of 20 questions becomes a game of 19 questions.

Option B: Give every child the points he or she would receive for a correct answer to the challenged question.

Option C: Replace the challenged question. Ask the quizzers a new question.

Option D: Let the children who gave the answer that was listed as the correct answer in the official questions keep their points. Give another question to the children who gave an answer that was an incorrect answer.

AWARD LEVELS

Children's Quizzing has the philosophy that every child has an opportunity to answer every question, and every child receives recognition for every correct answer he or she gives. Therefore, Children's Quizzing uses multiple-choice competition, and ties are never broken.

Children and churches do not compete against each other. They compete to reach an award level. All of the children and all of the churches who reach the same award level receive the same award. Ties remain as tied scores.

Recommended Award Levels:

> Bronze Award = 70-79% correct
>
> Silver Award = 80-89% correct
>
> Gold Award = 90-99% correct
>
> Gold All Star = 100% correct

Resolve all scoring and challenge decisions before presenting awards. The quizmaster and scorekeepers should be sure that all final scores are accurate prior to the presentation.

Never take an award from a child after the child receives an award. If there is a mistake, children may receive a higher award but not a lower award. This is true for individual awards and team awards.

COMPETITION ETHICS

The district Children's Quizzing director is the person on the district who has the responsibility to conduct the competitions in accordance with the Children's Quizzing Official Competition Rules and Procedures.

• *Hearing Questions Before the Competition.* Since competitions use the same questions, it is not appropriate for the children and the workers to attend another zone/area, district, or regional competition prior to their participation in their own competition of the same level. If an adult Quizzing worker attends another competition, the district Children's Quizzing director may choose to disqualify the church from participation in their competition. If a parent and/or child attends another competition, the district Children's Quizzing director may choose to disqualify the church from participation in their competition.

• *Worker's Conduct and Attitudes.* Adults are to conduct themselves in a professional and in a Christian manner. The discussions about disagreements with the district Children's Quizzing director, quizmaster, or scorekeepers are to be private. Adult Quizzing workers should not share information about the disagreement with the children. A cooperative spirit and good

sportsmanship are important. The decisions and the rulings of the district Children's Quizzing director are final. Relay these decisions in a positive tone to the children and to the adults.

CHEATING

Any cheating is serious. Treat the cheating seriously.

The district Children's Quizzing director, in discussion with the district Children's Ministries Council, determines the policy to follow in the event that a child or an adult cheats during a competition.

Make sure that all local children's ministries directors, children's pastors, and local Children's Quizzing directors receive the policy and the procedures of the district. Before accusing an adult or a child of cheating, have some evidence or a witness that the cheating occurred.

Ensure that the quiz continues and that the person accused of cheating does not suffer

embarrassment in front of other people. Here is a sample procedure.

• If you suspect that a child cheated, ask someone to serve as a judge to watch the areas, but do not point out any child whom you suspect. After a few questions, ask the opinion of the judge. If the judge did not see any cheating, continue with the quiz.

• If the judge saw a child who was cheating, ask the judge to affirm it. Do not act until everyone is sure.

• Explain the problem to the local Children's Quizzing director, and ask the director to talk with the accused person privately.

• The quizmaster, the judge, and the local Children's Quizzing director should watch for continued cheating.

• If the cheating continues, the quizmaster and the local Children's Quizzing director should talk with the accused person privately.

• If the cheating continues, the quizmaster should tell the local Children's Quizzing director that he or she will eliminate the score of the child from official competition.

• In the case that a scorekeeper cheated, the district Children's Quizzing director will ask the scorekeeper to leave, and a new scorekeeper will take his or her place.

• In the case that someone in the audience cheated, the district Children's Quizzing director will handle the situation in the most appropriate manner.

UNRESOLVED DECISIONS

Consult with the General Children's Quizzing Office regarding unresolved decisions.

Additional Resources

Additional resources can be downloaded at: *www.SdmiResources.MesoamericaRegion.org*

REVIEW QUESTIONS FOR BIBLE QUIZZING

QUESTIONS FOR BASIC LEVEL REVIEW (LESSON ONE: JOSHUA 1:1-18)

1. To whom did the Lord speak after Moses died? (1:1)

1. The people of Israel
2. The officers
3. **Joshua**

2. What did the Lord say that the people should do? (1:2)

1. Go back to the desert
2. **Get ready to cross the Jordan River**
3. Look for the Lord in the mountains

3. What did the Lord tell Joshua when he became the leader over Israel? (1:5)

1. I will help you for one year.
2. **I will never leave you nor forsake you.**
3. I will help you as long as you obey me.

4. Who would lead the people to inherit the land? (1:6)

1. Moses
2. **Joshua**
3. Aaron

5. What did God say Joshua needed to be? (1:6-7)

1. Brave and fearless
2. **Strong and courageous**
3. Safe and confident

6. When was Joshua supposed to meditate on the Book of the Law? (1:8)

1. **Day and night**
2. Once a year
3. Whenever he was in trouble

7. What did God say Joshua should not be? (1:9)

1. Frightened or weak
2. **Afraid or discouraged**
3. Fearful or shy

8. What were the fighting men supposed to do? (1:14)

1. Cross the Jordan River in their chariots
2. **Cross the Jordan River first, and be ready for battle.**
3. Send their families across the Jordan River first.

9. How did the officers serve Moses when he was alive? (1:17)

1. They obeyed Moses most of the time.
2. They did not obey Moses.
3. **They fully obeyed Moses.**

10. Finish this verse: "Have I not commanded you? Be strong and courageous. Do not be afraid; do not be discouraged, for the Lord your God ..." (Joshua 1:9)

1. "...will go with you always."
2. "...protects you from all harm."
3. **"...will be with you wherever you go."**

REVIEW QUESTIONS FOR BIBLE QUIZZING

QUESTIONS FOR ADVANCED LEVEL REVIEW (LESSON ONE: JOSHUA 1:1-18)

1. **What was Joshua's job before he became the leader of the Israelites? (1:1)**

1. He was a priest.
2. He was in charge of all the officers.
3. **He was Moses's aide.**
4. He was the chief judge.

2. **What did the Lord promise Joshua that he would do when the Israelites entered Canaan? (1:3)**

1. He would make Joshua king of the Israelites.
2. He would appoint a strong leader for the Israelites.
3. **He would give the Israelites every place where they set their feet.**
4. He would keep Joshua safe.

3. **Why did the Lord want Joshua to be strong and courageous? (1:6)**

1. Because he did not want Joshua to embarrass himself
2. Because he would become famous and the people would worship him
3. **Because he would lead the Israelites to inherit the land that the Lord swore to give to their ancestors**
4. All of the answers are correct.

4. **What did the Lord tell Joshua to do in order to be successful wherever he went? (1:7-8)**

1. Be strong and very courageous.
2. Obey all the law my servant Moses gave you.
3. Do not turn from the law, to the right or to the left.
4. **All of the answers are correct.**

5. **On what did God say Joshua should meditate day and night? (1:8)**

1. The plans to cross the Jordan River
2. **The Book of the Law**
3. The prayers of the Israelites
4. All of the answers are correct.

6. **What did the Lord tell Joshua not to be? (1:9)**

1. Strong and courageous
2. Obedient and brave
3. **Afraid and discouraged**
4. Lazy and unmotivated

7. **Who told the people to get ready to cross the Jordan River? (1:10-11)**

1. The Reubenites
2. **The officers of the people**
3. The priests
4. The Reubenites and Gadites

8. **What were the fighting men of the eastern tribes to do when they crossed the river? (1:14-15)**

1. Protect the tribes that did not have any fighting men.
2. **Help their fellow Israelites take possession of the land**
3. Train the people to fight.
4. All of the answers are correct.

9. **How did the officers respond to Joshua's instructions? (1:16)**

1. They hesitated.
2. **They said they would do what Joshua commanded.**
3. They rejected Joshua as their leader.
4. Half of the officers agreed to obey, but the others did not.

10. **Finish this verse: "Have I not commanded you? Be strong and courageous. Do not be afraid; do not be…" (Joshua 1:9)**

1. **"…discouraged, for the Lord your God will be with you wherever you go."**
2. "…worried, for I will help you."
3. "…scared, for I will defeat your enemies."
4. "…timid, for I will go with you.

REVIEW QUESTIONS FOR BIBLE QUIZZING

QUESTIONS FOR BASIC LEVEL REVIEW (LESSON TWO: JOSHUA 2:1-24)

1. **Who sent the two spies to Jericho? (2:1)**

1. The king of Jericho
2. Rahab
3. **Joshua**

2. **Where did the spies stay? (2:1)**

1. **Rahab's house**
2. The palace of the king
3. The inn

3. **What did Rahab tell the king of Jericho about the spies? (2:4-5)**

1. "I did not know where they came from."
2. "They left at dusk."
3. **Both answers are correct.**

4. **Where did Rahab hide the spies? (2:6)**

1. **On the roof**
2. In the basement
3. In her closet

5. **What happened as soon as the pursuers left the city? (2:7)**

1. All the people left the city.
2. **The gate was shut.**
3. The spies came back.

6. **What did Rahab tell the spies? (2:9)**

1. "The Lord is with us, not you."
2. "We are not afraid of you or your God."
3. **"I know that the Lord has given you this land."**

7. **What did the people of Jericho hear about the Lord and the Israelites? (2:10)**

1. The Lord dried up the water of the Red Sea.
2. The Israelites completely destroyed the two kings of the Amorites.
3. **Both answers are correct.**

8. **What did Rahab say about the God of the Israelites? (2:11)**

1. **"The Lord your God is God in heaven above and on the earth below."**
2. "Your God is not as powerful as our gods."
3. "We are not afraid of your God."

9. **How did the spies escape? (2:15)**

1. **Rahab let them down by a rope through the window.**
2. Rahab showed them a secret tunnel.
3. Rahab hid them in her wagon.

10. **What did the spies tell Rahab to tie in the window of her house? (2:17-18)**

1. A purple flag
2. A green banner
3. **A scarlet cord**

REVIEW QUESTIONS FOR BIBLE QUIZZING

QUESTIONS FOR ADVANCED LEVEL REVIEW (LESSON TWO: JOSHUA 2:1-24)

1. How did Joshua discover what Canaan and Jericho were like? (2:1)

1. He disguised himself and secretly went into the land.
2. **He secretly sent two spies.**
3. He and two spies went to spy out the land.
4. He captured the king of Jericho.

2. How did Rahab hide the spies? (2:6)

1. She hid them at her parents' house.
2. She sent them to secret tunnels.
3. **She hid them on the roof.**
4. She disguised them.

3. What happened after the pursuers left to look for the spies? (2:7-8)

1. The city gate was shut.
2. The spies lay down for the night on Rahab's roof.
3. Rahab went to the roof to talk with the spies.
4. **All of the answers are correct.**

4. What did the people of Jericho know about the Lord? (2:10)

1. He was the god of the Egyptians.
2. **He dried up the water of the Red Sea for the Israelites.**
3. They had only heard his name.
4. They did not know anything about the Lord.

5. What did Rahab say about the Lord? (2:11)

1. "The Lord is powerful, but not a god."
2. "The Lord your God has power over the weather."
3. "The Lord your God is not as powerful as our gods."
4. **"The Lord your God is God in heaven above and on the earth below."**

6. What did Rahab ask the spies to do for her? (2:12-13)

1. To spare only her when they attacked
2. To spare her family even if she must die
3. **To spare the lives of her and her family**
4. To spare all of Jericho

7. Where was Rahab's house located? (2:15)

1. It was located beside the river that flowed through the city.
2. **It was a part of the city wall.**
3. It was located outside the city wall.
4. It was located in the middle of the city.

8. How did Rahab help the spies? (2:4-6, 15)

1. She hid them from the king's men.
2. She said she did not know where they went.
3. She let them down by a rope through a window.
4. **All of the answers are correct.**

9. What did Rahab do so that the Israelites would spare her and her family? (2:17-18)

1. **Tie a scarlet cord in the window**
2. Put blood on the doorposts of her house
3. Paint her door black
4. Place a brown flag in her window

10. What did the spies say to Joshua about their trip to Jericho? (2:24)

1. "The king of Jericho planned an ambush for us."
2. **"All the people are melting in fear because of us."**
3. "Jericho is not as impressive as we thought."
4. "The people are so afraid that they have already left the city."

REVIEW QUESTIONS FOR BIBLE QUIZZING

QUESTIONS FOR BASIC LEVEL REVIEW (LESSON THREE: JOSHUA 3:1-17)

1. **Where did Joshua and the Israelites go early in the morning? (3:1)**

1. To Jericho
2. To the Jordan River
3. To the hills

2. **What were the people to do when they saw the Ark of the Covenant? (3:3)**

1. Bow before it.
2. Stop.
3. Follow it.

3. **How far away from the Ark were the Israelites to walk? (3:4)**

1. About two thousand cubits away
2. As far away as they wanted
3. About five hundred meters away

4. **What did Joshua tell the people? (3:5)**

1. "Tomorrow the Lord will do amazing things among you."
2. "Do not consecrate yourselves."
3. Both answers are correct.

5. **What were the priests supposed to do with the ark? (3:6)**

1. Walk behind the people
2. Walk among the people
3. Walk ahead of the people

6. **Where were the priests supposed to stand when they reached the Jordan River? (3:8)**

1. On the edge of the river
2. In the river
3. On the far side of the river

7. **To what were the Israelites to listen? (3:9)**

1. To the words of the Lord their God
2. To the words of their priests
3. To the words of Moses

8. **What was the Jordan River like during harvest time? (3:15)**

1. It was low.
2. It was at flood stage.
3. It was dry.

9. **What happened as soon as the priests' feet touched the water's edge? (3:15-16)**

1. The water stopped flowing.
2. The water piled up in a heap a great distance away.
3. Both answers are correct.

10. **What was the ground like when the priests stood in the middle of the Jordan River? (3:17)**

1. Dry ground
2. Damp ground
3. Muddy ground

REVIEW QUESTIONS FOR BIBLE QUIZZING

QUESTIONS FOR ADVANCED LEVEL REVIEW (LESSON THREE: JOSHUA 3:1-17)

1. Who went to the Jordan River early in the morning? (3:1)

1. Joshua and all the Israelites
2. All the Canaanites
3. Moses and all the Israelites
4. All of the answers are correct.

2. When were the people supposed to follow the ark? (3:3)

1. After three days.
2. When they saw the warriors.
3. When they saw the ark.
4. After Joshua blessed the ark.

3. Which tribe cared for the ark and carried it? (3:3)

1. The Reubenites
2. The Levites
3. The half-tribe of Manasseh
4. The Gadites

4. How far away from the ark did Joshua tell the people to stay? (3:4)

1. They could go near it, but they must not touch the ark.
2. They must walk three steps behind the half-tribe of Manasseh.
3. They must maintain a distance of about two thousand cubits from the ark.
4. The Lord did not care how far away they stood.

5. Why were the people supposed to consecrate themselves? (3:5)

1. Because they were sleepy
2. Because on the next day, the Lord would to do amazing things among them
3. So that they would not drown in the river
4. All of the answers are correct.

6. What was important about the Jordan River at that time of the year? (3:15)

1. The water in the Jordan River was very low.
2. The Jordan River was red.
3. The Jordan River split in two.
4. The Jordan River was at flood stage during harvest.

7. Where did the water go when it stopped flowing? (3:15-16)

1. It flooded nearby towns.
2. It flooded the fields and ruined the harvest.
3. It piled up in a heap at a town called Adam.
4. It flowed down a gully and formed a new river.

8. Where did the Israelites cross the Jordan River? (3:16)

1. Near the town of Harvest
2. Next to the town of Adam
3. Opposite the town of Jericho
4. Beside the Sea of Arabah

9. Who led the Israelites and were the first people to enter the Jordan River? (3:17)

1. The Israelite army
2. The priests who carried the ark
3. The Reubenites
4. All of the answers are correct.

10. What happened when the priests stood in the middle of the river? (3:5)

1. The water piled up in a heap at a town called Adam.
2. The priests stood on dry ground.
3. The whole nation of Israel passed by on dry ground.
4. All of the answers are correct.

REVIEW QUESTIONS FOR BIBLE QUIZZING

QUESTIONS FOR BASIC LEVEL REVIEW (LESSON FOUR: JOSHUA 4:1-24; 5:10-12)

1. How many men did Joshua choose from each tribe? (4:1-2)

1. One hundred
2. **One**
3. Three

2. What did the twelve men take from the middle of the Jordan River? (4:3)

1. **Twelve stones**
2. Twelve fish
3. A cup of water

3. For what did Joshua use the twelve stones? (4:7)

1. As a sign to warn the people of Jericho
2. As a marker to show the location of Gilgal
3. **As a memorial to remind the people of Israel forever**

4. How long did the priests stand in the middle of the Jordan River? (4:1, 10)

1. Until two days passed
2. **Until everything the Lord had commanded Joshua was done**
3. Until the water returned and threatened to drown them

5. Where did Joshua set up the twelve stones? (4:20)

1. At Jericho
2. On the bank of the Jordan River
3. **At Gilgal**

6. What were the Israelites to say when their descendants asked, "What do these stones mean?" (4:21, 22)

1. **Israel crossed the Jordan on dry ground.**
2. The Lord is the God of the Jordan River.
3. The Lord will never dry up the Jordan River again.

7. What bodies of water did the Lord dry up so that the Israelites could cross? (4:23)

1. The Red Sea
2. The Jordan River
3. **Both answers are correct.**

8. Why did God stop the flow of the Jordan so that the people could cross? (4:23-24)

1. So that all the peoples of the earth might know that the hand of the Lord is powerful
2. So that the Israelites might always fear the Lord their God
3. **Both answers are correct.**

9. What did the people eat the day after the Passover celebration? (5:11)

1. **Some of the produce of the land**
2. Manna
3. Meat from the sacrifice

10. What happened after the people ate the food from the land? (5:12)

1. **The manna stopped.**
2. The manna continued for a month, and then it stopped.
3. The manna came only to the people who were poor.

REVIEW QUESTIONS FOR BIBLE QUIZZING

QUESTIONS FOR ADVANCED LEVEL REVIEW (LESSON FOUR: JOSHUA 4:1-24; 5:10-12)

1. What special job did the Lord give to one man from each of the twelve tribes of Israel? (4:1-3)

1. To take turns with the other men and carry the ark
2. To take messages from Joshua to their tribes
3. **To choose a stone from the middle of the Jordan**
4. All of the answers are correct.

2. What was the purpose of the twelve stones? (4:6-7)

1. To build a bridge
2. **To be a memorial to the people of Israel forever**
3. To throw at the people of Jericho
4. All of the answers are correct.

3. How long did the priests stand in the middle of the Jordan River? (4:1, 10)

1. Until two days passed
2. **Until everything the Lord had commanded Joshua was done**
3. Until the water returned and drowned them.
4. Until Joshua lowered his arms

4. What happened as soon as the priests came out of the Jordan? (4:18)

1. They returned to their camp and rested.
2. The people cheered loudly.
3. **The Jordan River returned to flood stage.**
4. They prepared a sacrifice to the Lord.

5. What did Joshua do with the twelve stones? (4:20)

1. He set them up on the bank of the Jordan River.
2. He set them up at Jericho.
3. **He set them up at Gilgal.**
4. He set them in a circle around the campfire.

6. Why did the Lord dry up the Jordan in the same way he dried up the Red Sea? (4:23-24)

1. So that the Israelites could cross over.
2. So that all the peoples of the earth might know that the hand of the Lord is powerful
3. So that the Israelites might always fear the Lord
4. **All of the answers are correct.**

7. What happened on the evening of the fourteenth day of the month at Gilgal? (5:10)

1. **The Israelites celebrated the Passover.**
2. The people abandoned Joshua.
3. Joshua and his officers refused to eat some of the produce of the land.
4. All of the answers are correct.

8. What did the people eat the day after the Passover? (5:11)

1. Some leftover Manna
2. **Some produce from the land**
3. Fish from the Jordan
4. Meat from a sacrifice

9. When did the manna stop? (5:12)

1. Before they crossed the Jordan
2. **The day after they ate produce of the land**
3. Right before the Passover
4. The manna never stopped

10. Finish this verse: "He said to the Israelites, 'In the future when your descendants ask their parents,...'" (Joshua 4:21-22)

1. **"...What do these stones mean?" tell them, "Israel crossed the Jordan on dry ground."**
2. "...What happened to the sacrifice?" tell them, "We sacrificed to the Lord on these stones."
3. "...Did you honor the Lord?" tell them, "Yes, we built an altar to the Lord."
4. "...What did the Lord do?" tell them, "He gave us Manna."

REVIEW QUESTIONS FOR BIBLE QUIZZING

QUESTIONS FOR BASIC LEVEL REVIEW (LESSON FIVE: JOSHUA 5:13—6:25)

1. **Who stood in front of Joshua when he was near Jericho? (5:13-14)**

1. A man with a drawn sword in his hand
2. The commander of the army of the Lord
3. **Both answers are correct.**

2. **What did Joshua do when he realized that the commander of the army of the Lord stood in front of him? (5:14)**

1. He shook the commander's hand.
2. He saluted the commander.
3. **He fell facedown in reverence.**

3. **What did the Lord say to Joshua about Jericho? (6:2)**

1. **"See, I have delivered Jericho into your hands."**
2. "See, I want you to attack Jericho."
3. "You will spare ten people from Jericho."

4. **What was the Israelite army to do for six days? (6:3)**

1. **March around the city, once each day**
2. Stay in their tents all day and pray
3. Train to fight

5. **From what material were the trumpets made? (6:4)**

1. Cows' horns
2. **Rams' horns**
3. Bronze

6. **What did Joshua command the people to do as they marched around the city? (6:10)**

1. "Yell at the people of Jericho."
2. "Sing songs of praise to God."
3. **"Do not say a word until the day I tell you to shout."**

7. **How many times did the army march around Jericho on the seventh day? (6:15)**

1. Five times
2. Six times
3. **Seven times**

8. **What happened when the trumpets sounded and the people shouted? (6:20)**

1. The walls of Jericho collapsed.
2. Everyone charged straight in.
3. **Both answers are correct.**

9. **Where did Rahab and her family live after they left Jericho? (6:23)**

1. Inside the Israelite camp
2. **Outside the Israelite camp**
3. In the ruined city of Jericho

10. **Why did Joshua spare Rahab when he attacked Jericho? (6:25)**

1. **She hid the spies that Joshua had sent to Jericho.**
2. She knew where the king hid his treasure.
3. She ran away from the city.

REVIEW QUESTIONS FOR BIBLE QUIZZING

QUESTIONS FOR ADVANCED LEVEL REVIEW (LESSON FIVE: JOSHUA 5:13—6:25)

1. **Why did Joshua take off his sandals? (5:15)**

1. His feet were sore from the long journey.
2. **The commander of the Lord's army told him to.**
3. Moses taught him to do that every time the Lord appeared.
4. All of the answers are correct.

2. **What did the Lord say that the armed men should do for six days? (6:3)**

1. **March around the city once a day.**
2. Pray for the downfall of Jericho.
3. Use tools to break down the walls of Jericho.
4. Stay in their tents

3. **What were the Lord's instructions for how the Israelites should march? (6:3-5)**

1. Seven priests with trumpets would go in front of the ark.
2. Joshua would march around the city with all the armed men.
3. On the seventh day, they would march around the city seven times.
4. **All of the answers are correct.**

4. **What was the army to do when they heard the long trumpet blast on the seventh day? (6:4-5)**

1. Run back to their tents
2. Knock down the walls of Jericho
3. **Shout**
4. All of the answers are correct.

5. **What did the people do on the seventh day? (6:15)**

1. Stayed in their tents and prayed
2. **Marched around the city seven times**
3. Prepared a celebration feast
4. All of the answers are correct.

6. **What would happen to the people if they took the devoted things? (6:18)**

1. They would gain great riches.
2. They would receive honor.
3. **They would bring about their own destruction.**
4. They would divide the items with their neighbors.

7. **What happened when the trumpets sounded and the people shouted? (6:20)**

1. **The wall collapsed.**
2. The people of Jericho ran out of the city.
3. The people of Jericho blew their own horns.
4. All of the answers are correct.

8. **Who brought out Rahab and her family? (6:22-23)**

1. Joshua
2. The priests
3. **The two spies**
4. All of the answers are correct.

9. **Why did Joshua spare Rahab when he attacked Jericho? (6:25)**

1. **She hid the spies that Joshua had sent to Jericho.**
2. She knew where to find the king's treasure.
3. She fled the city.
4. All of the answers are correct.

10. **Finish this verse: "Obey the Lord your God and..." (Deuteronomy 27:10)**

1. "...listen to him so you will know how to live today."
2. **"...follow his commands and decrees that I give you today."**
3. "...listen to his voice so that you can hear what he wants you to do."
4. "...follow him always. Never turn from him."

REVIEW QUESTIONS FOR BIBLE QUIZZING

QUESTIONS FOR BASIC LEVEL REVIEW (LESSON SIX: JOSHUA 7:1-26)

1. Who acted unfaithfully with the devoted things? (7:1)

1. **The Israelites**
2. The people of Jericho
3. The Lord

2. Who took some of the devoted things? (7:1)

1. Joshua
2. **Achan**
3. The twelve elders

3. When Joshua sent men to Ai, what did he tell them to do? (7:2)

1. **Spy out the region of Ai.**
2. Spy out the Jordan River.
3. Spy out Jericho.

4. What happened when the Israelite warriors attacked Ai? (7:4-5)

1. The men of Ai routed the Israelites.
2. About 36 Israelites died.
3. **Both answers are correct.**

5. What did Joshua do after the defeat at Ai? (7:6)

1. He went outside the camp for thirty days.
2. **He fell facedown in front of the ark of the Lord until evening.**
3. He planned a feast.

6. Why did Israel not stand against their enemies? (7:10-12)

1. Israel had sinned and violated God's covenant.
2. Israel had stolen and lied.
3. **Both answers are correct.**

7. What did Israel need to do so that the Lord would stay with them? (7:12)

1. Say that they were sorry
2. **Destroy whatever they found among them that was devoted to destruction**
3. Take the devoted things back to Jericho

8. What would happen to the person who was caught with the devoted things? (7:15)

1. That person would be required to leave the Israelite camp.
2. **That person and all that belonged to him would be destroyed by fire.**
3. That person would be required to give back what he stole.

9. What happened when Joshua sent men to Achan's tent? (7:22)

1. They found Achan's children.
2. They did not find any stolen things.
3. **They found the robe, the silver, and the gold.**

10. What happened to Achan, his family and all of his possessions? (7:25)

1. **The Israelites stoned and burned them.**
2. The Israelites made them leave their camp.
3. The Israelites made them servants and gave his silver and gold to Joshua.

REVIEW QUESTIONS FOR BIBLE QUIZZING

QUESTIONS FOR ADVANCED LEVEL REVIEW (LESSON SIX: JOSHUA 7:1-26)

1. Who stole the devoted things? (7:1)

1. Joshua
2. The priests
3. **Achan**
4. Rahab

2. Why did Joshua send men to Ai? (7:2)

1. To find out how many people remained in Jericho
2. **To spy out the region of Ai**
3. To spy out the region of Shechem
4. All of the answers are correct.

3. Who told Joshua not to send the whole army against Ai? (7:2-3)

1. Achan
2. The priests
3. The elders
4. **The spies**

4. What happened after the Israelites were defeated at Ai? (7:5-6)

1. The hearts of all the Israelites melted.
2. Joshua and the elders fell facedown before the ark.
3. Joshua and the elders tore their clothes.
4. **All of the answers are correct.**

5. What would happen to the person who was caught with the devoted things? (7:15)

1. The Israelites would force him to leave the camp forever.
2. The Israelites would make him serve as Joshua's slave.
3. **The Israelites would destroy him and all that belonged to him by fire.**
4. The Israelites would require him to return what he stole.

6. What did Joshua tell Achan to do? (7:19)

1. Give glory to the Lord.
2. Admit what he did.
3. Hide nothing from Joshua.
4. **All of the answers are correct.**

7. What did Achan do with the stolen goods? (7:21)

1. **He hid them in the ground in his tent.**
2. He became nervous and threw them in the river.
3. He sold them to local merchants.
4. He displayed them in his tent.

8. Who took Achan and his family to the Valley of Achor? (7:24)

1. **Joshua, together with all of Israel**
2. King Carmi
3. Moses
4. The Lord

9. After Achan died, what happened? (7:26)

1. The Israelites divided his silver and gold.
2. Joshua held a feast.
3. **The Lord turned from his fierce anger.**
4. All of the answers are correct.

10. What does Proverbs 14:12 say?

1. "There is a good thought that a man thinks, but God knows the best way."
2. **"There is a way that appears to be right, but in the end it leads to death."**
3. "The faithless will be fully repaid for their ways, and the good man rewarded for his."
4. "He whose walk is upright fears the Lord."

REVIEW QUESTIONS FOR BIBLE QUIZZING

QUESTIONS FOR BASIC LEVEL REVIEW (LESSON SEVEN: JOSHUA 8:1-35)

1. What did the Lord tell Joshua to do? (8:1)

1. To take his whole army and attack Ai

2. To stay away from Ai

3. To take the spies and see how many men were in Ai's army

2. What was Joshua's plan to attack Ai? (8:3-6)

1. He planned to set an ambush behind the city.

2. He planned to lure the men away from the city.

3. Both answers are correct.

3. What happened when the king of Ai saw the Israelite army? (8:13-14)

1. He and his army stayed inside the city.

2. He and his army hurried to meet Israel in battle.

3. He ran away.

4. What did Joshua hold out toward Ai? (8:18)

1. A trumpet

2. A torch

3. A javelin

5. What happened when Joshua held out his javelin? (8:18-19)

1. The men who hid rose and rushed into Ai.

2. The men captured the city and set it on fire.

3. Both answers are correct.

6. How many people in the city of Ai survived the attack from the Israelites? (8:22-23)

1. No one except the king of Ai

2. Some fugitives

3. 100 men

7. What did Joshua build on Mount Ebal? (8:30-31)

1. An altar

2. A fortress

3. A monument

8. What did Joshua and the people offer to the Lord? (8:31)

1. Treasures from Ai

2. Burnt and fellowship offerings

3. All their cattle

9. What did Joshua write on the stones? (8:32)

1. The names of the bravest warriors

2. The cities that the Israelites conquered

3. A copy of the Law of Moses

10. What did Joshua read to all the Israelite people? (8:34-35)

1. The words of the Law

2. Blessings and curses

3. Both answers are correct.

REVIEW QUESTIONS FOR BIBLE QUIZZING

QUESTIONS FOR ADVANCED LEVEL REVIEW (LESSON SEVEN: JOSHUA 8:1-35)

1. Why did God send Joshua and the entire Israelite army to Ai? (8:1)

1. To make a treaty with Ai
2. **To attack Ai**
3. To have a meal with the men of Ai
4. All of the answers are correct.

2. What did the Lord say to Joshua when he commanded him to attack Ai? (8:1)

1. "Do not be afraid."
2. "Do not be discouraged."
3. "I have delivered into your hands the king of Ai, his people, his city and his land."
4. **All of the answers are correct.**

3. Why did Joshua send 30,000 Israelites out at night? (8:3-4)

1. To wait for a message from the angel of the Lord.
2. To set up an ambush behind the city.
3. **To wait for Joshua to signal the attack and hold up a torch.**
4. All of the answers are correct.

4. Where did the men in the ambush wait? (8:12)

1. At the foot of Mt. Ebal
2. Inside the city of Ai
3. **Between Bethel and Ai**
4. In the city of Bethel

5. What happened when Joshua raised his javelin? (8:18-19)

1. The soldiers of Ai saw the ambush and ran away.
2. The men in ambush rushed to Joshua's side.
3. **The men in ambush captured the city and set it on fire.**
4. All of the answers are correct.

6. What happened when the men of Ai saw the smoke from the city? (8:20)

1. **They had no chance to escape in any direction.**
2. They ran back to the city to save their families.
3. They fled to the mountains to escape the fire.
4. They turned on each other and killed one another.

7. After the battle in Ai, where did Joshua build an altar to the Lord? (8:30-31)

1. On Mount Ararat
2. **On Mount Ebal**
3. On top of the ruins of Ai
4. On Mount Sinai

8. What did the Israelites do on the altar? (8:31)

1. **They offered burnt offerings and sacrificed fellowship offerings to the Lord.**
2. They divided the treasures they stole from Ai.
3. They prayed to the Lord for forgiveness.
4. All of the answers are correct.

9. What did Joshua write on the stones? (8:32)

1. The date and time of the battle of Ai
2. **A copy of the Law of Moses**
3. The names of all the Israelite soldiers
4. The prayers that were lifted up to God

10. Finish this verse: "Be strong and very courageous. Be careful to obey all the law my servant Moses gave you; ..." (Joshua 1:7)

1. **"...do not turn from it to the right or to the left, that you may be successful wherever you go."**
2. "...do not disobey God. He desires his people to follow him."
3. "...do not turn away from the law. You will succeed if you follow him."
4. "...do not turn from it in any direction. God will bless you."

REVIEW QUESTIONS FOR BIBLE QUIZZING

QUESTIONS FOR BASIC LEVEL REVIEW (LESSON EIGHT: JOSHUA 9:1—10:15)

1. Who heard what Joshua did at Jericho and Ai? (9:3)

1. **The people of Gibeon**
2. No one
3. The Egyptians

2. To what did the Gibeonites resort? (9:3-4)

1. They planned an attack.
2. **They planned a ruse, or a trick.**
3. They planned to move away from the Israelites.

3. How did the Gibeonites convince the Israelites that they came from a distant country? (9:4-5, 12-13)

1. They showed the Israelites their dry and moldy bread.
2. They showed the Israelites their old wineskins and worn-out sacks and clothes.
3. **Both answers are correct.**

4. What did the Gibeonites want from the Israelites? (9:6)

1. Their gold and silver
2. To learn how to sacrifice offerings to the God of Israel
3. **To make a treaty with them**

5. What did the men of Israel fail to do before they made the treaty with the Gibeonites? (9:14)

1. Talk to Joshua
2. **Inquire of the Lord**
3. Ask the priests

6. What happened three days after Joshua and the leaders made a peace treaty with the Gibeonites? (9:16)

1. The Gibeonites attacked Israel.
2. They offered sacrifices to the Lord in honor of the treaty.
3. **They learned that the Gibeonites were their neighbors.**

7. Why did the Israelites not attack the Gibeonites? (9:17-18)

1. Because they were afraid
2. **Because of their oath**
3. Because they decided to trick the Gibeonites instead

8. What did Joshua do with the Gibeonites? (9:21)

1. **Let them live as woodcutters and water carriers**
2. Tricked them into breaking the treaty
3. Both answers are correct.

9. What happened when the Gibeonites asked for help from the Israelites? (10:6-8)

1. Joshua marched with his entire army to help Gibeon.
2. The Lord told Joshua, "Do not be afraid."
3. **Both answers are correct.**

10. What did Joshua say to the Lord when the Israelites fought the Amorites? (10:12)

1. **"Sun, stand still over Gibeon."**
2. "Lord, help me defeat the Amorites."
3. "Lord, what do I do?"

REVIEW QUESTIONS FOR BIBLE QUIZZING

QUESTIONS FOR ADVANCED LEVEL REVIEW (LESSON EIGHT: JOSHUA 9:1—10:15)

1. What did the Gibeonites hear about the Israelites? (9:3)

1. That Gilgal and Jordan had defeated them
2. **That the Israelites had defeated Jericho and Ai**
3. That the Israelites had defeated Adoni-Zedek and Pi
4. That the Israelites were weak

2. How did the Gibeonites deceive the Israelites? (9:4-6)

1. **They wore old clothes and said they were from a distant country.**
2. They pretended to be relatives of the Israelites.
3. They sent spies into the Israelite camp.
4. They made a peace treaty with Israel and then attacked them.

3. How was the Lord involved in the decision to make the treaty with Gibeon? (9:14)

1. Joshua inquired of the Lord and then made the treaty.
2. **The Israelites did not inquire of the Lord before they made the treaty.**
3. The Israelites asked the Lord and then ignored his commands.
4. The Lord did not respond to Joshua's prayer.

4. What happened three days after the Israelites made a peace treaty with Gibeon? (9:16)

1. They went to war with Gibeon.
2. The Amorites attacked them.
3. **They learned that the Gibeonites lived near them.**
4. They canceled the peace treaty with Gibeon.

5. Why did the Israelites decide not to attack the Gibeonites? (9:17-18)

1. They heard that Gibeon had many warriors.
2. They heard that Gibeon had made a treaty with the five Amorite kings.
3. They decided to attack later when Gibeon did not expect it.
4. **They honored the oath that they had sworn by the LORD.**

6. What happened when the five Amorite kings attacked Gibeon? (10:5-7)

1. Gibeon fought the Amorites bravely without the Israelites help.
2. Joshua helped the Amorite kings.
3. **Joshua and his army went to help Gibeon.**
4. The Israelites decided to make a treaty with Adoni-Zedek.

7. What did the Lord say to Joshua when he went to help Gibeon fight? (10:6-8)

1. "Do not be afraid of them."
2. "I have given them into your hand."
3. "Not one of them will be able to withstand you."
4. **All of the answers are correct.**

8. How was the Lord involved in the battle against the Amorites? (10:12-13)

1. **The Lord made the sun stand still.**
2. The Lord struck the Amorites with lightning.
3. The Lord gave courage to the Gibeonites.
4. All of the answers are correct.

9. How long did the sun stand still during the battle against the Amorites? (10:13)

1. About a full hour
2. **About a full day**
3. About two full days
4. About a full week

10. What does Psalm 25:10 say?

1. "All the ways of the Lord are sure. He knows what to do in times of trouble."
2. **"All the ways of the Lord are loving and faithful toward those who keep the demands of his covenant."**
3. "All the ways of the Lord are faithful and true to those who follow him."
4. "All of the ways of the lord are good for he is a good God."

REVIEW QUESTIONS FOR BIBLE QUIZZING

QUESTIONS FOR BASIC LEVEL REVIEW (LESSON NINE: JOSHUA 13:1-7; 14:1-15)

1. When Joshua had grown old, what did the Lord say to him? (13:1)

1. **"There are still very large areas of land to be taken over."**
2. "The land of the Philistines is too much to conquer."
3. Both answers are correct.

2. Who told Joshua that he would drive out the Sidonians for the Israelites? (13:6)

1. **The Lord**
2. Moses
3. Joshua's general

3. What did the Lord tell Joshua to allocate for Israel? (13:6)

1. Cattle and sheep
2. **The land of the Sidonians**
3. Both answers are correct.

4. Who came to see Joshua one day? (14:6)

1. **The people of Judah**
2. Joshua's wife
3. The king of Sidonia

5. What did Caleb tell Joshua? (14:7)

1. That Moses promised him the whole land of Canaan
2. **That Moses sent him from Kadesh Barnea to explore the land**
3. That Moses was a better leader

6. Who went up with Caleb to explore the land of Canaan? (14:7-8)

1. His enemies
2. **His fellow Israelites**
3. The priests

7. What did Caleb's companions do? (14:8)

1. They made Caleb bring a false report to the people.
2. They told the people to obey God and take over the land.
3. **They made the hearts of the people melt with fear.**

8. Who told Joshua that he followed the Lord wholeheartedly? (14:8)

1. **Caleb**
2. Moses
3. The high priest

9. Who gave Hebron to Caleb as his inheritance? (14:13)

1. **Joshua**
2. The priests
3. The elders

10. From what did the land have rest? (14:15)

1. From storms and earthquakes
2. **From war**
3. From poor crops

REVIEW QUESTIONS FOR BIBLE QUIZZING

QUESTIONS FOR ADVANCED LEVEL REVIEW (LESSON NINE: JOSHUA 13:1-7; 14:1-15)

1. What did the Lord say to Joshua after many years of battle and conquest? (13:1)

1. **"You are now very old, and there are still very large areas of land to be taken over."**
2. "It is time for you to rest from all your battles."
3. "The people must elect a new leader."
4. All of the answers are correct.

2. What did the Lord tell Joshua to do for the nine remaining tribes and the half tribe of Manasseh? (13:6-7)

1. Divide them into smaller tribes.
2. Give them all the cattle they needed.
3. **Divide the land among them as an inheritance.**
4. All of the answers are correct.

3. Who said, "I brought Moses back a report according to my convictions"? (14:7)

1. Joshua
2. **Caleb**
3. Moses
4. Joseph

4. How did Caleb follow the Lord? (14:9)

1. **Wholeheartedly**
2. Reluctantly at first, but faithfully after the battle of Jericho
3. With a sad heart
4. Joyfully

5. How strong did Caleb say he was? (14:11)

1. Strong enough to fight for three days and nights
2. As strong as the entire Israelite army
3. **As strong as he was the day that Moses sent him out**
4. All of the answers are correct.

6. What promise did the Lord give to Caleb? (14:12)

1. To give Caleb all the cattle and sheep of the land
2. **To give Caleb the hill country**
3. To show Caleb how to defeat the Canaanites
4. All of the answers are correct.

7. What land did Joshua give to Caleb? (14:13)

1. **Hebron**
2. Manasseh
3. The land of the Reubenites
4. The land of the Philistines.

8. Why has Hebron belonged to Caleb ever since? (14:14)

1. Caleb won the land in a battle.
2. Caleb served the gods of Hebron.
3. **Caleb served the Lord wholeheartedly.**
4. Caleb served the people well.

9. What had rest from war? (14:15)

1. **The land**
2. The Canaanites' cattle
3. The Canaanites' sheep
4. All of the answers are correct.

10. Finish this verse: "And whatever you do, whether in word or deed, do it all..." (Colossians 3:17)

1. "...with a good attitude and glorify the father."
2. **"...in the name of the Lord Jesus, giving thanks to God the father through him."**
3. "...wholeheartedly, but let your deeds speak for themselves."
4. "...to help others know the love of God."

REVIEW QUESTIONS FOR BIBLE QUIZZING

QUESTIONS FOR BASIC LEVEL REVIEW
(LESSON TEN: JOSHUA 20:1-9; 21:1-8, 43-45)

1. What did the Lord tell the Israelites to designate? (20:1-2)

1. **The cities of refuge**
2. The temples to the Lord on every hill
3. The camps around every city

2. Who may flee and find protection in a city of refuge? (20:3)

1. Anyone who killed a person accidentally
2. Anyone who killed a person unintentionally
3. **Both answers are correct.**

3. What were the elders of the city of refuge to do for anyone who accidentally killed someone? (20:4)

1. Give him some food, and then send him to another city.
2. **Admit him into their city and provide a place to live among them.**
3. Allow him to hide for one month and then conduct a trial.

4. What were the elders of the city to do if the avenger of blood pursued the one who was accused? (20:5)

1. **They must not surrender the fugitive.**
2. They must surrender the fugitive.
3. They must kill the fugitive.

5. Who approached Eleazar, Joshua, and the heads of the other tribal families of Israel? (21:1)

1. The five Canaanite kings
2. **The family heads of the Levites**
3. The enemies of Israel

6. Who said, "The Lord commanded through Moses that you give us towns to live in"? (21:1-2)

1. Joshua
2. Moses
3. **The heads of the Levite families**

7. What did the Israelites give to the Levites? (21:3)

1. Cattle and sheep
2. **Towns and pasturelands out of their own inheritance**
3. Tents

8. Who commanded through Moses that the Israelites should give towns and pasturelands to the Levites? (21:8)

1. Joshua
2. The priests
3. **The Lord**

9. What did Israel do when the Lord gave them all the land that he swore to give to their ancestors? (21:43)

1. **They took possession of it and settled there.**
2. They fought for more land.
3. Both answers are correct.

10. Who gave all the Israelites' enemies into their hands? (21:44)

1. Joshua
2. **The Lord**
3. Moses

REVIEW QUESTIONS FOR BIBLE QUIZZING

QUESTIONS FOR ADVANCED LEVEL REVIEW (LESSON TEN: JOSHUA 20:1-9; 21:1-8, 43-45)

1. Who said, "Tell the Israelites to designate the cities of refuge"? (20:1-2)

1. Eleazar
2. Joshua
3. **The Lord**
4. The priests

2. What was anyone who killed a person accidentally allowed to do? (20:3)

1. Find the avenger of blood
2. **Flee to a city of refuge and find protection from the avenger of blood**
3. Ask for forgiveness from the avenger of blood
4. All of the answers are correct.

3. What were the elders of the city of refuge to do with anyone who fled to that city? (20:4)

1. **Admit him into their city and provide him a place to live among them.**
2. Give him over to the avenger of blood.
3. Send him to hide in the hill country.
4. Give him one meal and then release him.

4. What did the family heads of the Levites say? (21:2)

1. "The Lord has forgotten us, so we will take your land."
2. **"The Lord commanded through Moses that you give us towns to live in, with pasturelands for our livestock."**
3. "The Lord told us that we would receive towns and wives from you."
4. All of the answers are correct.

5. What did the Israelites give to the Levites? (21:3)

1. Cattle and sheep
2. **Towns and pasturelands out of their own inheritance**
3. A temple for worshipping the Lord
4. Tents and camels

6. What did the Lord give to Israel? (21:43)

1. All the land east of the Red Sea
2. All the land west of the Red Sea
3. **All the land he had sworn to give their ancestors**
4. All of the answers are correct.

7. Who took possession of and settled in the land? (21:43)

1. **The Israelites**
2. The Canaanites
3. The Egyptians
4. The Gibeonites

8. Where did the Lord give Israel rest? (21:44)

1. **On every side**
2. In the cities of Ramoth and Golan only
3. In the city of Bezer only
4. In the north only

9. Whom did the Lord give into the Israelites' hands? (21:44)

1. Some of their enemies
2. Most of their enemies
3. **All of their enemies**
4. None of their enemies

10. Finish this verse: "Not one of all the Lord's good promises..." (Joshua 21:45)

1. **"...to Israel failed; every one was fulfilled."**
2. "...to his people succeeded; every one failed."
3. "...to the Israelites failed; they were all easy."
4. "...to the nation of Israel failed; he answered quickly."

REVIEW QUESTIONS FOR BIBLE QUIZZING

QUESTIONS FOR BASIC LEVEL REVIEW
(LESSON ELEVEN: JOSHUA 23:1-16; 24:14-32)

1. Who gave Israel rest from all their enemies? (23:1)

1. Joshua
2. Moses
3. **The Lord**

2. When did Joshua summon all Israel—their elders, leaders, judges and officials? (23:1-2)

1. **When he was old**
2. After the Israelites defeated the Egyptians
3. Before his first son was born

3. Who fought for the Israelites? (23:3)

1. Their women and children
2. **The Lord their God**
3. The Egyptians

4. What did Joshua warn the people? (23:6)

1. "Be very strong."
2. "Be careful to obey all that is written in the Book of the Law of Moses."
3. **Both answers are correct.**

5. Who were the Israelites told not to serve? (23:7)

1. The Egyptians
2. **The gods of the nations that remained among them**
3. Joshua

6. Who were the Israelites to be careful to love? (23:11)

1. **The Lord their God**
2. The Egyptians
3. Each other

7. What would happen if the Israelites served other gods? (23:16)

1. The Lord's anger would burn against them.
2. They would quickly perish.
3. **Both answers are correct.**

8. What were the Israelites supposed to throw away? (24:14)

1. The jars and jugs they did not use
2. **The gods their ancestors worshiped beyond the Euphrates River and in Egypt**
3. Any extra clothing they did not use

9. Who said, "But as for me and my household, we will serve the Lord"? (24:15)

1. Moses
2. The priests
3. **Joshua**

10. What did Joshua do when he made a covenant for the people? (24:25-27)

1. He wrote in the Book of the Law.
2. He set up a large stone as a witness to the covenant.
3. **Both answers are correct.**

REVIEW QUESTIONS FOR BIBLE QUIZZING

QUESTIONS FOR ADVANCED LEVEL REVIEW
(LESSON ELEVEN: JOSHUA 23:1-16; 24:14-32)

1. Who did the Lord give Israel rest from? (23:1)

1. The prophets of Baal
2. All their enemies
3. The Egyptians
4. All of the answers are correct.

2. What would happen if the Israelites served other gods? (23:16)

1. Joshua would serve other gods with them.
2. The Israelites would quickly perish from the land the Lord gave to them.
3. The Lord would still bless them.
4. The other gods would give the Israelites victory and prosperity.

3. Who told the Israelites to fear and serve the Lord? (24:14)

1. Joshua
2. The priests
3. The elders
4. All of the answers are correct.

4. Who said, "Choose for yourselves this day whom you will serve"? (24:15)

1. Moses
2. The priests
3. The elders
4. Joshua

5. Who did Joshua say that he and his household would serve? (24:15)

1. The gods of the Jebusites
2. The gods of the Egyptians
3. The gods of the Philistines
4. The Lord

6. What would happen to the Israelites if they forsook the Lord and served foreign gods? (24:20)

1. God would give their inheritance away.
2. God would appoint a new leader.
3. God would turn and bring disaster on them.
4. God would make them leave Canaan.

7. What did Joshua tell the people to do with their foreign gods? (24:23)

1. Give them away.
2. Hide them.
3. Throw them away.
4. Keep them.

8. What did Joshua do after the people said they would serve the Lord? (24:25-27)

1. He made a covenant.
2. He wrote in the Book of the Law.
3. He set up a large stone as a witness to the covenant.
4. All of the answers are correct.

9. How old was Joshua when he died? (24:29)

1. 110 years old
2. 100 years old
3. 95 years old
4. 90 years old

10. Quote Joshua 24:14a.

1. "Love the Lord with all your heart. Worship him alone."
2. "Now fear the Lord and serve him with all faithfulness."
3. "Live for God all the days of your life and obey all his rules."
4. "Now fear the Lord and obey all his commands."

1. Who said, "I brought you up out of Egypt and led you into the land I swore to give to your ancestors"? (2:1)

1. Deborah
2. Joshua
3. **An angel of the Lord**

2. What did the angel of the Lord tell Israel to do? (2:2)

1. **To break down the altars of the people of the land**
2. To break the promises they made to the people
3. To destroy the crops they grew

3. What would the gods of the people of the land be to the Israelites? (2:3)

1. **Snares**
2. Thorns in their sides
3. A stench in their nostrils

4. What did the Lord do to Israel because he was angry with them? (2:13-14)

1. He took away their land.
2. **He allowed raiders to plunder them.**
3. He rained down hailstones on Israel.

5. Whom did the Lord raise up for the Israelites when they were in great distress? (2:15-16)

1. Moses
2. Prophets
3. **Judges**

6. What did the judges do for the Israelites? (2:16)

1. They decided the punishments for their criminals.
2. **They saved them from the raiders.**
3. Both answers are correct.

7. When the people did not listen to their judges, what did they do instead? (2:17)

1. They worshiped other gods.
2. They quickly turned away from their obedience to the Lord.
3. **Both answers are correct.**

8. Who relented because the Israelites groaned when they were oppressed and afflicted? (2:18)

1. Their enemies
2. **The Lord**
3. The judges

9. Whom did the Lord use to test Israel? (2:21-22)

1. **Other nations**
2. Joshua
3. Pharaoh

10. Why did the Lord test Israel? (2:22)

1. To punish them for their disobedience
2. **To see if they would keep the way of the Lord and walk in it**
3. To scare them from the worship of idols

REVIEW QUESTIONS FOR BIBLE QUIZZING

QUESTIONS FOR ADVANCED LEVEL REVIEW (LESSON TWELVE: JUDGES 2:1-23)

1. What did the angel of the Lord say to the Israelites? (2:1-2)

1. "I brought you up out of Egypt."
2. "I will never break my covenant."
3. "You shall break down their altars."
4. **All of the answers are correct.**

2. What did the angel of the Lord tell the Israelites not to do? (2:2)

1. To build an altar to the Lord
2. **To make a covenant with the people of the land**
3. To make a covenant with the Lord
4. To build a temple to the Lord

3. Who wept and offered sacrifices to the Lord? (2:4-5)

1. Joshua
2. The Canaanites
3. **The Israelites**
4. The judges

4. What did the God of their ancestors do for the Israelites? (2:12)

1. He abandoned them in Egypt.
2. **He brought them out of Egypt.**
3. He left them in the wilderness.
4. He took them safely back to Egypt.

5. To whom did the Lord hand over the Israelites? (2:14)

1. **To raiders who plundered them**
2. To the Canaanite gods
3. To their priests
4. To the elders of the people

6. What did the Lord do when the people were in great distress? (2:15-16)

1. He ignored them because of their sins.
2. **He raised up judges for them.**
3. He asked them to sacrifice burnt offerings.
4. He sent them to battle against the raiders.

7. What did the judges do for the people? (2:16)

1. **They saved them out of the hands of the raiders.**
2. They sent them off to battle against their enemies.
3. They made them sacrifice to the Lord.
4. They sent raiders to steal from them.

8. When the people did not listen to their judges, what did they do instead? (2:17)

1. They listened to the Lord.
2. They listened to the priests.
3. **They worshiped other gods.**
4. They deceived the judges.

9. What did the people do when the judge died? (2:19)

1. They continued to follow the Lord.
2. **They returned to ways even more corrupt than those of their ancestors.**
3. They began to defeat all their enemies.
4. They elected another judge.

10. Why did the Lord test Israel? (2:22)

1. To punish them
2. So they would offer sacrifices to him
3. **To see if they would keep the way of the Lord and walk in it**
4. All of the answers are correct.

REVIEW QUESTIONS FOR BIBLE QUIZZING

QUESTIONS FOR BASIC LEVEL REVIEW (LESSON THIRTEEN: JUDGES 4:1-24)

1. Who was the Canaanite king who reigned in Hazor? (4:2)

1. **Jabin**
2. Sisera
3. Heber

2. Who oppressed the Israelites for 20 years? (4:3)

1. Dagon
2. **Sisera**
3. Barak

3. What did the Israelites do when Sisera oppressed them? (4:3)

1. They began to serve Baal.
2. **They cried out to the Lord for help.**
3. They joined his army.

4. Who led Israel during the time of Jabin's rule? (4:4)

1. Barak
2. Jael
3. **Deborah**

5. Who was Deborah? (4:4)

1. A prophet
2. A leader of the Israelites
3. **Both answers are correct.**

6. Why did the Israelites come to Deborah? (4:5)

1. To receive charity
2. **To settle their disputes**
3. To be healed

7. What did Barak request before he agreed to go to battle? (4:8)

1. Deborah must send 500 chariots with him.
2. **Deborah must go with him.**
3. Deborah must find him a wife.

8. Into whose hands would the Lord deliver Sisera? (4:9)

1. A young soldier
2. Barak
3. **A woman**

9. How many of Sisera's troops were left after the battle? (4:16)

1. Very few
2. **Not one man**
3. Only the men on chariots

10. What happened after God subdued Jabin? (4:23-24)

1. The Israelites grew fearful
2. **The Israelites destroyed Jabin.**
3. Both answers are correct.

REVIEW QUESTIONS FOR BIBLE QUIZZING

QUESTIONS FOR ADVANCED LEVEL REVIEW (LESSON THIRTEEN: JUDGES 4:1-24)

1. Who was the Canaanite king who reigned in Hazor? (4:2)

1. Jabin
2. Sisera
3. Heber
4. Joshua

2. After Ehud died, how did the Lord react when Israel once again did evil in his eyes? (4:1-2)

1. He sent a famine into the land.
2. He sold them into the hands of King Jabin.
3. He brought ten plagues on them.
4. He dried up the Jordan River.

3. Who led Israel during the time of Jabin's rule? (4:4)

1. Barak
2. Jael
3. Deborah
4. Joshua

4. Why did the Israelites come to Deborah? (4:5)

1. To receive charity
2. To settle their disputes
3. To be healed
4. All of the answers are correct.

5. To whom would the Lord deliver Sisera? (4:9)

1. A young soldier
2. Barak
3. A woman
4. Deborah

6. What did Deborah say to Barak before battle? (4:14)

1. "Go! This is the day the Lord has given Sisera into your hands."
2. "Stop! The Lord has turned his face from you."
3. "May the Lord bless and keep you."
4. All of the answers are correct.

7. How many of Sisera's troops were left after the battle? (4:16)

1. Very few
2. Not one man
3. Only the men on chariots
4. About 100

8. Who killed Sisera? (4:21-23)

1. Barak
2. Jael, Heber's wife
3. The army of Israel
4. A young soldier

9. What happened after God subdued Jabin? (4:23-24)

1. The Israelites did evil in the sight of the Lord.
2. The Israelites destroyed Jabin.
3. The Israelites held Jabin's family for ransom.
4. All of the answers are correct.

10. Finish this verse: "I know that you..." (Job 42:2)

1. "...save us with your plans. Every plan you make will be completed."
2. "...can do all things; no purpose of yours can be thwarted."
3. "...do everything and help us with this situation."
4. "...will come up with a plan that will help us defeat our enemies."

REVIEW QUESTIONS FOR BIBLE QUIZZING

QUESTIONS FOR BASIC LEVEL REVIEW (LESSON FOURTEEN: JUDGES 6:1-40)

1. **Where did the Israelites live when the Midianites oppressed them? (6:2)**

1. In the mountains
2. In caves
3. **Both answers are correct.**

2. **What did the Midianites do to the crops the Israelites planted? (6:3-4)**

1. **They ruined them.**
2. They ate them.
3. Both answers are correct.

3. **What did the Israelites do when the Midianites impoverished them? (6:6)**

1. Their army fought the Midianites.
2. **They cried out to the Lord for help.**
3. They moved to Egypt.

4. **What did Gideon do in the winepress? (6:11)**

1. **He threshed wheat.**
2. He ate lunch.
3. He read the Book of the Law.

5. **What did the angel of the Lord call Gideon? (6:12)**

1. An intelligent man
2. A scared man
3. **A mighty warrior**

6. **What did Gideon say to the angel of the Lord about himself? (6:15)**

1. "My clan is the strongest in Manasseh."
2. **"I am the least in my family."**
3. "I am the oldest in my family."

7. **Who did Gideon see face-to-face? (6:22)**

1. **The angel of the Lord**
2. The Midianite king
3. The Amorite god

8. **What did Gideon name the place where he built an altar to the Lord? (6:24)**

1. **"The Lord is Peace"**
2. "The Lord is Love"
3. "The Lord is Good"

9. **What did Gideon and the ten servants tear down? (6:25, 27)**

1. The winepress
2. The house where Gideon's family lived
3. **Baal's altar and the Asherah pole**

10. **What did Gideon put on the threshing floor for God to use as a sign? (6:36-37)**

1. A bushel of grain
2. A bowl of water
3. **A piece of fleece**

REVIEW QUESTIONS FOR BIBLE QUIZZING

QUESTIONS FOR ADVANCED LEVEL REVIEW (LESSON FOURTEEN: JUDGES 6:1-40)

1. Where did the Israelites live when the Midianites oppressed them? (6:2)

1. In the mountains
2. In the cities
3. In their fields
4. All of the answers are correct.

2. What did the Midianites do whenever the Israelites planted their crops? (6:3-4)

1. They camped on the land.
2. They ruined the crops.
3. They did not spare a living thing for Israel.
4. All of the answers are correct.

3. What did Gideon try to keep hidden from the Midianites? (6:11)

1. His money
2. His wine
3. His goats
4. His wheat

4. How did the angel of the Lord greet Gideon in the winepress? (6:12)

1. "Greetings, Prince of Israel."
2. "The Lord is with you, mighty warrior."
3. "Gideon, why are you in the winepress?"
4. All of the answers are correct.

5. What did the angel of the Lord do with the offering that Gideon prepared for God? (6:19-21)

1. He did not touch it.
2. He touched it and fire consumed it.
3. He ate it.
4. He ignored it.

6. What did Gideon name the place where he built an altar to the Lord? (6:24)

1. "The Lord is Good"
2. "The Lord is Gracious"
3. "The Lord is Peace"
4. "The Lord is Love"

7. What did Gideon do at night because he was afraid? (6:25-27)

1. He pressed grapes into wine.
2. He tore down Baal's altar and the Asherah pole.
3. He argued with the angel of the Lord.
4. All of the answers are correct.

8. What did Joash say Baal could do if he was really a god? (6:31)

1. Rebuild the altar
2. Defend himself
3. Know who tore down his altar
4. All of the answers are correct.

9. What was the first sign Gideon asked for? (6:36-37)

1. That the dew would cover the fleece and the ground would be dry.
2. That the dew would only appear on the ground.
3. That the fleece would disappear.
4. That the Lord would appear beside the fleece.

10. What was the second sign Gideon asked for? (6:39-40)

1. That the fleece would be dry, and the dew would cover the ground.
2. That the Lord would appear beside the fleece.
3. That the fleece would disappear.
4. That a larger fleece would appear.

REVIEW QUESTIONS FOR BIBLE QUIZZING

QUESTIONS FOR BASIC LEVEL REVIEW (LESSON FIFTEEN: JUDGES 7:1-25; 8:28)

1. What did the Lord tell Gideon about the size of the army? (7:2)

1. Your army is too small.
2. Your army is just the right size.
3. **You have too many men.**

2. Why did God want to reduce the number of men in Gideon's army? (7:2)

1. **God did not want Israel to boast that their own strength had saved them.**
2. God did not want that many Israelites to die in battle.
3. Gideon's army was too strong.

3. How many men lapped water from their cupped hands? (7:6)

1. 10,000 men
2. **300 men**
3. 22,000 men

4. Who was Gideon's servant? (7:10)

1. **Purah**
2. Tarah
3. Obed

5. What did one of the men in the Midianite camp dream? (7:13-14)

1. **That Gideon defeated the Midianites**
2. That the Midianites defeated the Israelites
3. That Gideon spied on the Midianite camp

6. What did Gideon call out when he returned to the Israelite camp? (7:15)

1. "Get up!"
2. "The Lord has given the Midianite camp into your hands."
3. **Both answers are correct.**

7. How did Gideon divide the 300 men? (7:16)

1. Into groups of ten
2. **Into three groups**
3. Into five groups

8. What did Gideon give each of the 300 men? (7:16)

1. **A trumpet and an empty jar with a torch inside**
2. A sword and a torch
3. Both answers are correct.

9. What did the Midianites do when the 300 trumpets sounded? (7:22)

1. They fought the Israelites.
2. **They turned on each other with their swords.**
3. Both answers are correct.

10. During Gideon's lifetime, how long did the land enjoy peace? (8:28)

1. Fifty years
2. **Forty years**
3. Twenty years

REVIEW QUESTIONS FOR BIBLE QUIZZING

QUESTIONS FOR ADVANCED LEVEL REVIEW (LESSON FIFTEEN: JUDGES 7:1-25; 8:28)

1. What did the Lord tell Gideon about the size of his army? (7:2)

1. Your army is too small.
2. Your army is just the right size.
3. **You have too many men.**
4. Your men are too small.

2. Why did God want Gideon to reduce the size of his army? (7:2)

1. **God did not want Israel to boast that their own strength had saved them.**
2. God did not want that many Israelites to die in battle.
3. Gideon did not have enough weapons.
4. Many of Gideon's men needed to be with their families.

3. How many men lapped water from their cupped hands? (7:6)

1. 500 men
2. 3000 men
3. **300 men**
4. 30,000 men

4. To what were the number of the Midianites' camels compared? (7:12)

1. Locusts
2. **The sand on the seashore**
3. The number of camels the Israelites had
4. The number of Midianites

5. What did Gideon call out to the Israelite camp after he spied on the Midianites? (7:15)

1. "The Lord does not want us to fight."
2. "We must leave this area."
3. **"The Lord has given the Midianite camp into your hands."**
4. "Be prepared to fight."

6. How did Gideon divide the 300 men? (7:16)

1. Into companies of ten
2. **Into three companies**
3. Into five companies
4. into two equal companies

7. What did Gideon give each man? (7:16)

1. A sword
2. A camel and a sword
3. **A trumpet and an empty jar with a torch inside**
4. A rock and a slingshot

8. What did the three companies do after they heard Gideon and the men with him blow their trumpets and break their jars? (7:19-20)

1. They blew their trumpets.
2. They smashed their jars.
3. "They shouted, 'A sword for the Lord and for Gideon!'"
4. **All of the answers are correct.**

9. What did the Midianites do when the 300 trumpets sounded? (7:22)

1. They fought the Israelites.
2. **They turned on each other with their swords.**
3. They began to burn down the Israelite camp.
4. All of the answers are correct.

10. During Gideon's lifetime, how long did the land enjoy peace? (8:28)

1. Fifty years
2. **Forty years**
3. Twenty years
4. Seven years

REVIEW QUESTIONS FOR BIBLE QUIZZING

QUESTIONS FOR BASIC LEVEL REVIEW (LESSON SIXTEEN: JUDGES 13:1-25)

1. Into whose hands did the Lord deliver the Israelites for 40 years? (13:1)

1. The Egyptians
2. **The Philistines**
3. The Jebusites

2. What did Manoah and his wife not have? (13:2)

1. **Children**
2. A home of their own
3. Cattle

3. Who appeared to Manoah's wife? (13:3)

1. The Philistine king
2. **The angel of the Lord**
3. A soldier

4. What did the angel tell Manoah's wife? (13:3)

1. **"You will become pregnant and give birth to a son."**
2. "Your clan is the weakest in Israel."
3. "Your husband will die soon."

5. What would never touch the boy's head? (13:5)

1. Shampoo
2. **A razor**
3. Both answers are correct.

6. What did Manoah do after his wife told him what the angel said? (13:7-8)

1. **He prayed and asked the Lord to send the man of God again to teach them how to bring up the boy.**
2. He fled to the mountains and hid.
3. Both answers are correct.

7. What did the angel of the Lord say was beyond understanding? (13:18)

1. **His name**
2. The ways of the Lord
3. His thoughts

8. What amazing thing happened while Manoah and his wife watched the burnt offering? (13:19-20)

1. The Lord appeared in a flame.
2. **The angel of the Lord ascended in the flame.**
3. Both answers are correct.

9. What did Manoah's wife name her son? (13:24)

1. Gideon
2. Manoah, Jr.
3. **Samson**

10. What happened to Samson while he was in Mahaneh Dan? (13:25)

1. He fell in love.
2. **The Spirit of the Lord began to stir him.**
3. Both answers are correct.

REVIEW QUESTIONS FOR BIBLE QUIZZING

QUESTIONS FOR ADVANCED LEVEL REVIEW (LESSON SIXTEEN: JUDGES 13:1-25)

1. **What did Manoah's wife not have? (13:2)**

1. **Children**
2. A house
3. Cattle
4. Land

2. **Who told Manoah's wife she would give birth to a son? (13:3)**

1. **The angel of the Lord**
2. Manoah
3. A midwife
4. The priest

3. **What did the angel tell Manoah's wife? (13:4-5)**

1. Do not drink wine.
2. Do not eat anything unclean.
3. Do not ever allow a razor to touch her son's head.
4. **All of the answers are correct.**

4. **Why should a razor not touch the boy's head? (13:5)**

1. It would be too cold to shave his head.
2. **He would be a Nazirite, dedicated to God from the womb.**
3. He would not resemble his father.
4. All of the answers are correct.

5. **What did Manoah's wife tell her husband about the man of God? (13:6)**

1. **"He looked like an angel of God, very awesome."**
2. "He looked hungry, so I offered him some food."
3. "He looked tired, so I gave him a place to sleep."
4. "He looked thirsty, so I gave him some water."

6. **Who came to Manoah's wife when she was out in the field? (13:9)**

1. **The angel of God**
2. A judge
3. All of Manoah's servants
4. The priest

7. **What was beyond understanding? (13:18)**

1. The Lord's power
2. **The angel of the Lord's name**
3. His thoughts
4. The ways of the Lord

8. **What did the Lord do while Manoah and his wife watched the burnt offering? (13:19-20)**

1. He sent another angel to tell them what to do.
2. **As the flame blazed up toward heaven, the angel of the Lord ascended in the flame.**
3. He came down from heaven in a cloud.
4. All of the answers are correct.

9. **What did Manoah's wife name her son? (13:24)**

1. Gideon
2. Moses
3. **Samson**
4. Joshua

10. **When did the Spirit of the Lord begin to stir Samson? (13:25)**

1. When he got married
2. When he turned 25
3. While he traveled to Jericho
4. **While he was in Mahaneh Dan**

REVIEW QUESTIONS FOR BIBLE QUIZZING

QUESTIONS FOR BASIC LEVEL REVIEW (LESSON SEVENTEEN: JUDGES 16:1-31)

1. Whom did Samson love? (16:4)

1. Deborah
2. Delilah
3. Darla

2. Who wanted Delilah to find out the secret of Samson's strength? (16:5)

1. Samson's mother
2. God
3. The rulers of the Philistines

3. What did Samson first tell Delilah would cause him to lose his strength (16:7)

1. If she tied him with seven bowstrings
2. If she unbraided his hair
3. Both of the answers are correct

4. What would happen to Samson if someone shaved his head? (16:17)

1. He would become stronger.
2. He would become taller.
3. He would lose his strength.

5. How did Samson's strength leave him? (16:19)

1. Someone tied him with special ropes.
2. Someone wove his braids into fabric.
3. Someone shaved off his seven braids.

6. What did Samson do while someone shaved off his braids? (16:19)

1. He read.
2. He slept.
3. He ate.

7. Why did the Philistines assemble? (16:23)

1. To offer a sacrifice to their god, Dagon
2. To celebrate Samson's defeat
3. Both answers are correct.

8. What did Samson ask the Lord to do for him once more? (16:28)

1. Give him his sight
2. Help him escape
3. Give him his strength

9. What did Samson do to kill the Philistines? (16:29-30)

1. He collapsed Dagon's temple on them.
2. He burned down Dagon's temple.
3. Both answers are correct.

10. How many years did Samson lead Israel? (16:31)

1. Twenty
2. Thirty
3. Forty

REVIEW QUESTIONS FOR BIBLE QUIZZING

QUESTIONS FOR ADVANCED LEVEL REVIEW (LESSON SEVENTEEN: JUDGES 16:1-31)

1. What did Samson carry to the top of the hill at Gaza? (16:3)

1. The doors and two posts of the city gate
2. Five men
3. A lion he killed
4. Delilah

2. Whom did Samson love? (16:4)

1. The king's daughter
2. Doris
3. **Delilah**
4. Deborah

3. What did the Philistine rulers offer Delilah in return for her help? (16:5)

1. 100 shekels of gold
2. Her own house
3. **1,100 shekels of silver from each ruler**
4. Her own land

4. What did Samson say would cause him to lose his strength? (16:11, 13, 17)

1. If anyone tied him with new ropes
2. If anyone wove his seven braids into the fabric of a loom
3. If anyone shaved off his seven braids
4. **All of the answers are correct.**

5. What happened each time Samson told Delilah a false source of his strength? (16:9, 12, 14)

1. Samson would pretend to be asleep.
2. **Samson broke free and the Philistines did not subdue him.**
3. Samson hated Delilah.
4. All of the answers are correct.

6. How did Delilah finally subdue Samson? (16:19)

1. She did not let him sleep.
2. **She called for someone to shave off his braids while he slept.**
3. She told him the truth.
4. All of the answers are correct.

7. What did the Philistines do when they captured Samson? (16:21)

1. They gouged out his eyes.
2. They put shackles on him.
3. They put him in prison.
4. **All of the answers are correct.**

8. Why did the Philistine rulers assemble? (16:23)

1. To celebrate the battle they won over the tribe of Dan
2. **To celebrate the defeat of Samson and to offer a sacrifice to their god, Dagon**
3. To celebrate Samson's triumph over Dagon
4. All of the answers are correct.

9. After he performed, what did Samson ask the Lord to do? (16:28)

1. To remember him
2. To strengthen him once more
3. To let him get revenge on the Philistines with one blow for his two eyes
4. **All of the answers are correct.**

10. What does Judges say about Samson's last show of great strength? (16:30)

1. "Thus Samson the Nazirite died a slave in the land of Philistia."
2. "Thus he killed only a few compared to when he led Israel."
3. **"Thus he killed many more when he died than while he lived."**
4. "Thus Samson obeyed the Lord and did a great deed for Israel."

REVIEW QUESTIONS FOR BIBLE QUIZZING

QUESTIONS FOR BASIC LEVEL REVIEW (LESSON EIGHTEEN: RUTH 1:1-22)

1. How many sons did Naomi have? (1:1)

1. One
2. Two
3. Three

2. Where was Naomi originally from? (1:2)

1. Moab
2. Jerusalem
3. Bethlehem

3. What happened while Naomi lived in Moab? (1:2-4)

1. Her husband died.
2. Her sons married Moabite women.
3. Both answers are correct.

4. What were the names of Naomi's daughters-in-law? (1:4)

1. Orpah and Ruth
2. Ruth and Kilion
3. Kilion and Orpah

5. Who came to the aid of the Israelites and provided food for them? (1:6)

1. The Lord
2. The Moabites
3. The people of Bethlehem

6. What did Naomi say she hoped the Lord would give her daughters-in-law? (1:9)

1. A safe journey to their fathers' houses
2. Good health and long life
3. Rest in the home of another husband

7. What did Naomi's daughters-in-law first say to her? (1:9-10)

1. "We will go to our mothers' homes."
2. "We want to stay here with you."
3. "We will go back with you to your people."

8. Why did Naomi say Orpah and Ruth should not go with her? (1:11)

1. Because she had no money to care for them.
2. Because she was unable to produce more sons who could be their husbands.
3. Both answers are correct.

9. Who stayed with Naomi? (1:14)

1. Ruth
2. Orpah
3. Both of them

10. What did Ruth tell Naomi when Naomi asked her to go with Orpah? (1:15-16)

1. "Where you go I will go."
2. "Your people will be my people and your God my God."
3. Both answers are correct.

REVIEW QUESTIONS FOR BIBLE QUIZZING

QUESTIONS FOR ADVANCED LEVEL REVIEW (LESSON EIGHTEEN: RUTH 1:1-22)

1. **Why did Naomi and her family leave Bethlehem to go to Moab? (1:1)**

1. They wanted to leave Moab and go home.
2. They were not welcome in Bethlehem.
3. **There was a famine in Bethlehem.**
4. There were no wives for their sons in Bethlehem.

2. **What happened while Naomi and her family lived in Moab? (1:3-5)**

1. Her husband died.
2. Her two sons got married.
3. Her two sons died.
4. **All of the answers are correct.**

3. **How did the Lord come to the aid of his people in Bethlehem? (1:6)**

1. **He provided them with some food.**
2. He subdued the Israelites' enemies.
3. He provided a new judge for them.
4. He provided rest from the Philistines.

4. **What did Orpah and Ruth first tell Naomi they would do? (1:9-10)**

1. They would stay with Naomi in Moab.
2. They would find new husbands.
3. **They would go with Naomi back to her people.**
4. They wanted to go home to their mothers.

5. **What did Orpah do? (1:14-15)**

1. She went with Naomi to the land of Judah.
2. **She left Naomi and went back to her people.**
3. She found another husband.
4. She decided to go to Bethlehem on her own.

6. **What did Ruth say when Naomi asked her to go with Orpah? (1:15-16)**

1. "Don't urge me to leave you."
2. "Where you go I will go."
3. "Your people will be my people and your God my God."
4. **All of the answers are correct.**

7. **What did Ruth decide to do? (1:18)**

1. She went back to her people and her gods.
2. She hoped to find another husband in Moab.
3. **She was determined to go with Naomi.**
4. She decided to go with Orpah.

8. **What did the women in Bethlehem say when Naomi and Ruth arrived? (1:19)**

1. "Who is that woman with Naomi?"
2. "Why is Naomi here? She left us ten years ago."
3. "Why would Naomi bring Ruth with her?"
4. **"Can this be Naomi?"**

9. **What did Naomi think the Lord did to her? (1:20-21)**

1. He withheld his love from her.
2. He gave her too many sons.
3. **He made her life very bitter.**
4. He sent her away poor and brought her back rich.

10. **What time of year did Naomi and Ruth arrive back in Bethlehem? (1:22)**

1. Planting time
2. **Harvest time**
3. Winter time
4. Spring time

REVIEW QUESTIONS FOR BIBLE QUIZZING

QUESTIONS FOR BASIC LEVEL REVIEW (LESSON NINETEEN: RUTH 2:1-23)

1. Who was a relative of Naomi's husband? (2:1)

1. Judah
2. Boaz
3. Elimelech

2. Why did Ruth go to the fields? (2:2)

1. To plant corn
2. To pick flowers
3. To gather the leftover grain

3. In whose field did Ruth work? (2:3)

1. Boaz's field
2. Naomi's field
3. An ownerless field

4. How did Boaz greet his harvesters? (2:4)

1. "The Lord be with you!"
2. "You need to work harder!"
3. Both answers are correct.

5. How did Ruth work while in the fields? (2:7)

1. She worked hard for most of the day.
2. She did not work very long and was lazy.
3. She spent most of her time in the shelter.

6. What did Boaz ask the Lord to do for Ruth? (2:11-12)

1. Give her another husband
2. Repay her and richly reward her
3. Both answers are correct.

7. Where did Boaz say Ruth came to take refuge? (2:12)

1. In Naomi's field
2. In his home
3. Under the Lord's wing

8. What instructions did Boaz give to the harvesters about Ruth? (2:15-16)

1. "Gather up some sheaves for her."
2. "Leave some stalks for her to pick up."
3. Both answers are correct.

9. Why did Naomi say it was a good idea for Ruth to work in Boaz's field? (2:22)

1. Ruth might be harmed in someone else's field.
2. Ruth would gather the most grain from Boaz's field.
3. Both answers are correct.

10. With whom did Ruth stay close while she gleaned in Boaz's field? (2:23)

1. Boaz
2. The overseer
3. The women of Boaz

REVIEW QUESTIONS FOR BIBLE QUIZZING

QUESTIONS FOR ADVANCED LEVEL REVIEW (LESSON NINETEEN: RUTH 2:1-23)

1. Who was Boaz? (2:1)

1. A wealthy relative of Naomi's husband.
2. A wealthy storekeeper.
3. A servant boy.
4. All of the answers are correct.

2. Where did Ruth work? (2:3)

1. In a store that belonged to Elimelek's mother
2. In a mill where people brought their grain
3. In a field that belonged to Boaz
4. All of the answers are correct.

3. How did Boaz greet his harvesters when he returned from Bethlehem? (2:4)

1. "The Lord be with you!"
2. "The Lord repay you!"
3. "May God bless you richly!"
4. "Good afternoon, hard workers."

4. What instructions did Boaz give to Ruth about how to harvest in his field? (2:9)

1. Ask the foremen where to harvest.
2. Harvest after the women and drink water whenever she was thirsty.
3. Harvest only on the south side of the field.
4. Avoid the servant girls.

5. What did Boaz hear about Ruth? (2:11)

1. He heard that she left her parents and her homeland.
2. He heard about all that she did for Naomi.
3. He heard that she came to live with a people she did not know.
4. All of the answers are correct.

6. Whom did Boaz ask to reward Ruth richly? (2:12)

1. Naomi
2. The God of Israel
3. The god of the Moabites
4. The servant girls

7. What did Boaz say about what Ruth had done? (2:12)

1. She came to take refuge under the Lord's wings
2. She did honorable deeds for the Lord.
3. She followed the Lord wholeheartedly.
4. She helped Naomi leave Bethlehem.

8. What did Ruth take back to town after her day in the fields? (2:17-18)

1. Boaz's servants
2. The barley she had gathered
3. Fruits and vegetables
4. All of the answers are correct.

9. What did Naomi call Boaz? (2:20)

1. A friendly overseer
2. One of her guardian-redeemers
3. A greedy man
4. A landowner

10. How did Ruth take care of Naomi while they lived in Bethlehem? (2:23)

1. She worked at Boaz's house.
2. She gleaned grain.
3. She worked at the mill.
4. She helped Naomi plant their own wheat field.

REVIEW QUESTIONS FOR BIBLE QUIZZING

QUESTIONS FOR BASIC LEVEL REVIEW (LESSON TWENTY: RUTH 3:1-12; 4:1-17)

1. What did Naomi say that she would try to find for Ruth? (3:1)

1. A home
2. A job
3. Land

2. What would Boaz do that night? (3:2)

1. Work in his garden at home
2. Winnow barley on the threshing floor
3. Meet with the elders at the city gate

3. What did Naomi tell Ruth to do when Boaz lay down to sleep? (3:4)

1. Uncover his feet, lie down, and wait for him to tell her what to do
2. Help him thresh the wheat completely
3. Both answers are correct.

4. What did Boaz do after he finished eating and drinking? (3:7)

1. He was angry and he decided to burn the wheat.
2. He was in good spirits and lay down near the grain pile.
3. He was very sad and wept in the corner.

5. What did the townsmen of Bethlehem think of Ruth? (3:11)

1. They thought that she ran after younger, rich men as she searched for a husband.
2. They thought that she was a woman of noble character.
3. They thought that she was a cautious person.

6. What did Boaz give to Ruth? (3:15)

1. Some barley
2. A shawl
3. Both answers are correct

7. In earlier times in Israel, how did the transfer of property become final? (4:7)

1. One person took off a sandal and gave it to the other person.
2. Both people signed a contract.
3. They shook hands.

8. What did Boaz tell the elders when the first guardian-redeemer did not want the land? (4:9-10)

1. Boaz would buy the property and take Ruth as his wife.
2. Boaz would buy the property and take Naomi as his wife.
3. Both answers are correct.

9. What was the name of Boaz's and Ruth's son? (4:17)

1. Obed
2. Jesse
3. David

10. Finish this verse: "For the Lord is good and his love endures forever;..." (Psalm 100:5)

1. "...his grace covers all our sins."
2. "...his power and might protect us."
3. "...his faithfulness continues through all generations."

REVIEW QUESTIONS FOR BIBLE QUIZZING

QUESTIONS FOR BLUE LEVEL REVIEW (LESSON TWENTY: RUTH 3:1-12; 4:1-17)

1. What was Naomi's plan to find a home for Ruth? (3:1-3)

1. She planned to send Ruth back to Moab.
2. **She planned to send Ruth to see Boaz.**
3. She planned to plant barley.
4. She had no plan.

2. What happened while Boaz was at the threshing floor? (3:7)

1. He finished eating and drinking and was in good spirits.
2. He lay down near the grain pile.
3. Ruth approached quietly, uncovered his feet and lay down.
4. **All of the answers are correct.**

3. What did Boaz say after Ruth asked him to cover her with his garment? (3:9-10)

1. Why are you here? Leave before someone sees you.
2. Why do you want to be with me?
3. **This kindness is greater than that which you showed earlier.**
4. All of the answers are correct.

4. Why did the other guardian-redeemer have the opportunity to buy Naomi's land before Boaz? (4:3-4)

1. Boaz was scared of him.
2. **The other guardian-redeemer was a closer relative than Boaz.**
3. Boaz did not want the land.
4. All of the answers are correct.

5. Why did the other guardian-redeemer decide not to buy the land? (4:5-6)

1. He did not need more land.
2. He did not have money to buy the land.
3. **He did not want to take Ruth as his wife and endanger his estate.**
4. All of the answers are correct.

6. In earlier times in Israel, how did the transfer of property become final? (4:7)

1. **One person took off a sandal and gave it to the other person.**
2. He spoke in front of the town elders.
3. He signed a contract
4. All of the answers are correct.

7. How would Boaz make sure Mahlon's name would not disappear? (4:9-10)

1. He would name his first child Mahlon.
2. **He would marry Ruth.**
3. He would name his farm Mahlon.
4. All of the answers are correct.

8. What did the women say that the Lord did for Naomi? (4:13-14)

1. The Lord provided a great daughter for Naomi.
2. The Lord was with Naomi in the good times and the bad.
3. The Lord did not forget Naomi's troubles.
4. **The Lord did not leave Naomi without a guardian-redeemer.**

9. What did the women say to Naomi about Ruth? (4:15)

1. Ruth was lucky to marry a rich husband.
2. **Ruth was better to her than seven sons.**
3. Ruth was a great daughter.
4. Ruth was now a real relative to her.

10. What was the name of Ruth's and Boaz's son? (4:17)

1. Jesse
2. Mahlon
3. **Obed**
4. David

MEMORY VERSES—PROGRESS CHART

EVENT: _____ CHILD'S NAME: _____ SCORE _____

1 Have I not commanded you? Be strong and courageous. Do not be afraid; do not be discouraged, for the Lord your God will be with you wherever you go. Joshua 1:9

DATE MEMORIZED: ....

2 Then Peter began to speak: "I now realize how true it is that God does not show favoritism but accepts from every nation the one who fears him and does what is right." Acts 10:34-35

DATE MEMORIZED: ....

3 Joshua told the people, "Consecrate yourselves, for tomorrow the Lord will do amazing things among you." Joshua 3:5

DATE MEMORIZED: ....

4 He said to the Israelites, "In the future when your descendants ask their parents, 'What do these stones mean?'

tell them, 'Israel crossed the Jordan on dry ground.'" Joshua 4:21-22

DATE MEMORIZED: ....

5 Obey the Lord your God and follow his commands and decrees that I give you today. Deuteronomy 27:10

DATE MEMORIZED: ....

6 There is a way that appears to be right, but in the end it leads to death. Proverbs 14:12

DATE MEMORIZED: ....

7 Be strong and very courageous. Be careful to obey all the law my servant Moses gave you; do not turn from it to the right or to the left, that you may be successful wherever you go. Joshua 1:7

DATE MEMORIZED: ....

8 All the ways of the Lord are loving and faithful toward those who keep the demands of his covenant. Psalm 25:10

DATE MEMORIZED: ....

9 And whatever you do, whether in word or deed, do it all in the name of the Lord Jesus, giving thanks to God the Father through him. Colossians 3:17

DATE MEMORIZED: ....

10 Not one of all the Lord's good promises to Israel failed; every one was fulfilled. Joshua 21:45

DATE MEMORIZED: ....

11 Now fear the Lord and serve him with all faithfulness. Joshua 24:14a

DATE MEMORIZED: ....

12 Lord our God, you answered them; you were to Israel a forgiving God, though you punished their misdeeds. Psalm 99:8

DATE MEMORIZED: ....

13 I know that you can do all things; no purpose of yours can be thwarted. Job 42:

DATE MEMORIZED: ....

14 The Lord your God is with you, the Mighty Warrior who saves. He will take great delight in you; in his love he will no longer rebuke you, but will rejoice over you with singing. Zephaniah 3:17

DATE MEMORIZED: ....

15 Wait for the Lord; be strong and take heart and wait for the Lord. Psalm 27:14

DATE MEMORIZED: ....

16 The Lord delights in those who fear him, who put their hope in his unfailing love. Psalm 147:11

DATE MEMORIZED: ....

17 Hear my voice when I call, Lord; be merciful to me and answer me. Psalm 27:7

DATE MEMORIZED: ....

18 But Ruth replied, "Don't urge me to leave you or to turn back from you. Where you go I will go, and where you stay I will stay. Your people will be my people and your God my God." Ruth 1:16

DATE MEMORIZED: ....

19 Share with the Lord's people who are in need. Practice hospitality. Romans 12:13

DATE MEMORIZED: ....

20 For the Lord is good and his love endures forever; his faithfulness continues through all generations. Psalm 100:5

DATE MEMORIZED: ....

CHILDREN'S QUIZZING SCORE SHEET

Basic Quizzing uses only questions 1-15. Advanced quizzing uses 20 questions. Read the Official Rules and Procedures for complete instructions.

CHURCH/TEAM NAME:

ROUND 1

Names:	1	2	3	4	5	6	7	8	9	10	11	12	13	14	15	16	17	18	19	20	Total
Team Bonus:																					

Team Total:

ROUND 2

Names:	1	2	3	4	5	6	7	8	9	10	11	12	13	14	15	16	17	18	19	20	Total
Team Bonus:																					

Team Total:

ROUND 3

Names:	1	2	3	4	5	6	7	8	9	10	11	12	13	14	15	16	17	18	19	20	Total
Team Bonus:																					

Team Total:

ATTENDANCE SHEET

Write the children's names in the lines provided. Place an X in the column for each lesson the child is in attendance. You may reproduce this attendance sheet if you need more lines.

CHILD	1	2	3	4	5	6	7	8	9	10	11	12	13	14	15	16	17	18	19	20

THE STORY BEHIND
KIDZFIRST BIBLE STUDIES FOR CHILDREN
AND QUIZ EVENTS

The Kids Reaching Kids Mission Offering Project is designed to encourage children to give sacrificially to meet the needs of other children. Aptly named, it focuses on Kids… Reaching… Kids.

Kids Reaching Kids challenges children, churches, districts, fields and regions, to meet children's needs in every world region.

- Mentally through education to enrich children's minds.
- Physically through compassion to meet children's basic needs.
- Spiritually through evangelism to reach children for Christ.
- Socially through discipleship to strengthen children's faith.

This biblical approach is modeled on the life of Jesus. Luke 2:52 reveals how Jesus' life was shaped in a holistic fashion. Jesus grew in wisdom(mentally) and stature(physically), and in favor with God(spiritually) and men (socially).

Each year a project is chosen that addresses a vital need of children across the globe. The proceeds are available for a variety of ministries with children in all six Nazarene world regions.

The D-Code Challenge: Bible Quizzing – Unlocked, Unlimited, and Understood

In 2008-2009, the Kids Reaching Kids Mission Offering Project, the D-Code Challenge, raised funds for the translation, production and distribution of Children's Bible Quizzing materials.

The book you are holding originated from materials produced by The Nazarene Publishing House.

It was translated into Global English, French, Korean, Portuguese, and Spanish through Children's Ministries International, Global Nazarene Publications, and a team of translators around the world.

CERTIFICATE OF COMPLETION

presented to

Congratulations for successfully completing

Bible Studies for Children
Joshua, Judges, & Ruth

LOCATION

TEACHER

DATE

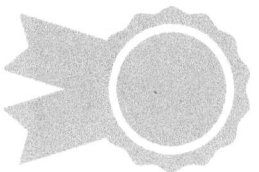

AWARD FOR EXCELLENCE

presented to

Great job! We recognize your outstanding achievement in

Bible Studies for Children

Joshua, Judges, & Ruth

TEACHER

LOCATION

DATE